Social Security in the 21st Century

Social Security in the 21st Century

Edited by
Bertil Holmlund
Agnar Sandmo
and
Erling Steigum

BLACKWELL
Publishers

First Published 2000
ISBN 0-631-22587-0

Blackwell Publishers Ltd
108 Cowley Road
Oxford OX4 1JF, UK

Blackwell Publishers Inc
350 Main Street
Malden, Massachusetts 02148, USA

British Library Cataloguing in Publication Data has been applied for

Library of Congress Cataloguing in Publication Data has been applied for

Typeset by Keytec Typesetting
Printed and bound in Great Britain by
MPG Books, Bodmin, Cornwall

This book is printed on acid-free paper

Contents

Editors' Preface.
Bertil Holmlund, Agnar Sandmo and Erling Steigum vii

Authors' Affiliations. ix

1 Economic and Social Security in the Twenty-first Century, with Attention to Europe.
Jacques H. Drèze 1

2 Social Security Reform and National Wealth.
John Laitner 23

3 Adverse Selection in the Annuities Market and the Impact of Privatizing Social Security.
Jan Walliser 47

4 The Financial Stability of Notional Account Pensions.
Salvador Valdés-Prieto 67

5 Pension Reform during the Demographic Transition.
Hans Fehr 91

6 The Welfare State, Budgetary Pressure and Labour Market Shifts.
Anthony B. Atkinson 115

7 Unskilled Migration: A Burden or a Boon for the Welfare State?
Assaf Razin and Efraim Sadka 133

8 Early Retirement and Economic Incentives.
Erik Hernæs, Marte Sollie and Steinar Strøm 149

9 The Political Economy of Social Security.
Georges Casamatta, Helmuth Cremer and Pierre Pestieau 171

10 A Positive Theory of Social Security.
Guido Tabellini 191

Editors' Preface

As the twenty-first century begins, social security is once again the focus of an important economic and political debate. It is widely recognized that the public provision of social security can be justified for reasons of both equity and efficiency; the questions for public policy are: how much and in what forms? While the provision of increased economic security in itself is a good thing and may lead to improved functioning of the economy in the presence of incomplete and imperfect insurance markets, social security may also create incentives that are harmful for the efficient functioning of the economy. This may occur either through the design of the benefit system or through the taxes or social security premiums that are necessary to finance it. The financial aspects have recently been given much attention in view of the demographic development in many Western countries with an increasing share of old-age pensioners in the population. There have also been concerns that the shifts in the population will create a political majority in favour of a level of social security which is not sustainable in the long run.

The topic of this special issue of *The Scandinavian Journal of Economics* is therefore a timely one, with all of the above themes reflected in the ten papers that it contains. The response of the authors whom we invited to submit papers (which all underwent a normal refereeing process) has confirmed our belief that this is an area where the rate of return to research, both theoretical and empirical, is very high. We hope that the present selection of articles will stimulate further work in the area.

Bertil Holmlund
Agnar Sandmo
Erling Steigum

Author Affiliations

Anthony B. Atkinson:
Nuffield College, Oxford, England

Georges Casamatta:
Université de Toulouse, Toulouse, France

Helmuth Cremer:
Université de Toulouse, Toulouse, France

Jacques H. Drèze:
Université Catholique de Louvain, Louvain-la-Neuve, Belgium

Hans Fehr:
University of Wuerzburg, Wuerzburg, Germany

Erik Hernæs:
Ragnar Frisch Centre for Economic Research, Oslo, Norway

John Laitner:
University of Michigan, Ann Arbor, MI, USA

Pierre Pestieau:
Université de Liège, Liège, Belgium

Assaf Razin:
Tel-Aviv University, Tel-Aviv, Israel

Efraim Sadka:
Tel-Aviv University, Tel-Aviv, Israel

Marte Sollie:
Statistics Norway, Oslo, Norway

Steinar Strøm:
Ragnar Frisch Centre for Economic Research and University of Oslo, Oslo, Norway

Guido Tabellini:
Università Bocconi, Milan, Italy

Salvador Valdés-Prieto:
Catholic University of Chile, Santiago, Chile

Jan Walliser:
International Monetary Fund, Washington, DC, USA

1

Economic and Social Security in the Twenty-first Century, with Attention to Europe

*Jacques H. Drèze**

I. Looking Ahead

The ex ante Viewpoint

The Scandinavian Journal of Economics invites us to look ahead into a future that is unusually distant from the viewpoint of standard economic thinking. The brief is particularly challenging when emphasis is placed on coping with uncertainty: the future tends to become more uncertain, the farther ahead we look. Looking into the twenty-first century is very different from looking at a stationary state.

There is, however, a saving grace. As we look into a more distant future, we become increasingly concerned with as yet unborn individuals, or with young individuals whose future characteristics and opportunities remain largely unknown. For that group of young or unborn individuals, the natural goal of alleviating future uncertainties can be fostered through mutual insurance. A system whereby the lucky ones who will do well tomorrow help out those who will do poorly enhances *ex ante* the prospective welfare of *all*, at a gain of overall efficiency. In contrast, when the lucky ones of today are taxed to help out the less fortunate, the transfers are seen as redistributive, needing justification on ethical rather than on efficiency grounds.

The *ex ante* viewpoint was initially introduced in a pioneering contribution by William Vickrey (1945), further extended by John Harsanyi (1953) and James Mirrlees (1971). Under the name "veil of ignorance", it was built into the foundations of *A Theory of Justice* by John Rawls (1971). It is also the viewpoint underlying the present essay.

As spelled out in Section III, the *ex ante* viewpoint suggests a high degree

*This contribution and introduction to *The Scandinavian Journal of Economics* millennium special issue was initially submitted as an extension of Drèze (1999), but revised as per helpful suggestions of two anonymous referees who recommended a non-technical exposition and the inclusion of some topics in Sections III, IV and V.

of *ex post* equality, driven by considerations of risk-sharing efficiency. But *ex post* equalizing transfers raise issues of moral hazard, productive efficiency, time consistency, fiscal competition, etc. Reconciling the two conflicting efficiency motivations brings us into the realm of second-best analysis, beset with the difficulties of modelling distortions, designing and implementing suitable policies or turning qualitative prescriptions into quantified decisions. By necessity, my discussion of so many issues will remain general, with some attention to identifying research priorities.

Application of the *ex ante* viewpoint calls for defining the proper reference group. Logically, that group consists of all economic agents apt to participate in a common program. Traditionally, such a group is identified with the citizens (to be) of a given country. I will argue in Section II that reasoning at the world level would be meaningful; but that goal remains unrealistic. There is, however, an intermediate level, namely that of the European Union. I will start at the more familiar national level, then move on the EU level. Given the long-run perspective, it is then relevant to anticipate some consequences of further economic integration and to take enlargement prospects into account.

Long-run Economic Uncertainties

Although the topic of this special issue is "social security", I refer in my title to "*economic and social* security". The basic concern of most households lies with their income prospects, as related in the first place to employment prospects, and subsidiarily (by default) to replacement incomes. Today we regard both employment and social security—the welfare state—as problematic: unemployment is too high and not abating significantly; social security is too costly, yet not fully effective; European integration is seen as a threat to the welfare state, through fiscal competition. The natural human quest for economic security, as a basis for the attainment of deeper goals (building a family, a home, a network of relationships etc.), is thus threatened today on two fronts: the perspective of finding or keeping a job yielding a stable income, and the perspective of relying on a solvent social security system for a substitute income in case of need.

The uncertainties with which I am concerned are those surrounding the real incomes of individuals and families. These uncertainties arise mainly from two sources, which it is helpful to separate logically, even if the distinction is often blurred in concrete instances. One source concerns a person's ability, and determination, to earn an income through the supply of labour services. Individuals are born with endowments of characteristics (health, intelligence, skills, emotional stability, willpower etc.) which are relevant to performance on the labour market. A person's native endowment is a matter of luck, even though there are significant statistical regularities.

Births do not occur in a vacuum, but rather in a social setting where individual characteristics develop more or less felicitously depending on surroundings. As a life unfolds, chance intervenes repeatedly. A person may opt for training which later developments reward or not. A professional career may start in a sector, or in a firm, later crowned with success or again stricken with failure. The statistical distributions of relative labour incomes summarize the outcomes of these life histories.

The chance events include specific contingencies, like illness, premature death or other circumstances which keep a person out of the labour force. To the extent that these circumstances are observable, they are typically covered by contingency-related programs, which are an essential component of existing safety nets. To minimize dispersion, I ignore that kind of uncertainties here (except for Remark 4 in Section III below), and concentrate on lifetime earnings.

Another source of income uncertainties is of a macroeconomic nature. It is captured by the growth rates of national incomes per capita. Looking back at the twentieth century, these growth rates have varied substantially, both across countries over the whole century, and over time within the century for individual countries. As we look ahead today into successive decades of the twenty-first century, there is considerable uncertainty about the prospective growth rates of national incomes.

The two sources of uncertainty correspond to individual risks, that affect individuals but not aggregates, and macroeconomic or aggregate risks, that society must bear. The former correspond roughly to the place of an individual worker within the distribution of labour incomes. The latter concern the properties, especially the location, of the whole distribution. Using the standard description of future uncertainties by an event tree, the latter concern event-dependent *overall shifts* in the distribution of labour incomes; the former concern event-dependent *individual places* in event-dependent income distributions. A detailed modelling of these uncertainties is complex, and I will streamline these aspects. It is helpful, however, to distinguish successive levels of aggregation, and to reflect on their quantitative significance. The following features stand out.

(i) The variability due to an individual's place in the distribution of disposable incomes, as measured by the ratio of the 90th to the 10th percentile, has a country median in the EU of 3.4; it ranges from 2.6 (Finland) to 4.4 (Spain), still well below the US figure (5.9), but somewhat above the Eastern Europe figures which range from 2.6 (Hungary) to 3.3 (Estonia).[1] Individual uncertainties are thus substan-

[1] See Atkinson (1995b, p. 47) and Atkinson and Micklewright (1992, p. 103); the data mostly refer to the mid-1980s; the trend since then has been one of increasing inequality.

tial. In particular, the income prospects of low-skilled workers have deteriorated over the past decade in industrialized countries, under the joint influence of globalization and skill-biased technological progress.[2]

(ii) The labour share is not trended and hovers around 70 percent. Thus the average value for EU15 in 1998 was 68 percent, with values ranging from 60 percent in Ireland to 75 percent in Portugal. (It is 72 percent in the US and 73 percent in Japan.[3]) Still, variations over time in individual European countries (but not the US) have often been as high as 10 percentage points within a decade or two.

(iii) GDP per capita, adjusted for purchasing power and expressed in percentages of the EU15 average, range from 68 percent in Greece and Portugal to 112 percent in Belgium or Austria and 116 percent in Denmark (Luxembourg is an outlier at 164 percent); they reach 65 percent in the Czech Republic and Slovenia, but less than 30 percent in Bulgaria, Latvia, Lithuania and Romania.[4]

(iv) National incomes typically grow at positive rates that are, however, subject to sizeable long-run uncertainties. In the EU15, it has been estimated that some 45 percent of medium-term income risks could be eliminated through mutual insurance.[5]

Accordingly, I will be concerned successively with the uncertainty affecting individual incomes at a point in (future) time (Section III, extended to the EU dimension in Section IV), with national macroeconomic uncertainties (Section V), and with the prospects for international risk sharing within the EU (Section VI).

II. Sharing Risks

To set the stage for my discussion of economic security, I record concisely some properties of efficient risk sharing among a set of agents maximizing expected utility.

Let a set of n individuals $i = 1 \ldots, n$ each be endowed with a given risky prospect – say a random wealth level y^i with S alternative values y_s^i,

---

[2]This development takes the form of increased income inequality in the US and of persistent unemployment of low-skilled workers in Europe; see Drèze and Sneessens (1994), or Feenstra (1997) for recent references.

[3]See *European Economy 65*, pp. 292–293. The precision of these figures is imperfect; compare *ibid. 60*, pp. 164–165 and *63*, pp. 276–277.

[4]Without the purchasing power adjustment, incomes per capita in the last four countries average a mere 10 percent of the EU15 level.

[5]See Forni and Reichlin (1999).

$s = 1 \ldots, S$, corresponding to alternative "states of the world" of respective probabilities $\pi_s \geqslant 0$, $\sum_s \pi_s = 1$. The preferences of agent i are represented by the state-independent cardinal utility function $U_i(y^i)$, with absolute and relative risk-aversion functions $R_A^i = -U_i''/U_i'$ and $R_R^i = y^i R_A^i$; the corresponding risk-tolerance functions are

$$T_A^i = \frac{1}{R_A^i}, \qquad T_R^i = \frac{1}{R_R^i}.$$

Aggregate risk tolerance is $T_A = \sum_i T_A^i$ and average relative risk aversion is usefully measured by the harmonic mean

$$\hat{R}_R = \frac{\sum_i y^i}{\sum^i (y^i/R_R^i)} = \frac{Y}{T_A}.$$

An efficient mutual insurance scheme calls for pooling all the individual risks and letting each individual receive a share z_s^i of the aggregate wealth $Y_s = \sum_i y_s^i$, $s = 1 \ldots, S$. Efficiency further requires that marginal shares $\beta_s^i = \mathrm{d}z_s^i/\mathrm{d}Y_S$, $\sum_i \beta_s^i = 1$ be proportional to risk tolerances. For $z_s = (z_s^1 \ldots, z_s^n)$, two alternative formulations are

$$\beta_s^i = \frac{T_A^i(z_s^i)}{T_A(z_s)} = \frac{\hat{R}_R(z_s)}{R_R^i(z_s^i)} \cdot \frac{y_s^i}{Y_s}. \tag{1}$$

The special case of linear sharing rules, where $z_s^i = \alpha^i + \beta^i Y_s$, $\sum_i \alpha^i = 0$, $\sum_i \beta^i = 1$, provides an instructive benchmark, popularized through the CAPM.[6] Relatively risk-tolerant individuals will have relatively high marginal coefficients β^i and correlatively low (possibly negative) fixed wealth components α^i.[7]

There exists a system of prices q_s for unit insurance contracts on the occurrence of Y_s, given by the formula

$$q_s = \pi_s \left[1 - \frac{Y_s - \overline{Y}}{T_A}\right], \quad \sum_s q_s = 1, \quad \sum_s q_s Y_s = \overline{Y} - \frac{\sigma_Y^2}{T_A} = \overline{Y} - \hat{R}_R \frac{\sigma_Y^2}{\overline{Y}}. \tag{2}$$

[6]The benchmark is a first approximation, exact when individual utilities are quadratic or negative exponential, or again when individual relative risk aversions are constant and common; see e.g. Eeckhoudt and Gollier (1992).

[7]In the case of common constant relative risk aversion, $\overline{y}^i = \beta^i \overline{Y}$ so that $\alpha^i = (\beta^i \sigma_Y^2 - \sigma_{y^i Y})/T_A$; α^i is equal to the difference between the premium corresponding to the risk $\beta^i \sigma_Y^2$ borne by i and the risk $\sigma_{y^i Y}$ contributed by i.

The aggregate risk premium $\overline{Y} - \sum_s q_s Y_s = \hat{R}_R(\sigma^2_Y/\overline{Y})$ is thus proportional to average relative risk aversion and inversely proportional to aggregate (expected) wealth. The latter feature underscores the desirability of maximizing the wealth base over which risks are shared. *In principle, risks should be pooled and shared worldwide and over the infinite future.*

For further reference (in Section VI), I add that an efficient linear risk-sharing arrangement can always be implemented in two stages. Let P: $\{P_1 \ldots, P_k\}$ define a partition of the set $I = \{1 \ldots, n\}$ of agents. The subset of agents P_j has aggregate endowment $Y^j = \sum_{i \in P_j} y^i$ and aggregate absolute risk tolerance $\mathcal{T}^j_A = \sum_{i \in P_j} T^i_A$. Let the k subsets P_j, $j = 1 \ldots, k$, organize a risk exchange, resulting in shares $Z^j_s = A^j + B^j Y_s$, with

$$B^j = \frac{\mathcal{T}^j_A}{T_A} \quad \text{and} \quad A^j = \overline{Y}^j - \frac{\sigma_{Y^j Y}}{T_A} - B^j\left(\overline{Y} - \frac{\sigma^2_Y}{T_A}\right).$$

Next, let the individual agents in P_j organize a risk exchange, resulting in shares $\hat{z}^i_s = \hat{\alpha}^i + \hat{\beta}^i Z^j_s$, with

$$\hat{\beta}^i = \frac{T^i_A}{\mathcal{T}^j_A} \quad \text{and} \quad \hat{\alpha}^i = \overline{y}^i - \frac{\sigma_{y^i Z^j}}{\mathcal{T}^j_A} - \hat{\beta}^i\left(\overline{Z}^j - \frac{\sigma^2_{Z^j}}{\mathcal{T}^j_A}\right).$$

Then, for each $i = 1 \ldots, n$, for each $s = 1 \ldots, s$, $\hat{z}^i_s = z^i_S$ as defined above. Thus, in particular, an efficient linear sharing of income risks among all citizens of a set of countries could be implemented through efficient international sharing of national income risks, coupled with efficient risk-sharing arrangements among citizens of each country separately.

III. Individual Risks: National Analysis

Social Insurance

Individual risks concern the place of a future entrant to the labour market in the wage distribution. Individual risks are *by definition* uncorrelated with macroeconomic risks. If they could be exchanged on the market, no risk premium would be required.[8] A risk-averse individual would then be happy to exchange her uncertain lifetime income for its expected value. Of course,

[8] Some doubt on the realism of this conclusion is cast by the observation that "catastrophe bonds", covering risks seemingly uncorrelated with market risks, yield a significant risk premium; see Froot (1999).

this is unrealistic for reasons of moral hazard and enforceability, compounded by adverse selection.

First, having exchanged her lifetime income for its expected value, the individual would have no incentive to perform well and, in particular, could not convince the market that she will perform. She might then prefer to bear the risk and reap the benefits of effort, rather than selling at a loss to eliminate the uncertainty. Second, if the individual proves successful, she might be tempted to default on the insurance contract and keep for herself the excess of her income over the expected value; while she would insist on collecting the insurance if she fails. Thus she could not convince the market of her honesty, and might again prefer to bear the risk rather than selling at a loss. Because individuals differ in their unobservable motivations and honesty, an adverse selection problem arises.

A compulsory social insurance scheme avoids the problem of enforceability (taxes are legally binding—up to evasion); it does not avoid the moral hazard problem, but mitigates it by taking out the adverse selection element. Social security design thus calls for a second-best compromise between risk-sharing efficiency and productive efficiency.

Some characterization of the second-best compromise has been offered for alternative specifications of the source of moral hazard. *Ex post* taxes and transfers may distort *ex ante* decisions: about savings as in Varian (1980); about labour supply as in Eaton and Rosen (1980); about risk taking as in Sinn (1995)—to cite a few standard references. In Diamond, Helms and Mirrlees (1980), the labour-supply decision is made after the uncertainty has been resolved, but remains distorted by an income tax. In all these contributions, wages or labour productivity are exogenous. A related contribution, Drèze and Gollier (1993), treats wages as endogenous but subject to policy intervention, and studies the trade-off between *ex ante* insurance through restricted wage flexibility, and *ex post* productive efficiency impaired by unemployment at downward rigid wages. Clearly, realistic modelling of the social security design problem should include most of the elements listed above, and still others. For the long run, investment in education (see Remark 3 below), or norms and habit formation matter.[9] But modelling the diffused influence of the social security design on education, labour supply and effort in a lifetime framework with endogenous wage formation is hardly tractable.

Instead of modelling distortions explicitly, one can adopt a short-cut fruitfully exploited by Barro (1979) in a related context and, through (quadratic) convex functions of the transfers, capture the global deadweight costs of *ex post* redistribution—whether due to administrative costs, incen-

---

[9] Cf. Lindbeck *et al.* (1999).

tive effects on labour supply, effort, education ... or fraud. This leads to defining two reference wage levels, say y_0 and $y_1 > y_0$, and a policy whereby wages $y_s < y_0$ are subsidized and wages $y_s > y_1$ are taxed, while wages intermediate between y_0 and y_1 are neither taxed nor subsidized.[10]

The fact that the redistributive policy is costly explains why y_0 should be less than the mean wage $\overline{y}$ suggested by full insurance. From y_0 upward, the gain in risk-sharing efficiency is no longer sufficient to absorb the deadweight costs of redistribution, which comes to a halt. Yet, the positive transfers at the low end must be financed. Positive prudence ($u''' > 0$), implied by diminishing absolute risk aversion, makes it efficient to concentrate tax collection on the higher incomes, namely those exceeding y_1.[11]

A simple schedule of proportional subsidies or taxes would generate disposal incomes z_s defined by ($1 \geqslant \sigma > 0$, $1 > \tau \geqslant 0$):

$$\begin{aligned} z_s &= y_s + \sigma(y_0 - y_s) = (1 - \sigma)y_s + \sigma y_0 \quad \text{if } y_s < y_0 \\ &= y_s \quad \text{if } y_0 \leqslant y_s \leqslant y_1 \\ &= y_s - \tau(y_s - y_1) = (1 - \tau)y_s + \tau y_1 \quad \text{if } y_s > y_1. \end{aligned}$$

The reference wages should be such that the ratio of marginal utilities $u'(y_0)/u'(y_1)$ is equal to the ratio of the marginal cost of subsidies at y_0 to the marginal yield of taxes at y_1, a ratio exceeding unity under distorting taxation.[12] The absolute levels (y_0, y_1) should be such that the program is self-financing, at the second-best subsidy and tax rates; these rates would normally be increasing in the degree of risk aversion of the hypothetical wage earner and decreasing in the convexity of the deadweight cost functions. At a first (gross) approximation, these rates might be equal to the ratio of relative risk aversion R_R to the sum of R_R and the corresponding measure of curvature for the deadweight cost functions (defined separately for the subsidies and taxes). These guidelines are also indicative of the parameters that must be estimated if one wishes to translate qualitative prescriptions into

[10] See the appendix to Drèze (1999); the quadratic utility assumption used there is unnecessary for the characterization in the text. The non-linear feature also emerges in Varian (1980) or Drèze and Gollier (1993); it is not brought out in contributions that impose a linear tax structure.

[11] This is at variance with the results obtained by Mirrlees (1971) under different modelling assumptions; see also the discussion in Varian (1980).

[12] A marginal cost (resp. yield) equal to one plus (resp. minus) some "marginal cost of public funds" would lead to a ratio $u'(y_0)/u'(y_1)$ between 2 and 4; for plausible values of relative risk aversion (assumed constant), the ratio y_0/y_1 would fall between 0.7 and 0.9, implying a fairly high degree of *ex ante* insurance. See below, however, in particular footnote 17.

an actual social security design – an issue to which I return later in this section.

Implementation

The characterization just outlined is no more than an abstract guideline. It serves as a reminder of two principles: (i) risk aversion and absence of private markets for ensuring *ex ante* the uncertainties affecting future lifetime incomes provide a strong rationale for extensive transfers, aimed ideally at substantial *ex post* equality of incomes; (ii) administrative costs and moral hazard entail serious limitations on the effective prospects for such transfer policies; attention should be focused on how to bypass or minimize these limitations. The following remarks do not aim at exhausting the topic.

Remark 1. The form of redistributive transfers emerging from the preceding subsection is quite simple: negative (resp. positive) labour taxes on the difference between actual income y_s and a reference level y_0 (resp. $y_1 > y_0$). Implementing such transfers is a matter of routine for the positive labour taxes, but less familiar for the negative ones, up to the occasional (but spreading) recourse to employment subsidies. Negative (resp. positive) labour taxes should be understood relative to the actuarial value of associated benefits; thus, the negative taxes might simply take the form of reduced social insurance contribution on low wages, as suggested in Drèze and Sneessens (1994) and elsewhere. Negative labour taxes are described and strongly advocated in Phelps (1997, Ch. 8), to which I refer readers.[13] That proposal deserves more attention than it has received, as an alternative to minimum wages, earned-income tax credits, negative income taxes or participation incomes.[14]

Remark 2. In several of the contributions quoted above, the admissible tax structure is a combination of a proportional income or labour tax and a flat lump-sum transfer. A lump-sum transfer, unrelated to employment, is called "social dividend" by Meade (1989) or "unconditional basic income" by Van Parijs (1992); it was termed "demogrant" by George McGovern during the 1972 presidential campaign in the US. It is also advocated as "participation income" by Atkinson (1995a), who opens the door to restricting eligibility

[13] Phelps advocates non-proportional negative labour taxes, but that refinement introduces only a second-order modification.

[14] I generally share the view expressed by Phelps (1997) that negative labour taxes are in principle more appealing than these alternatives. See also Solow (1998) and Van der Linden (2000).

to those who work (possibly outside the market sphere) or are involuntarily unemployed. The idea is to let wages clear the labour market, while reforming the tax system to pay an unconditional basic income to all. This also frees some (like single mothers of young children)[15] from the need to work in order to survive, and provides correct incentives to work all around; indeed, wages should measure marginal productivity[16] and could be earned without giving up benefits. It lies beyond my purpose to discuss in detail these—or other still—alternative measures. To repeat, reconciling income protection (insurance) with full employment and incentives while minimizing deadweight costs is an elusive art; further investigations and experiments remain desirable.

Remark 3. It may be objected that, from a long-run viewpoint, the main distortion introduced by income protection policies comes from reduced incentives to invest in education. The point is well taken, but invites the comment that income protection, progressive taxation *and subsidized education* go hand in hand. As a general first principle, private decisions to invest in education are undistorted if the tax rate on the additional earnings associated with education is equal to the share of subsidies in the total investment cost. That principle remains valid regardless of whether the tax takes the form of reduced benefits (at the low end) or direct contributions (at the upper end). Its application may call for differentiating subsidy rates by types of education (e.g. vocational versus college, etc.).

Remark 4. My discussion of individual risks has been couched in terms of income uncertainty, meaning labour–income uncertainty. A similar reasoning could be applied to *ex ante* choices about different forms of contingent income protection, such as disability allowances versus unemployment benefits versus pension rights. The same principle of risk sharing would work in the direction of equalizing the levels of all forms of income protection (up to the ancillary qualification that benefits tied to special circumstances might be adjusted to special needs). This principle is advocated in e.g. Lindbeck *et al.* (1994). I concur.

---

[15]Cf. Blank (1996).

[16]Minimum wages may result in overemployment of those not entitled to unemployment or welfare benefits, if their marginal product falls short of disutility of work. On the other hand, it remains doubtful that competitive wage formation would emerge naturally under the proposed scheme.

Political Economy Considerations

The *ex ante* argument for social insurance introduced earlier rests on hypothetical reasoning, on a *gedankenexperiment.* But any program conceived today for the *ex ante* benefit of future generations could be voted down and repealed tomorrow, if it lacks *ex post* political support. There is a *time-consistency* issue. Thus, my hypothetical workers will know tomorrow where they stand in the wage distribution, and will evaluate the costs and benefits of the programme accordingly. To use a "median voter" illustration, if the reference wage y_1 were lower than the median, it would be in the interest of a majority to repeal the programme, or at least modify it so as to push y_1 up to the median. There is no logical difficulty in introducing into the formal analysis a *constraint* to the effect that, say, y_1 should be greater than or equal to the median wage. That would be an instructive exercise.

More realistically, it must be recognized that a social security system is the outcome of a political decision-making process, hopefully guided by economic reasoning and quantitative empirical research, but still reflecting in the end political leadership and bargaining. Economic analysis supplies political decision-makers with some guidelines on desirable policies. Translating such guidelines into quantified policy instruments raises a serious accuracy problem. We do not have a sufficiently convincing model of the economy, nor sufficiently accurate estimates of several key parameters (elasticities of labour supply and demand, risk tolerances etc.),[17] to propose a specific design with confidence that it is close to being *ex ante* second best. This is not to say that estimation is worthless. On the contrary, it says that experience should be sought and accumulated, so that we become less ignorant tomorrow than we are today. The quantitative design of a social insurance system is not yet reducible to economic calculation. It remains a major policy decision, that should be in the foreground of both public debate and scientific research.

IV. Individual Risks: the European Dimension

I mentioned in Section II that efficient risk sharing calls for pooling all risks and sharing them on the basis of risk tolerances. An efficient national social security system aims at doing precisely that, for the nationals covered by the system. The logic of global pooling would seem to plead for setting up an

[17]Numerical estimates of relative risk aversion are revealing of our uncertainties. Friend and Blume (1975), later confirmed by Szpiro (1986), suggest values between 1 and 2; more recently, Blake (1996) provides estimates ranging between 8 and 48 (*sic*!) as the size of financial portfolios varies between £35.000 and £500. In footnote 12 above, I use values of 4 and 8, for indicative purposes.

integrated social security system at the EU level. That conclusion is unwarranted, however: Section III concerns microeconomic risks, which are globally non-existent. There is no insurance gain from pooling non-existent risks.

Of course, it could be claimed that the reasoning of Section III should be applied directly to the European level. That is, the "reference group" mentioned in the introduction should be the EU, not some member state. The hypothetical worker, whose *ex ante* preferences are considered behind the veil of ignorance, would then be modelled as having equal probabilities of landing in the shoes of any worker *in the EU,* rather than any worker *in a given member state.* Such an approach calls for equalizing opportunities across the Union, in spite of the substantial differences in initial conditions among member states. From an analytical viewpoint, Section III would stand—with a broadened domain of application: it would suggest guidelines for a Union-wide social security system. In the short and medium run, this would result in substantial redistribution between member states—exactly the kind of transfers which the Union has rejected so far—limiting itself instead to the targeted programs covered by the so-called "structural funds". I do not discuss this broad political problem any further; see however, Section VI below.

There is another Union-wide issue related to individual risks, namely fiscal competition. The process of European integration carries the threat of depriving national member states of the ability to pursue autonomous social insurance policies. The argument to that effect is expounded, in particular, by Sinn (1990, 1998); see also Atkinson (1995b, Ch. 14). From the long-run viewpoint adopted here, it does not help to remark that labour mobility remains limited in Europe today. First, *marginal* mobility is the more relevant phenomenon, and it is rising. Second, Europe may be expected to attain a high degree of labour market integration before the end of the twenty-first century. The issue of fiscal competition should thus be faced squarely.

In an integrated labour market, real net earnings at a given skill level should be approximately equalized across locations. The implications of labour taxes or subsidies cannot be studied without modelling wage formation, as done for instance in Wildasin (1991, 1995). One significant feature of such models is the following: a member country implementing a social insurance scheme which redistributes incomes from the high-skilled to the low-skilled induces at equilibrium a more compressed wage distribution *in the Union as a whole,* thereby reducing the cost of implementing similar policies in other member countries. *There is an externality,* not captured by the first country, and apt to result in an insufficient degree of redistribution, at a non-cooperative (Nash) equilibrium. Superior equilibria require cooperation, either in the form of an integrated Union-wide social insurance scheme, or in the form of lump-sum or matching grants (some positive, some negative) from the Union to member states.

Sooner or later, the EU will have to face that thorny problem. Promoting efficiency on markets for private goods while accepting inefficiency in an area as important as social security would not make sense. In the meantime, specific labour taxes in individual member states are compatible with labour market integration—in the same way, *and subject to the same limitations* that, say, different mixes of direct and indirect taxes are compatible with economic integration. What matters to firms choosing their location is overall cost considerations. If one country adopts (relative to its neighbours) lower taxes on unskilled labour but higher taxes on skilled labour, it will attract firms which use more intensively unskilled labour. If the country's labour force is biased towards low skills, such a policy may be advisable; it is definitely compatible with equilibrium of an integrated labour market (with equalized net earnings at each skill level).

V. Macroeconomic Risks: National Analysis

The subject matter of Section III was the uncertainty faced by a future entrant to the labour market regarding her position in the wage distribution at the time of entry. A static analysis is broadly suitable for this topic. Moreover, the zero-sum property (through *ex ante* insurance) of the suggested policies leaves out the uncertainties affecting the overall wage distribution, i.e., the macroeconomic uncertainties, to which I now turn. The more interesting domestic issues concern risk sharing between capital and labour on the one hand, and between successive generations on the other hand. My concern is with how they affect the lifetime earnings of individuals.

The main channel of risk sharing between capital and labour in advanced economies is the government budget. Let a government tax capital incomes and labour incomes, to finance public goods or services which benefit all citizens independently of their actual tax liabilities. *Fluctuations in the labour share* are reduced by tax collections, thereby reducing the variability of real incomes (net of taxes but inclusive of public services). Given the size of the public sector in Europe, this channel is significant (though limited by fiscal competition for capital income taxation).

A more ambitious program of risk sharing between capital and labour would call for linking the tax rates on profits negatively, and the tax rates on labour incomes positively, to the labour share. With a labour share averaging, say, 70 percent of national income and oscillating between 65 and 75 percent, full stabilization of the after-tax labour share would result from adjustments in the tax rates on profits (resp. labour) not exceeding 14 (resp. 7) percentage points. A practical difficulty would come from the fact that the capital share does not consist solely of profits but also of real estate income, rents of all kinds, incomes of self-employed and the like, all of which are subject to distinct tax regimes. I have not pursued this matter, which is of limited long-run relevance given that the labour share is not trended. But I take this opportunity to raise the issue and invite further research.[18]

Intergenerational risk sharing is an interesting subject in its own right. A seminal paper by Gordon and Varian (1988) develops a very natural idea. Living generations cannot participate in bearing risks that will materialize beyond their own horizon. But they can share with future generations the risks (as yet pending) that will be resolved during their own lifetime. This simply calls for making positive or negative additions to the capital stock which they bequeath to future generations – positive if the realization is more favourable than expectations, negative otherwise, balanced on average (subject to a suitable risk premium). As this forward-shifting affects a growing number of future generations, the risks borne by each generation are spread increasingly thinly, and the associated risk premium falls *pari passu*. Asymptotically the risk premium could vanish.

Gordon and Varian illustrate the principle for an overlapping-generations economy where the (otherwise stationary) endowment of each generation is subject to a random shock. The successive shocks are i.i.d. with mean 0 and variance σ^2. If each shock is spread evenly over n generations, then in steady state each generation shifts forward a fraction $(n-1)/n$ of its own shock and bears a risk equal to the average shock of its own and of the preceding $n-1$ generations, which has mean 0 and variance σ^2/n (thanks to the independence assumption). Had the realizations been perfectly correlated, there would be no reduction in variance; realism lies somewhere in between.

Such a scheme requires public intervention, because private agents would find it difficult to finance a contemporaneous negative shock through bonds to be redeemed by their heirs.[19] It is accordingly doubtful that private capital markets support an efficient intergenerational sharing of risks—as confirmed by the surprisingly high-risk premia prevailing on these markets (the so-called "equity premium puzzle").[20] The public sector does engage in some intergenerational burden sharing, for instance when financing wars. Here again, a time-consistency problem arises: a generation experiencing a favourable outcome may decide to keep the benefits to itself, putting the

---

[18] In Drèze (1993), I considered the related issue of linking labour taxes to the rate of unemployment.

[19] In my home country Belgium, heirs have the standard option of rejecting an inheritance of negative net value.

[20] See e.g. Kocherlakota (1996). It may be remarked that models with an infinitely-lived representative agent implicitly assume full intergenerational risk sharing.

scheme in jeopardy.[21] I have not investigated this problem, which I bequeath to future researchers. It is an important problem, as we may be missing an opportunity to reduce risk premia significantly.

VI. International Sharing of Macroeconomic Risks

New Financial Instruments

Everywhere in the world, social security, where it exists, is a national responsibility. In federal political entities, some responsibilities are delegated to member states, but a form of mutual insurance is typically present at the federal level. Social security improves risk sharing among the citizens of a nation, but these bear in common the nation's macroeconomic uncertainties. To a limited extent, international capital markets enable individuals to diversify the risks of their non-human wealth. The extent is limited because many assets are non-marketed (real estate, unincorporated businesses, etc.). Where markets exist, few asset-holders own internationally diversified portfolios; see Baxter and Jehrman (1997).

As noted in Section II, international risk sharing could be achieved on a two-tier basis, with countries sharing macroeconomic risks among themselves in addition to organizing domestic social security. A simple way of implementing international risk sharing is described as follows: *each participating country issues perpetual bonds paying annual dividends proportional to the country's national income; countries exchange these bonds among themselves so as to end up with efficient portfolios.*[22] The principle is straightforward. The implementation raises a number of issues which are better understood in the light of the explicit formula for efficient portfolios corresponding to linear sharing rules.

Linear sharing rules are efficient if all participants in the exchange have the same, constant relative risk aversion. I am concerned here with risk sharing among member countries, the upper tier of a two-tier arrangement. In part for simplicity of a tentative first exploration, in part for lack of good reasons to proceed otherwise, I assume in what follows that aggregate relative risk aversion is identical for all member countries and constant. The efficient portfolios are then easily characterized. Each country should hold a fraction of the pooled risks equal to its share of expected aggregate income,

---

[21] Kimball (1988) discusses in greater depth a simple example where time consistency appears plausible.

[22] This suggestion was formulated in 1997 independently by Drèze (1999) and (in a somewhat different guise) by Obstfeld and Peri (1998). An independent rationale for issuing such bonds, and an analysis of some of their properties, appear in Shiller (1993), whose work has influenced my own thinking in this area.

and a (positive or negative) safe asset (indexed bond) amounting to its specific risk premium (the difference between the risk premium corresponding to its share of the pool and the risk premium defined by the covariance of its own national income with the aggregate). Thus, each country would exchange its entire national income Y^j against a share of the aggregate income Y, namely a share given by $B^j = \overline{Y}^j/\overline{Y}$, and a transfer A^j representing a positive or negative risk premium.[23]

The first and foremost conclusion to be drawn is that such an exchange raises at the national level the same moral hazard problem which stands in the way of private insurance of individual income risks. Having transferred the entirety of its national income to a pool, of which it owns a small share, a country would have no incentive to pursue growth-promoting economic policies. The efficient risk-sharing arrangement is not feasible, on this ground of moral hazard.

I do not think that we are ready to model formally the implications of mutual insurance for the choices of economic policies and ultimately for growth rates of national incomes. The analogy with individual expected utility maximization is too remote. The only benchmark that I can think of is the record of federal nations, like the US, Canada, Germany, etc. Federal tax-and-benefit systems imply a form of mutual insurance among the member states. A standard reference figure for the US is that 30–35 percent of idiosyncratic shocks affecting value added in an individual state are absorbed by the federal tax-and-benefit system. In other words, there is a mutual insurance scheme pooling 30–35 percent of state incomes.[24] The literature on fiscal federalism does not allude to a serious moral hazard problem tied to this level of insurance.[25] Instead, it is commonly claimed that a comparable degree of mutual insurance would be desirable in the European Monetary Union (EMU), to alleviate the impact of idiosyncratic shocks. I shall accordingly be pragmatic and regard as realistic an arrangement whereby European countries issue bonds indexed on their own national incomes, to the tune of 30 percent of these incomes, and exchange such instruments among each other.

[23] Whether a government should allocate the net yield of its portfolio to its overall budget, or earmark it for special purposes (like the social security budget), is for that government to decide, as part of its lower-tier risk allocation policy.

[24] This proportion characterizes gross risk pooling. Because the citizens of each state are affected by federal revenues and expenditures, which include 30 percent of the risks affecting all states, the extent of net risk pooling is lower (and not ascertained with full accuracy); see Fatás (1998) and references therein.

[25] See Persson and Tabellini (1996) for a positive discussion.

Open Questions

Even under the pragmatic arrangement just described, a number of questions must be faced.

(i) *Moral hazard* is a more pervasive issue than just growth policies. In an international context, exchange rates come in. One exception is the European Monetary Union with its single currency, the euro. I propose aiming at a first risk-sharing arrangement as described above among the members of the EMU only. Otherwise, special precautions have to be taken, to prevent a national government from manipulating exchange rates to its benefit.[26] Also, idiosyncratic shocks can be met through real adjustments – from price flexibility to factor mobility. Mutual insurance reduces the incentives for these adjustments, thereby creating another moral hazard problem.

(ii) *Trade*. Should the indexed perpetuities be tradable and quoted on stock exchanges? A first reaction is affirmative, on the grounds that the new assets would enlarge the opportunity sets of private traders. Shiller (1993) makes his case for the creation of such bonds entirely on the basis of trading (hedging) opportunities for households and corporations.[27]

There are some dangers, however. First, trading on financial markets would enable governments to float additional issues, thereby creating the moral hazard problem mentioned above. Second, market prices for assets indexed on a country's national income could be interpreted by voters as measuring a government's performance; or politicians might anticipate such an interpretation, with the same consequences. Welfare-enhancing policies like health care for the elderly, that do not affect national income positively, would then be penalized. And the excess volatility of financial markets would introduce noise into policy appraisal. All this is clearly undesirable.[28]

These objections do not apply to market trading of the pooled security paying dividends indexed on the EMU aggregate income. Such a market would enlarge individual opportunities; it would also enable national govern-

---

[26] Another moral hazard issue concerns income reporting. Clearly, common accounting standards should be followed by all participating countries, and should be monitored. This problem is largely resolved inside the European Union, which has adopted common accounting standards (SEC). Possibly, monitoring should be tightened. The problem is akin to that of monitoring accounts of firms traded on the stock exchange.

[27] Shiller's case rests in particular on the observation that marketed assets account for a very small fraction of a country's GNP: in the US, which has the most developed set of financial markets, that fraction is only 7 percent, according to Shiller (1998). Shiller (1993) also addresses the question as to why the proposed securities have not been issued by the private sector. I am not surprised either, given that indexed bonds are not issued privately; see Drèze (1992, Sec. 12) for an explanation.

[28] Obstfeld and Peri (1998) argue that countries would feel motivated to pursue growth-enhancing policies so as to increase the market price at which they could float new bonds. I am reasoning for initial trades, limited to 30 percent of GDP.

ments to reallocate their portfolios between that security and other assets, at market prices.

(iii) *Pricing.* If EMU member countries were to exchange among themselves securities indexed on national incomes and not traded on financial markets, at what prices should the exchange take place? This is a genuine issue, which invites further research. The purpose of the scheme is to organize efficient sharing of long-term income risks, not to smooth short-run fluctuations. The problem in defining initial prices is to estimate, for each country, the ratio of its expected long-term income to the EMU aggregate, and the covariance between these two variables. This problem must be solved now for the existing members of EMU, then again for each new member. There are basically two approaches to the problem.

The first analyses historical data in the framework of a theoretical model of asset pricing. This is done by Shiller (1993, Table 4.1), who calculates the present value (in 1990) of perpetual claims to national incomes of 54 countries, by means of the "log-linearised present value model" of Campbell and Shiller (1988).[29] His analysis could be updated and replicated for EMU member countries.[30] Shiller's 54 countries do not include East European candidates to E(M)U, however; owing to lack of data and to structural transformation, the approach is not directly applicable to these countries.

A second approach would recognize that there is convergence in the EU. The member countries whose per capita incomes were much lower than the EU average 30 or 40 years ago grew faster than the average.[31] This catching-up process is bound to slow down as convergence improves. Forecasting the ratio of expected income $\overline{Y}^j$ in country j to the EMU average $\overline{Y}$ amounts to forecasting country j''s convergence (or lack thereof). A general model of long-run convergence could be estimated from regional data for a set of countries, and applied to new entrants from Eastern Europe. In its simplest form, such a model might assert that the percentage gap between per capita income in country j and in EMU is expected to close down at some fixed annual rate (like 1.5 or 2 percent per annum). Risk sharing would then call for transferring to the Union 30 percent (in my proposal) of the difference between *actual* and *predicted* convergence. The analytics of a specific scheme remain to be worked out, as this approach extends the simple portfolio formula above to treat the ratio $\overline{Y}^j/\overline{Y}$ as time dependent.

The numbers suggest that a pragmatic approach might work.[32] For current

---

[29] This calculation includes a risk premium, which could be extracted to define the safe asset component of each country's efficient portfolio.

[30] Covariances with EMU aggregates will differ from covariances with world aggregates.

[31] The process is roughly comparable to that observed in the US over the past century; see Wildasin (1991, p. 767) and references therein.

[32] It may be remarked that the estimation difficulties mentioned in the text could not be eluded by private agents participating in stock-exchange trading.

members of EMU, convergence is already substantial, and national incomes display high correlations. Thus for eight of eleven EMU countries representing 97 percent of aggregate EMU income, the historical correlations (R^2) between the annual growth rates (per capita) of Y^j and Y range between 0.7 and 0.9; the ratios $\overline{Y}^j/\overline{Y}$ could thus be estimated more precisely than the numerators and denominator separately. Using current values, averaged over a few years, for Y^j and Y might provide a tolerable approximation to $\overline{Y}^j/\overline{Y}$ for these eight countries. This could be complemented by a generous treatment of the remaining three countries (Ireland, Luxembourg and Finland), which together account for a mere 3 percent of Y. Similarly, the aggregate income of Eastern European candidates is but a small percentage of the EMU aggregate.[33] The EMU members could thus provide insurance to these candidates at little exposure, and this would be desirable on two grounds: the uncertainty is high, and it is currently borne by the relatively poor.

VII. Conclusions

In this chapter, I have surveyed a number of issues related to economic and social security in the long run. Some general conclusions emerge, and a number of open problems stand out. I summarize these under two headings—individual then macroeconomic risks—distinguishing conclusions (C1, C2) and problems (P1, P2).

C1. *Individual risks*—a person's place in the wage distribution—loom large among the uncertainties surrounding the incomes of future entrants to the labour market. Income prospects for workers who will end up with low skills relative to market demand are a source of long-run concern in Europe. Efficient risk sharing calls for wage subsidies at the low end of the wage distribution financed by labour taxes at the upper end, or some equivalent thereof. Such a policy goes beyond a safety net geared to individual contingencies, though these two forms of insurance should be integrated in a consistent design with related levels of income protection. The main limitation to *ex ante* insurance comes from incentives (moral hazard) and other distortions created by *ex post* transfers. Full income equality, to implement *ex ante* risk-sharing efficiency, and absence of distorting taxes and transfers, to implement *ex post* productive efficiency, define the two poles between which a second-best compromise must be sought.

P1. The precise design of a second-best policy raises a number of

[33] It is about 5 percent, at official exchange rates, for the 10 leading candidates combined; and the insurance would be limited to 30 percent of GDP.

problems that remain on the research agenda. One set of problems concerns the choice of instruments (wage subsidies, minimum wages, tax credits, participation income etc.) apt to minimize distortions. A second set of problems concerns the estimation of parameters entering the definition of second-best policies (risk aversion, elasticity of labour supply, marginal costs of public transfers etc.). A third set of problems concerns political feasibility, in particular time consistency and fiscal competition in the EU. On all these fronts, there exist well-defined research challenges.

C2. *Macroeconomic risks* raise the issue of organizing efficient risk sharing along three dimensions: between capital and labour, across successive generations and among EU member countries. Given that the labour share is not trended, improved risk sharing between capital and labour concerns mostly temporary fluctuations, not the long-run uncertainties on which this chapter focuses. The prospects for improved intergenerational risk sharing are possibly more significant, though less well understood. They suggest a potential for lower risk premia. The international dimension is particularly significant for Eastern European countries aspiring to join the EU; their current income levels are relatively much lower, and there is substantial uncertainty about the rate at which their incomes will converge. A rather simple scheme would call for each EMU member country to issue bonds indexed on the country's nominal national income and to exchange these for a diversified portfolio of similar bonds issued by the other members. Such a scheme offers scope for improved international risk sharing. The extent to which this scheme could be implemented remains limited by moral hazard considerations.

P2. The positive and normative analysis of intergenerational risk sharing deserves research attention. So does the prospect for improved international risk sharing through exchange of bonds indexed on national incomes. One important open question is the desirability, or not, of trading such bonds on stock exchanges. In the absence of market prices, the initial valuation of such bonds requires quantitative investigation.

I have been treading uncharted territory here. It takes an occasion like this millennium special issue to allow oneself to air such speculative ideas. I am grateful for the opportunity.

References

Atkinson, A. B. (1995a), *Public Economics in Action*, Clarendon Press, Oxford.

Atkinson, A. B. (1995b), *Incomes and the Welfare State,* Cambridge University Press, Cambridge.

Atkinson, A. B. and Micklewright, J. (1992), *Economic Transformation in Eastern Europe and the Distribution of Income,* Cambridge University Press, Cambridge.

Barro, R. J. (1979), On the Determination of the Public Debt, *Journal of Political Economy 87*, 940–971.

Baxter, M. and Jehrman, U. J. (1997), The International Diversification Puzzle Is Worse Than You Think, *American Economic Review 87* (1), 170–180.

Blake, D. (1996), Efficiency, Risk Aversion and Portfolio Insurance: An Analysis of Financial Asset Portfolios Held by Investors in the United Kingdom, *Economic Journal 106*, 1175–1192.

Blank, R. M. (1996), Labor Markets and Public Assistance Programs, *NBER Reporter*, Fall, 11–13.

Campbell, J. Y. and Shiller, R. J. (1988), Stock Prices, Earnings, and Expected Dividends, *Journal of Finance 43*, 661–676.

Diamond, P. H., Helms, L. J. and Mirrlees, J. A. (1980), Optimal Taxation in a Stochastic Economy, *Journal of Public Economics 14*, 1–29.

Drèze, J. H. (1992), *Money and Uncertainty: Inflation, Interest, Indexation*, Banca d'Italia, Lezioni Paolo Baffi di Moneta e Finanza, Edizioni Dell' Elefante, Roma.

Drèze, J. H. (1993), Can Varying Social Insurance Contributions Improve Labour Market Efficiency? in A. B. Atkinson (ed.), *Alternatives to Capitalism: The Economics of Partnership*, Macmillan, London.

Drèze, J. H. (1999), Jobs and Economic Security in the 21st Century, in H. Löffer and E. W. Streissler (eds.), *Sozialpolitik und Ökologieprobleme der Zukunft*, 65–96, Österreichische Akademie der Wissenschaften, Wien.

Drèze, J. H. and Gollier, C. (1993), Risk Sharing on the Labour Market and Second-best Wage Rigidities, *European Economic Review 37*, 1457–1482.

Drèze, J. H. and Sneessens, H. (1994), Technical Development, Competition from Low-wage Economies and Low-skilled Unemployment, *Swedish Economic Policy Review 1*, 185–214.

Eaton, J. and Rosen, H. S. (1980), Labour Supply, Uncertainty, and Efficient Taxation, *Journal of Public Economics 14*, 357–364.

Eeckhoudt, L. and Gollier, C. (1992), *Risk: Evaluation, Management and Sharing*, Harvester Wheatsheaf, New York.

Fatás, A. (1998), Does EMU Need a Fiscal Federation?, *Economic Policy 26*, 163–192.

Feenstra, R. C. (1997), International Trade and Investment, *NBER Reporter*, Summer, 1–10.

Forni, M. and Reichlin, L. (1999), Risk and Potential Insurance in Europe, *European Economic Review 43*, 1237–1256.

Friend, I. and Blume, M. E. (1975), The Demand for Risky Assets, *American Economic Review 65*, 900–922.

Froot, K. A. (1999), The Market for Catastrophe Risk: A Clinical Examination, NBER Working Paper no. 7286, Cambridge, MA.

Gordon, R. H. and Varian, H. R. (1988), Intergenerational Risk Sharing, *Journal of Public Economics 37*, 185–202.

Harsanyi, J. R. (1953), Cardinal Utility in Welfare Economics and in the Theory of Risk Taking, *Journal of Political Economy 61*, 434–435.

Kimball, M. S. (1988), Farmers' Cooperatives as Behavior Toward Risk, *American Economic Review 78*, 224–232.

Kocherlakota, N. R. (1996), The Equity Premium: It's Still a Puzzle, *Journal of Economic Literature XXXIV*, 42–71.

Lindbeck, A., Molander, P., Persson, T., Sandmo, A., Swedenborg, B. and Thygesen, N.

(1994), *Turning Sweden Around*, MIT Press, Cambridge, MA.
Lindbeck, A., Nyberg, S. and Weibull, J. W. (1999), Social Norms and Economic Incentives in the Welfare State, *Quarterly Journal of Economics 114* (1), 1–35.
Meade, J. E. (1989), *Agathotopia: The Economics of Partnership*, Aberdeen University Press, Aberdeen.
Mirrlees, J. A. (1971), An Exploration in the Theory of Optimum Taxation, *Review of Economic Studies 38*, 175–208.
Obstfeld, M. and Peri, G. (1998), Regional Non-adjustment and Fiscal Policy, *Economic Policy 26*, 205–247.
Persson, T. and Tabellini, G. (1996), Fiscal Federal Constitutions: Risk Sharing and Redistribution, *Journal of Political Economy 104*, 979–1009.
Phelps, E. S. (1997), *Rewarding Work: How to Restore Participation and Self-Support to Free Enterprise*, Harvard University Press, Cambridge, MA.
Rawls, J. (1971), *A Theory of Justice*, Harvard University Press, Cambridge, MA.
Shiller, R. J. (1993), *Macro Markets: Creating Institutions for Managing Society's Largest Risks*, Clarendon Press, Oxford.
Shiller, R. J. (1998), Institutions for Managing Risks to Living Standards, *NBER Reporter*, Spring, 17–20.
Sinn, H. W. (1990), Tax Harmonization or Tax Competition in Europe, *European Economic Review 34*, 489–504.
Sinn, H. W. (1995), A Theory of the Welfare State, *Scandinavian Journal of Economics 97* (4), 495–526.
Sinn, H. W. (1998), European Integration and the Future of the Welfare State, *Swedish Economic Policy Review 5*, 113–132.
Solow, R. M. (1998), *Work and Welfare*, Princeton University Press, Princeton, NJ.
Szpiro, G. G. (1986), Measuring Risk Aversion: An alternative Approach, *Review of Economics and Statistics LXVIII*, 156–159.
Van der Linden, B. (2000), Fighting Unemployment Without Worsening Poverty: Basic Income versus Reductions of Social Security Contributions, forthcoming in W. Saverda, B. Nolan and C. Lucifora (eds.), *Policy Measures for Low Wage Employment in Europe*, Edward Elgar, Cheltenham.
Van Parijs, P. (1992), *Arguing for Basic Income*, Verso, London.
Varian, H. R. (1980), Redistributive Taxation as Social Insurance, *Journal of Public Economics 14*, 49–68.
Vickrey, W. (1945), Measuring Marginal Utility by Reactions to Risk, *Econometrica 13*, 215–236.
Wildasin, D. E. (1991), Income Redistribution in a Common Labour Market, *American Economic Review 81*, 757–774.
Wildasin, D. E. (1995), Factor Mobility, Risk and Redistribution in the Welfare State, *Scandinavian Journal of Economics 97* (4), 527–546.

2

Social Security Reform and National Wealth

*John Laitner**

I. Introduction

On the one hand, the US stock market has appreciated enormously since the early 1980s without inducing a boom in gross investment; see, for example, McGrattan (1998, Table 3). Such a scenario suggests rising demand for financial assets in the face of inelastic supply. On the other hand, commentators decry low and falling US private saving rates, and economists propose social security reform as one way of increasing private incentives for accumulating wealth; see e.g. Feldstein (1998), Feldstein and Samwick (1998), Kotlikoff (1998), Kotlikoff *et al.* (1998), and others. This chapter attempts to study the relationship of these ideas—the possible implications for policy reform of the recent patterns in financial markets. It asks, to what extent might social security reform merely raise the price of existing assets rather than induce new physical investment?

To study the issue, a neoclassical model is constructed which incorporates an inelastically supplied factor as well as elastically supplied reproducible capital. The inelastic factor arises from proprietary technologies: firms own portions of society's stock of technical know-how, and the know-how arises exogenously (see Section III). The price of existing assets can, in principle, change relative to the price of output without stimulating an increase or contraction in physical investment.[1]

While the analysis suggests that social security reform can indeed raise incentives for private saving, it shows a non-trivial part of the stimulus of reform dissipating in price inflation of the stocks of inelastic factors, leaving less growth in the national base of physical capital than would have otherwise occurred. Physical investment expands the economy's production possibilities set, of course, while price inflation of existing assets does not. Although the overall case for social security reform is not overturned, gains may be smaller than expected: for elimination of unfunded social security,

*I owe thanks to two referees for helpful suggestions on an earlier draft of this paper.

[1]An earlier version of this paper considered land as an inelastic factor as well; see e.g. Feldstein (1977) and Chamley and Wright (1987). Results were very similar.

the long-run increase in the physical capital stock is 35 per cent larger without inelastic factors than in the baseline case with such assets (see Section IV). The analysis also shows that asset-price inflation can affect intergenerational equity during an economy's course of adjustment after reform, with unanticipated capital gains perhaps mitigating welfare losses for cohorts relatively old at the moment of a policy change.

The organization of this chapter is as follows. Data on the magnitude of US private net worth relative to the stock of reproducible capital are examined in Section II, with the goal of beginning to assess the possible empirical fraction of wealth stemming from the capitalized value of inelastically supplied factors. In Section III we study the theoretical effects of social security reform in an overlapping generations model in which private firms own part of society's stock of technology. Section IV reports numerical analysis of a more detailed, realistic specification.

II. US Net Worth and Reproducible Capital

We begin by presenting US data on overall private net worth and on the replacement cost of the stock of reproducible capital. A comparison of the two provides a measure of the possible market value of what are later referred to as inelastically supplied assets.

Column 1 of Table 1 reports estimates of the replacement cost of the US domestic stock of plant and equipment, houses and business inventories. (The column excludes consumer durables and government capital.) The data come from the Bureau of Economic Analysis; see US Department of

Table 1. *US household net worth and the stock of reproducible capital (billions US dollars)*

Year	Private sector reproducible capital stock	Household and non-profit organization net worth	Column 2 ÷ GDP
1961	1,284.20	1,481.70	2.72
1966	1,699.30	1,945.20	2.47
1971	2,598.80	2,954.70	2.63
1976	4,641.60	4,401.70	2.42
1981	8,654.00	8,003.90	2.57
1986	11,038.20	12,321.90	2.79
1991	14,013.30	17,432.50	2.95
1996	17,803.00	24,704.40	3.22

Sources: Column 1: Table 1, "fixed private capital", US Department of Commerce (1997, p. 38); plus current dollar business inventories (see text). Column 2: US Federal Reserve Flow of Funds (http://www.bog.frb.fed.us)—Table B.100, row 43 less rows 6 and 7; minus L.106, rows 14 and 15; plus L.106, row 19; L.105, row 18; plus L.105, rows 7 and 10; minus L.108, row 15; plus L.108, rows 10 and 22; plus L.107, row 1; minus L.107, row 23.

Commerce (1997). Using resale prices and engineering life spans for equipment and structures, geometric depreciation and constant-dollar investment streams from the National Income and Product Accounts, the BEA derives stocks of domestic plant and equipment and residential structures from perpetual inventory equations.[2] Column 1 shows totals in current dollar units. It augments the BEA series with current-dollar business inventories from the *Economic Report of the President* (1997).

Column 2 of Table 1 provides estimates of US household and non-profit institution net worth from the Federal Reserve's Flow of Funds tables. To construct the column, we began with total household and non-profit institution net worth. We then excluded consumer durables and the equipment of non-profit institutions; we subtracted federal, state and local government debt and currency; we added total assets located in the US but owned by the rest of the world; and we subtract rest-of-world liabilities held in the US. Column 2 presents, therefore, the aggregate market value of domestic US businesses and residential houses, including the land on which the latter are situated and the value of intangible assets.

Figure 1 shows the difference between column 2 and column 1 as a percentage of column 1.[3] The wedge between market value and replacement cost has risen considerably in the last two decades. Nevertheless, except for low values in the late 1970s and exceptionally high values very recently, it arguably centres at 15–25 per cent. Here, the wedge is viewed as a measure of the capitalized value of inelastically supplied factors. To the extent that column 2 reflects investments in advertising or systematic R&D, our estimates overstate the significance of inelastic factors. On the other hand, the subsequent text includes reasons why our estimates may be understatements as well.

The ratio of column 2 to column 1 is a measure of Tobin's average q. It differs from series in Von Furstenberg (1977), Hayashi (1982), Blanchard *et al.* (1993), and Poterba and Samwick (1995) in its data sources; see also Hall (1993). It also differs in composition: the other series consider non-financial corporations, whereas our data cover all corporate and non-corporate business and include private residences. Our q tends to be somewhat higher than those in the preceding chapters. In column 6 of Hayashi (1982, Table I), for instance, average q varies from 0.842 in 1960, to 1.116 in 1966, to 0.623 in 1976. The extended sequence in Blanchard *et al.* (1993, Figure 1) dips to about 0.4 in 1980, before rising to about 0.9 in 1990. In Poterba and Samwick (1995, Table 2), it rises from 0.9 to almost 1.5 by 1995. In our table, the ratio of column 2 to column 1 is 1.17 for 1990 and 1.3 for 1995.

---

[2]For a discussion and comparisons with older data, see Katz and Herman (1997) and Fraumeni (1997).

[3]Although, to save space, Table 1 lists data at five-year intervals, Figure 1 uses annual data.

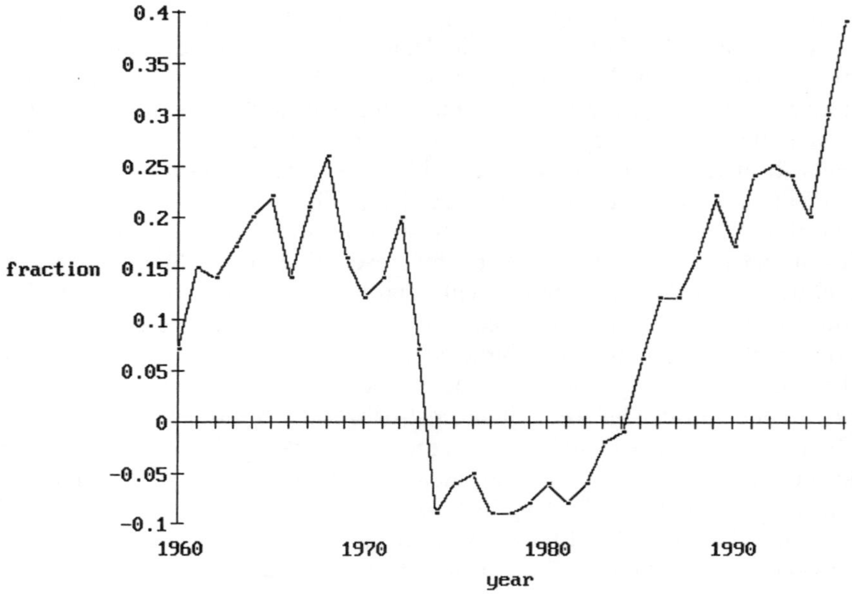

Fig. 1. Net worth less reproducible capital as a fraction of the latter (Table 1, column 2 – column 1)/column 1

Since our chapter lacks Hayashi's (1982) sophisticated treatment of taxes, our assessment of inelastically supplied assets tends to be understated. Hayashi's theoretical model implies a steady-state value for average q of $h = \psi_I \cdot (1 - k - z) + a$, with $\psi_I \in (0, 1]$ the marginal yield of new capital from investment spending, k the investment tax credit, z the present value of current and future tax deductions on new investment, and a the present value of corresponding deductions on past investments. As Hayashi's z considerably exceeds a for every year in his table, and $k > 0$, his data suggest $h < 1$; thus, since Figure 1 uses $q - 1$ but a more detailed treatment of taxes would call for $q - h$, our approach tends to lead to understatements.

III. Private Ownership of Technology

In modelling a possible explanation for Figure 1, we assume (i) that improvements in technology arise exogenously and (ii) that individual firms control new technologies for a time. For concreteness, assume firms accomplish this control with patents. Although in practice some innovations flow from costly, systematic R&D efforts (as in the pharmaceutical industry), in other cases inspired (or lucky) individuals or companies seem to effect change with modest inputs of resources, sometimes amassing very large payoffs (e.g. Henry Ford or Steve Jobs). Our model incorporates the second description. We assume that companies, rather than individuals, receive inspiration and obtain the patents. The capitalized value of patents constitutes an asset in addition to reproducible physical capital. Since inspiration is exogenous, changes in the value of existing patents do not affect the supply of new patents. In support of our assumptions, note that if common stock prices in the US reflect the value of patents, and if (valuable) patents routinely emerge from systematic R&D efforts, the run-up in stock prices over the last two decades should have induced a research boom. Arguably that has not happened; see, for instance, National Science Foundation (1996, Chart 6, p. 17), where the US trend in R&D spending as a fraction of GDP was slightly negative over the period 1960–1996.[4]

The Model

We use an overlapping generations framework. Households live two periods, each inelastically supplies one unit of labour in its first period of life and no labour in its second period, and there are no inheritances or bequests. If $C(t, 1)$ is first-period-of-life consumption for a household born at t, and $C(t, 2)$ is its second-period-of-life consumption, the household's lifetime utility is

$$(1-\theta)\cdot \ln(C(t, 1)) + \theta \cdot \ln(C(t, 2)). \tag{1}$$

The corresponding lifetime budget constraint is

$$C(t, 1) + \frac{C(t, 2)}{R(t+1)} \leqslant (1-\sigma)\cdot W(t) + \frac{\sigma \cdot W(t+1)}{R(t+1)}, \tag{2}$$

where the consumption good is the numeraire of the economy, $W(t)$ is the time-t wage, and $R(t+1)$ is one plus the interest rate on savings carried from t to $t+1$. There is a proportional social security tax at rate σ on wages. The social security system is unfunded, with tax revenues immediately passed to elderly households as retirement benefits. There is no population growth.

For future reference, let $S(t)$ be savings in youth for a household born at t. Provided households maximize utility, treating factor prices as given, $S(t)$

[4]Note that the trend is partly due to falling government R&D spending on defence and space exploration. Non-federal R&D/GDP rose from 0.01 to about 0.015 over the period.

equals $(1-\sigma)\cdot W(t)$ minus first-period-of-life consumption, which is $(1-\theta)$ times the RHS of (2); thus,

$$S(t) = (1-\sigma)\cdot\theta\cdot W(t) - \frac{\sigma\cdot(1-\theta)\cdot W(t+1)}{R(t+1)}. \tag{3}$$

Turning to production, firms build and finance reproducible physical capital at $t-1$ to use at t. For simplicity, physical capital fully depreciates after one period of use. Think of each firm as issuing one-period bonds to finance its physical investments at $t-1$. Each firm also has equity shares. Firms own part of the available technology, through patents, and ownership generates fees. A firm uses its fees to pay dividends to its shareholders. The capitalized value of future fees determines the market price of the firm's equity shares. The aggregate value of equity shares after payment of time-t dividends is $E(t)$.

The value of equity shares reflects the value of both current and future patents. We assume agents accurately anticipate the overall flow of new patents (which is non-stochastic). Think of a fixed universe of firms. Even if agents do not know which firm will innovate next period, they can secure a share of all future dividends by holding a diversified portfolio.

Suppose a firm has an inspiration which improves society's time-t stock of knowledge by the amount Δ. Assume there are many small, price-taking producers of output, and that an inventor licenses his discovery to all who wish to use it. With the new invention, a producer with reproducible capital K, labour L, and public-domain technology a can increase its output, and hence its revenues, from $a\cdot K^{\alpha}\cdot L^{1-\alpha}$ to $(a+\Delta)\cdot K^{\alpha}\cdot L^{1-\alpha}$. We assume the licenser appropriates all of the licensee's benefits, $\Delta\cdot K^{\alpha}\cdot L^{1-\alpha}$. In view of this the producer chooses its K and L to maximize

$$a\cdot K^{\alpha}\cdot L^{1-\alpha} - R(t)\cdot K - W(t)\cdot L.$$

Let $A(t)$ register society's overall technology at time t, with part $B(t)$ privately owned, and $A(t)-B(t)$ in the public domain. The aggregate production function is

$$Q(t) = A(t)\cdot K(t)^{\alpha}\cdot L(t)^{1-\alpha}, \quad \alpha\in(0,1). \tag{4}$$

For simplicity, normalize

$$L(t) = 1 \quad \text{all } t.$$

Competition and profit maximization yield

$$R(t) = [A(t) - B(t)] \cdot \alpha \cdot K(t)^{\alpha - 1}, \tag{5}$$

$$W(t) = [A(t) - B(t)] \cdot (1 - \alpha) \cdot K(t)^{\alpha}. \tag{6}$$

Aggregate returns to patent owners are

$$B(t) \cdot K(t)^{\alpha}.$$

Assume that overall technological progress occurs deterministically with $A(t) = g^t$, $g > 1$, that all new ideas are initially owned by firms, and that ideas drift at rate δ into the public domain, so that

$$B(t+1) = (1 - \delta) \cdot B(t) + A(t+1) - A(t), \quad \delta \in (0, 1). \tag{7}$$

Then

$$B(t+1) = (1 - \delta) \cdot B(t) + (g - 1) \cdot g^t.$$

Back substituting,

$$B(t) = B \cdot g^t \quad \text{with} \quad B \equiv \frac{(g-1)/g}{1 - [(1-\delta)/g]}. \tag{8}$$

Definition 1. An "equilibrium" is a sequence

$$\{Q(t), K(t), E(t), C(t, 1), C(t, 2), S(t), W(t), R(t)\}_{t \geqslant 0}$$

of positive values consistent with household utility maximization (i.e., (3)), with (4)–(8), with

$$K(t+1) + E(t) = S(t), \quad t \geqslant 0, \tag{9}$$

and with

$$E(t) = \frac{B(t+1) \cdot K(t+1)^{\alpha}}{R(t+1)} + \frac{E(t+1)}{R(t+1)}, \quad t \geqslant 0. \tag{10}$$

The RHS of (9) is the net worth which the household sector carries from t to $t+1$; the LHS sums the bonds and equities of the business sector. Equation (10) requires that equities and physical capital pay the same rate of return at all times after 0.

Definition 2. A "steady-state equilibrium" is an equilibrium with $R(t)$ constant all t

Steady-state Equilibrium

Our long-run analysis focuses on steady-state equilibria. For a constant interest rate, (5) requires $K(t+1) = x \cdot K(t)$ with $x \equiv g^{1/(1-\alpha)}$. For a steady state, the aggregate production function then implies that $Q(t)$ has a constant growth factor x, (6) shows the same is true for the wage, (3) shows it holds for $S(t)$, and (9) shows it holds for $E(t)$. Summarizing:

Proposition 1. *In any steady state, $Q(t)$, $K(t)$, $C(t, 1)$, $C(t, 2)$, $S(t)$, $W(t)$, and $E(t)$ have a constant growth factor $x \equiv g^{1/(1-\alpha)}$.*

Proposition 1 shows that transformed variables $k(t) \equiv K(t)/x^t$ and $e(t) \equiv E(t)/x^t$ will be constant in an SSE. Letting asterisks denote steady–state values, (10) implies

$$R^* > x \quad \text{and} \quad e^* = \frac{x \cdot B \cdot [k^*]^\alpha}{R^* - x}. \tag{11}$$

The first is necessary for finite equity values (infinite values would exceed the carrying capacity of private portfolios). From (9),

$$x \cdot k^* + \frac{x \cdot B \cdot [k^*]^\alpha}{R^* - x} = (1-\sigma) \cdot \theta \cdot (1-\alpha) \cdot (1-B) \cdot [k^*]^\alpha - \frac{\sigma \cdot (1-\theta) \cdot (1-\alpha) \cdot x \cdot k^*}{\alpha}.$$

Moving the last term to the LHS, and dividing through by k^* and then R^*, we have

$$\frac{x}{R^*} + \frac{x \cdot B}{\alpha \cdot (1-B) \cdot (R^* - x)} + \frac{\sigma \cdot (1-\theta) \cdot (1-\alpha) \cdot x}{\alpha \cdot R^*} = \frac{(1-\sigma) \cdot \theta \cdot (1-\alpha)}{\alpha}. \tag{12}$$

Figure 2 shows that (12) has one, and only one, root $R^* > x$.

Thus, we have:

Proposition 2. *The model has a unique steady-state equilibrium. Equation*

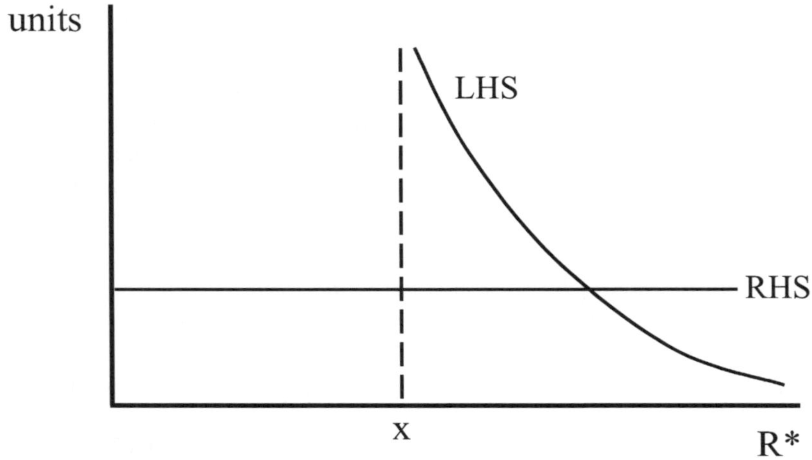

Fig. 2. The LHS and RHS of equation (12) for $R^* > x$

(12) determines the unique $R^* > x$. Given R^*, (5) implies k^*, (6) implies $W(t)$, (11) implies e^*, and (4) implies $Q(t)$.

Turning to dynamics, we can reduce our model to two first-order difference equations in $k(t)$ and $e(t)$. The former is a predetermined variable, but $e(t)$ is a jump variable. We have:

Proposition 3. *The local phase diagram surrounding the model's steady-state equilibrium is a saddle point—as required for stability and determinacy.*

The proof of Proposition 3 is omitted from this paper but is available from the author on request.

Social Security Reform

We now show that $E(t)$ may tend to reduce the absolute and relative impact of social security reform on an economy's steady–state stock of physical capital.

Equities crowd out the economy's accumulation of reproducible capital:

Proposition 4. *A larger B leads to a larger R^* and a smaller k^*.*

Proposition 4 follows from (12), Figure 2 and (5).

An increase in σ reduces life–cycle saving, raising R^* and lowering k^*:

Proposition 5. *Raising σ raises R^* and lowers k^*.*

This also follows from (12), Figure 2, and (5).

More subtly, having $B > 0$ as opposed to $B = 0$ lowers the long–run responsiveness of the economy's physical capital stock to changes in σ: reductions (increases) in σ lose part of their force as they inflate (deflate) the price of equities.

Proposition 6. *Having $B > 0$ makes the steady-state elasticities for R^* and k^* with respect to σ smaller in absolute value than when $B = 0$.*

To prove Proposition 6, differentiate (12) with respect to $\ln(\sigma)$, yielding

$$\frac{x}{R^*} \cdot \frac{\mathrm{d}\ln(R^*)}{\mathrm{d}\ln(\sigma)} + \frac{x \cdot B}{\alpha \cdot (1-B) \cdot (R^* - x)} \cdot \frac{R^*}{R^* - x} \cdot \frac{\mathrm{d}\ln(R^*)}{\mathrm{d}\ln(\sigma)} + \frac{\sigma \cdot (1-\theta) \cdot (1-\alpha) \cdot x}{\alpha \cdot R^*} \cdot \frac{\mathrm{d}\ln(R^*)}{\mathrm{d}\ln(\sigma)} = \frac{\sigma \cdot (1-\theta) \cdot (1-\alpha) \cdot x}{\alpha \cdot R^*} + \frac{\sigma \cdot \theta \cdot (1-\alpha)}{\alpha}.$$

Collecting terms,

$$\frac{\mathrm{d}\ln(R^*)}{\mathrm{d}\ln(\sigma)} = \frac{\dfrac{\sigma \cdot (1-\theta) \cdot (1-\alpha) \cdot x}{\alpha \cdot R^*} + \dfrac{\sigma \cdot \theta \cdot (1-\alpha)}{\alpha}}{\dfrac{x}{R^*} + \dfrac{x \cdot B}{\alpha \cdot (1-B) \cdot (R^* - x)} \cdot \dfrac{R^*}{R^* - x} + \dfrac{\sigma \cdot (1-\theta) \cdot (1-\alpha) \cdot x}{\alpha \cdot R^*}} > 0. \quad (13)$$

Since $R^*/(R^* - x) > 1$, the denominator of (13) is larger than the LHS of (12)—hence than the RHS of (12). So,

$$\frac{\mathrm{d}\ln(R^*)}{\mathrm{d}\ln(\sigma)} \leqslant \frac{\dfrac{\sigma \cdot (1-\theta) \cdot (1-\alpha) \cdot x}{\alpha \cdot R^*} + \dfrac{\sigma \cdot \theta \cdot (1-\alpha)}{\alpha}}{\dfrac{(1-\sigma) \cdot \theta \cdot (1-\alpha)}{\alpha}}. \quad (14)$$

If $B = 0$, we have equality in (14) (e.g. the second term of the denominator in (13) entirely disappears); when $B > 0$, we have strict inequality in (14). In the latter case, it is also true that the RHS of (14) is lower, because, as Proposition 4 shows, R^* is higher. Proposition 6 follows.

Propositions 4–6 show that results from reforming an unfunded social security system might be disappointing to adherents of conventional models. Suppose we permanently reduce σ by enough to raise the steady-state capital stock for the model without inelastic assets by \$1. Consider the same percentage change in σ for the specification in this section. By Proposition 6, the percentage change in k^* will be lower with equities than without; by Proposition 4, the magnitude of k^* with equities will be lower as well. In the end, the absolute change in k^* for a model with equities will be a fraction of \$1.

Transitions

Inelastically supplied assets can affect intergenerational equity during the transition to a new steady state. Consider a surprise, permanent reduction in σ at time 0, supposing the economy had attained the steady–state equilibrium consistent with its old σ prior to time 0. Figure 3 presents a phase diagram. The steady state before reform is (k_0^*, e_0^*); after reform it is (k^*, e^*). Proposition 3 guarantees a saddle point about (k^*, e^*), with a positively sloped stable arm. As government announces reform, we must vertically jump to this arm, subsequently converging to the new steady state. The jump must be upward: the shape of the stable arm implies that all future

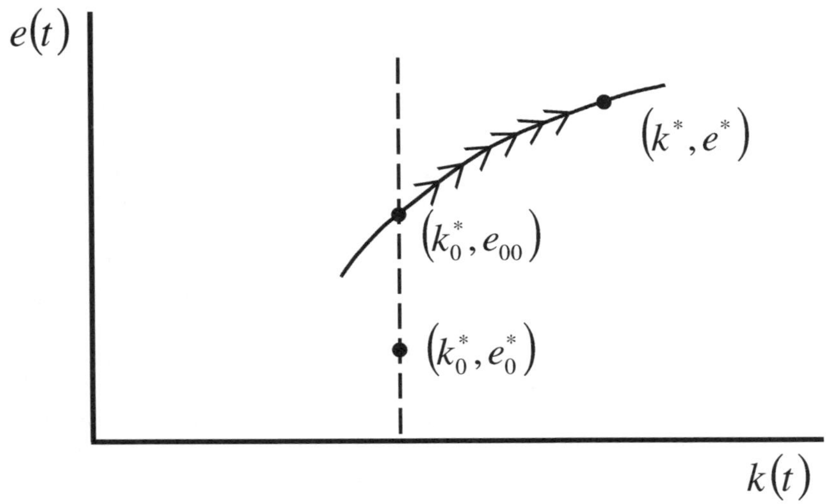

Fig. 3. The transition of $k(t)$ and $e(t)$ following a reduction in σ at $t = 0$

fees on proprietary technologies will be higher and all future interest rates lower than at the old steady state; thus, the present value of fees must rise after reform. Retired households at time 0 have paid social security taxes under the old system but now find their benefits reduced; however, the skip from e_0^* to e_{00} gives the elderly unanticipated capital gains which, at least in part, offset their lost benefits.

The details of the political process through which social security reform is carried out will be important. Since our model incorporates rational expectations, the jump in $e(t)$ occurs as soon as private agents foresee reform. If legislators move slowly, or if they choose phased reforms, a cohort would conceivably enjoy price appreciation on its equities but die before government actually implemented reductions in social security benefits. A subsequent cohort would then endure diminished retirement benefits yet miss a reform–induced jump in the price of its equities.

IV. Simulations

We now turn to quantitative results. We elabourate the model of Section III so that households have multiperiod life spans and reproducible capital has a depreciation rate under 100 percent. We study the effect of social security reform on the economy's steady-state equilibrium, and we examine transition paths between steady states.

Framework

Households begin with a 21-year-old male and female. The male and female retire at age 63 and die after age 78. Time is discrete. Life spans are deterministic. As there will be no population growth, without loss of generality think of the economy as always having 1 household of each age 21, . . . , 78.

Men and women inelastically supply labour until retirement. Their "effective" labour supplies rise with age (from experiential human capital), mimicking empirical age/earnings profiles from the US Department of Health and Human Services (1993, Table 4B5–6). We weight earnings for men and women by numbers in each age/sex category, convert household age/earnings profiles for 1970, 1980 and 1990 to 1992 dollars with the GDP deflator, and average for each age over the three years. Table 2 reports our figures. If $L(s)$ is household labour (with experience) at age s, the table gives values of $W(1992) \cdot L(s)$.

A household born at t maximizes

Table 2. *Household earnings*

Age	Earnings	Age	Earnings	Age	Earnings
21	8,428.0	41	31,238.0	61	31,180.0
22	11,273.0	42	31,982.0	62	29,022.0
23	12,917.0	43	32,451.0	63	11,779.0
24	14,592.0	44	32,927.0	64	11,779.0
25	16,299.0	45	33,409.0	65	11,779.0
26	18,038.0	46	33,897.0	66	11,779.0
27	19,811.0	47	34,392.0	67	11,779.0
28	20,705.0	48	34,504.0	68	11,779.0
29	21,615.0	49	34,615.0	69	11,779.0
30	22,541.0	50	34,724.0	70	11,779.0
31	23,483.0	51	34,833.0	71	11,779.0
32	24,442.0	52	34,940.0	72	11,779.0
33	25,203.0	53	34,770.0	73	11,779.0
34	25,977.0	54	34,594.0	74	11,779.0
35	26,763.0	55	34,410.0	75	11,779.0
36	27,563.0	56	34,219.0	76	11,779.0
37	28,376.0	57	34,022.0	77	11,779.0
38	29,075.0	58	33,530.0	78	11,779.0
39	29,784.0	59	33,025.0	79	0.0
40	30,505.0	60	32,507.0	80	0.0

Source: See text.

$$\sum_{s=21}^{78} u(C(t, s), s), \tag{15}$$

where

$$u(C, s) = \beta^s \cdot \frac{C^\gamma}{\gamma}, \qquad \gamma < 1, \beta > 0.$$

As in Auerbach and Kotlikoff's (1987) and Kotlikoff's (1998) "baseline case", we set $\gamma = -3$. Letting $NW(t, s)$ be the net worth the household carries to age s, σ the (proportional) social security tax, $SSB(t, s)$ social security benefits, τ the (proportional) income tax and $R(t)$ one plus the after–tax interest rate, the household's budget constraint is

$$NW(t, s+1) = R(t+s+1) \cdot NW(t, s) + W(t+s) \cdot (1 - \tau - \sigma) \cdot L(s) + SSB(t, s) - C(t, s), \tag{16}$$

$$NW(t, 21) = 0 \quad \text{and} \quad NW(t, 79) = 0.$$

Bankruptcy laws leave creditors unwilling to make loans to households with negative net worth, so

$$NW(t, s) \geqslant 0 \quad \text{all} \quad s. \tag{17}$$

Social security benefits net of income taxes—assuming half of benefits are taxable—are split among retirees in proportion to their final earnings:

$$SSB(t, s) = \sum_{v=21}^{62} \sigma \cdot W(t+s) \cdot L(v) \cdot \frac{W(t+62)}{\sum_{v=63}^{78} W(t+s-v+62)} \cdot (1 - 0.5 \cdot \tau),$$

$$s = 63, \ldots, 78.$$

Our social security tax equals the average over 1970, 1980 and 1990 of US OASI tax rates on employers and individuals: $\sigma = 0.0918$.

There is a Cobb–Douglas aggregate production function with capital's share $\alpha = 0.25$ and labour's share 0.75. It takes one year to build new reproducible capital. Calculations from US Department of Commerce (1997) data suggest a depreciation rate for reproducible capital of $\mu = 0.0389$. We set the economy's steady-state growth factor $x = 1.01$. There is proportional tax τ on all factor payments and rents. The average of US federal, state and local tax collections as a percent of NNP for 1970, 1980 and 1990 gives $\tau = 0.2648$. We treat all taxes other than social security as user fees, so the simulations below do not change τ after social security reform.

Letting $W(t)$ be the gross-of-tax wage, $R(t)$ be one plus the net-of-tax interest rate, and

$$L \equiv \sum_{v=21}^{62} L(v), \tag{18}$$

competitive factor pricing yields

$$W(t) = (1 - B) \cdot (1 - \alpha) \cdot A(t) \cdot K(t)^{\alpha} \cdot L^{-\alpha}, \tag{19}$$

$$R(t) = 1 + (1 - \tau) \cdot [(1 - B) \cdot \alpha \cdot A(t) \cdot K(t)^{\alpha - 1} \cdot L^{1-\alpha} - \mu], \tag{20}$$

with B as in Section III. Also as in Section III, $E(t)$ stands for the aggregate value of equities at the end of period t, and

$$E(t) = \frac{(1-\tau) \cdot B \cdot A(t+1) \cdot K(t+1)^{\alpha} \cdot L^{1-\alpha}}{R(t+1)} + \frac{E(t+1)}{R(t+1)}. \tag{21}$$

The reproducible capital stock which households finance to period $t+1$ is $K(t+1)$.

Steady States

Table 3 presents steady-state equilibria. Given Figure 1, our baseline case assumes a steady-state ratio

$$\frac{E(t)}{K(t+1)} = 0.2. \tag{22}$$

To calibrate subjective discount factor β, we measure household consumption $C(t, s)$ from the 1984 Consumer Expenditure Survey and $C(t, s+13)$ from the 1997 Consumer Expenditure Survey.[5] The average rate of growth for $s = 22, \ldots, 53$ is 2.56 percent per year.

Our computations are as follows. First, we derive a steady-state equilibrium for our baseline case, solving simultaneously for R^*, B, and β which satisfy the conditions for a steady state, (22), and

$$[R^* \cdot \beta]^{1/(1-\gamma)} = 1.0256, \tag{23}$$

which comes from our consumption survey data and the fact that first–order conditions for an unconstrained household imply

$$C(t, s+1) = [R^* \cdot \beta]^{1/(1-\gamma)} \cdot C(t, s). \tag{24}$$

(Despite the approximation implicit in assuming non-binding constraints for (23), in all other computations we use Mariger's (1986) algorithm to solve (15) with liquidity constraint (17).) The steady-state wage, Table 2 and (18) determine the aggregate labour supply at time 0. All subsequent computations keep the same β and the same total labour supply. Second, holding B

[5]We used 1984 and 1997 Consumer Expenditure Survey consumption-by-age tables from http://stats.bls.gov/csxhome.htm. For both years, we classified survey consumption components into National Income and Products Account categories. Component amounts were normalized to the NIPA totals. For owner–occupied housing, we imputed service flows for different age groups by apportioning the NIPA total flow of services from houses in proportion to average housing market values reported in the survey. We then extrapolated from the survey age categories to yearly ages, and converted to 1992 dollars with the NIPA consumption price deflator.

Table 3. *Steady-state simulations*

	Ratio $\frac{E^*}{x \cdot K^*}$:					
Variable[a]	0.01	0.10	0.20	0.30	0.40	0.50
			Prior to social security reform			
R	1.043	1.048	1.053	1.058	1.063	1.067
$E(-1)$	0.007	0.649	1.174	1.602	1.954	2.246
$K(0)$	7.222	6.490	5.869	5.340	4.886	4.492
$NW(0)$	7.229	7.139	7.043	6.942	6.840	6.738
$Q(0)$	2.808	2.734	2.666	2.604	2.547	2.494
			After social security reform			
R	1.025	1.031	1.037	1.041	1.046	1.050
$E(-1)$	0.017	1.255	2.043	2.612	3.043	3.376
$K(0)$	10.643	9.047	7.952	7.101	6.407	5.825
$NW(0)$	10.660	10.302	9.995	9.713	9.450	9.201
$Q(0)$	3.094	2.971	2.877	2.797	2.726	2.661
			Percentage change due to reform			
E	140.844	93.418	74.078	63.031	55.682	50.318
K	47.368	39.391	35.488	32.981	31.142	29.668
NW	47.461	44.303	41.920	39.916	38.153	36.551

[a] $NW(0)$ is aggregrate net worth carried into period 0: $NW(0) = E(-1) + K(0)$.

fixed as well, we solve for a new steady-state R^* with the social security tax set to 0. For other columns in Table 3, with $\sigma = 0.0918$ we solve for R^* and B from the steady–state conditions and the appropriate version of (22); then, keeping the same B, we solve for a new R^* with $\sigma = 0$.

Column 3 at the top of Table 3 reports our baseline simulation. The net worth to GDP ratio for the economy is 2.64, roughly at the average for Table 1.[6] The net-of-tax steady-state interest rate is 5.3 percent, and the gross rate is 7.2 percent. The latter compares, for example, with 6.7 percent in Auerbach and Kotlikoff's (1987, Table 5.1) base case. The fraction of output flowing to patent owners is $B = 2.6$ percent. Liquidity constraint (17) binds for ages 21–26. Household net worth rises to a peak of \$411,900 at age 63. The values of B for columns 1–6, respectively, are 0.000, 0.012, 0.025, 0.039., 0.054 and 0.069.

[6]In general the life-cycle model has trouble accounting for empirical wealth levels; see e.g. Kotlikoff and Summers (1981), Hubbard and Judd (1987), Auerbach and Kotlikoff (1987, Ch. 9), Modigliani (1988), Kotlikoff (1988) and Laitner (1992). To meet this difficulty, we assume relatively long retirement spans, constraint (17), no public debt and no special provision for children's consumption.

As Proposition 4 predicts, patent wealth crowds out reproducible capital. At the top of Table 3, as we move from the negligible $E^*/(x \cdot K^*)$ ratio of column 1 to column 2's ratio of 0.10, K^* falls more than 10 percent. As we raise the equity ratio to 0.20, K^* falls another 8–9 percent. At a ratio of 0.50, K^* has fallen almost 40 percent from column 1.

Eliminating social security yields percentage increases in steady–state private net worth of 37–47 percent in columns 1–6. This is somewhat less than Kotlikoff's (1998, Fig. 7.6) 57 percent increase—presumably because Kotlikoff's model has an elastic labour supply, with work hours expanding 6 percent after social security taxes on earnings fall. However, each dollar's change in Kotlikoff's net worth increases the national stock of reproducible capital by one dollar. For columns 2–6 of Table 3, in contrast, 13–24 percent of the increase dissipates into inflation of equity prices. Consistent with Proposition 6, Table 3 shows that social security reform yields higher percentage gains in steady-state reproducible capital for cases in which inelastically supplied assets have a smaller role. In column 1, eliminating social security raises the steady-state capital stock by 47 percent; in column 2, the increase in capital is 39 percent; in column 3 it is 35 percent; and in column 6 it is less than 30 percent. Price appreciation on inelastically supplied assets greatly exceeds expansion in the stock of reproducible capital in all cases. Combining the impacts of Propositions 4 and 6, in column 1 the increase in k^* after reform is 3.4 units, whereas it is just 2.1 units in column 3—only 62 percent as great.

Transitions

An important practical obstacle to social security reform is that some birth cohorts may be hurt during the transition to the steady state of a new regime, even if many others are helped. We now examine the transitions of our model using Laitner's (1990) methodology based on linearizations, or variational equations. Even with saddle-point dynamics, the procedure can handle the very high dimensionality of a multiperiod-life-span overlapping generations model.

We compute dynamic elasticities

$$\frac{d\ln(k(t))}{d\ln(\sigma)} \quad \text{and} \quad \frac{d\ln(e(t))}{d\ln(\sigma)}$$

measuring the change in $k(t)$ and $e(t)$ (recall the notation of Section III) following a permanent, surprise increase in social security taxes at time 0. The Appendix provides details. Prior to time 0 the economy rested in the steady–state equilibrium for $\sigma = 0.0918$. We assume that all household portfolios have the same ratios of reproducible capital to equities. We scale our results to reflect a complete elimination of the social security system, multiplying all point elasticities by -100.

Our baseline case (i.e., column 3 at the top of Table 3) generates a system of first-order difference equations of dimension 104 (see Appendix). Half of the variables are jump variables and half are predetermined. In each computation, the eigenvalues have the correct pattern for saddle-point stability.

Baseline results for our normalized, aggregative variables $k(t)$ and $e(t)$ are as follows. Since reproducible capital is a predetermined variable, the elasticity of $k(t)$ is zero at time 0. It steadily climbs to 33.7, reaching one-half the final value in 12–13 years. Aggregate equity value, on the other hand, is a "jump variable". It leaps at time 0 to about 60 percent of its new steady-state level. The final elasticity for e is 56.4, and its approach to that level is monotonic. The outcomes bear out the simpler analysis of Figure 3.[7]

To study the welfare of individual birth cohorts during the transition to the new steady state, consider a household born at time t. For each age s, our variational equations yield the derivative of $C(t, s)$ with respect to the time-0 social security tax change. Call the derivative $\mathrm{d}C(t, s)/\mathrm{d}\sigma$. The corresponding change in a household's lifetime utility is

$$\sum_{s=21}^{78} \frac{\partial u(C^*(t, s), s)}{\partial C(t, s)} \cdot \frac{\mathrm{d}C(t, s)}{\mathrm{d}\sigma},$$

where $C^*(t, s)$ are values from the initial steady state. To deduce an equivalent variation, we ask what equal percentage change, say, $\mathrm{d}\xi(T)/\mathrm{d}\sigma$, for a household dying at time T, in all of the original consumption figures would yield the same change in utility as an increase in social security taxes of $\mathrm{d}\sigma$. Noting that a household's life span is 57 years,

$$\frac{\mathrm{d}\xi(t+57)}{\mathrm{d}\sigma} = \frac{\sum_{s=21}^{78} \frac{\partial u(C^*(t, s), s)}{\partial C(t, s)} \cdot \frac{\mathrm{d}C(t, s)}{\mathrm{d}\sigma}}{\sum_{s=21}^{78} \frac{\partial u(C^*(t, s), s)}{\partial C(t, s)} \cdot C^*(t, s)}. \tag{25}$$

Below, we rescale outcomes to $-100 \cdot \sigma \cdot \mathrm{d}\xi(T)/\mathrm{d}\sigma$.

---

[7] In terms of accuracy, the final elasticity for $k(t)$ from the linear approximations is very close to the non-linear elasticity at the bottom of Table 3: 35.5. The approximation is less exact for $e(t)$: the linearized long-run elasticity of 56.4 is somewhat small in comparison to the percentage at the bottom of Table 3, 74.1.

In fact, we split the equivalent variation into three parts. Write the indirect utility function of a household dying at time T as

$$V_T = V(\vec{\sigma}_T, \vec{W}_T, \vec{R}_T, NW_T),$$

where $\vec{\sigma}_T$ is the vector of (*ex post*) social security taxes over the household's lifetime, $\vec{W}_T$ and $\vec{R}_T$ are corresponding wage and interest rates, and NW_T is the household's net worth at the date the social security system changes. Differentiating,

$$\frac{\mathrm{d}V_T}{\mathrm{d}\sigma} = \frac{\partial V}{\partial \vec{\sigma}_T} \cdot \frac{\mathrm{d}\vec{\sigma}_T}{\mathrm{d}\sigma} + \left[\frac{\partial V}{\partial \vec{W}_T} \cdot \frac{\mathrm{d}\vec{W}_T}{\mathrm{d}\sigma} + \frac{\partial V}{\partial \vec{R}_T} \cdot \frac{\mathrm{d}\vec{R}_T}{\mathrm{d}\sigma} \right] + \frac{\partial V}{\partial NW_T} \cdot \frac{\mathrm{d}NW_T}{\mathrm{d}\sigma} \tag{26}$$

where $\mathrm{d}\vec{\sigma}_T/\mathrm{d}\sigma$, $\mathrm{d}\vec{W}_T/\mathrm{d}\sigma$, $\mathrm{d}\vec{R}_T/\mathrm{d}\sigma$ and $\mathrm{d}NW_T/\mathrm{d}\sigma$ reflect general equilibrium changes from social security reform, with $\mathrm{d}NW_T/\mathrm{d}\sigma$ capturing the particular household's unanticipated capital gains from the jump in $E(-1)$. We call the first RHS side term the "direct effect" of social security reform, the second the "factor-price effect" and the third term the "asset effect". Expression (25) measures their sum—in elasticity form. The "direct effect" captures the effect on each cohort's lifetime welfare of social security tax and benefit changes, holding factor prices constant and omitting unanticipated capital gains at time 0. The "factor-price effect" measures the welfare consequences of general equilibrium wage and interest rate changes induced by social security reform. The "asset effect" captures the impact of time-0 unanticipated capital gains on privately owned technologies. For each birth cohort, we can compute all three "effects" using $\mathrm{d}k(t)/\mathrm{d}\sigma$ and $\mathrm{d}e(t)/\mathrm{d}\sigma$ from our variational equations.

Suppose we discontinue the social security system at time 0. The "direct effect" should certainly be negative for all households dying up to time 15—these households paid taxes under the old regime, but find their benefits cancelled. Households dying at later dates will suffer less, as reform will lower their social security taxes before retirement. Young households, and households beginning after time 0, will have a positive "direct effect": because $R^* > x$ (recall Section III), the lifetime present value of their social security benefits under the old regime fell short of the present value of their social security taxes; hence, reductions in social security taxes and benefits provide a net gain for them.

To understand the "factor-price effect", recall that social security reform causes the capital stock to rise monotonically. Thus, the wage component of the factor-price effect should be positive for all cohorts. The interest-rate component will eventually be negative: in all of our simulations, the preponderance of consumption falls later in life than earnings; hence, a fall in the interest rate raises the present value of the lifetime consumption stream at the old steady state more than it raises the present value of lifetime earnings, ultimately forcing households to reduce their consumption.

Finally, households alive at time 0 enjoy an unanticipated capital gain from the time-0 jump in the price of equities. This constitutes their "asset effect". Given (17), it will be non-negative. Households which are either very old or quite young at time 0 will not have enough net worth to realize a large asset effect. The primary beneficiaries will be those households relatively near retirement age at time 0.

Figure 4 graphs the three effects at different ages for our baseline case. We convert all effects to equivalent variation form, using the same scaling and units as in (25).

In Figure 4, the "direct effect" is generally the largest of the three. It falls to a trough of −3.47 percent of lifetime resources for households dying after 15 years. It eventually rises to 10.20 percent. The profile of the factor-price effect is slightly more complicated: it briefly rises, then falls to a trough at year 43, and then steadily rises to its final contribution of 3.27 percent.

The asset effect rises steadily to a peak of 0.55 percent at year 23, and then it falls monotonically to 0. It is opposite in sign and about 20 percent as large as the direct effect for households dying in years 0–20; it becomes a larger percentage thereafter, exceeding 100 percent of the direct effect in

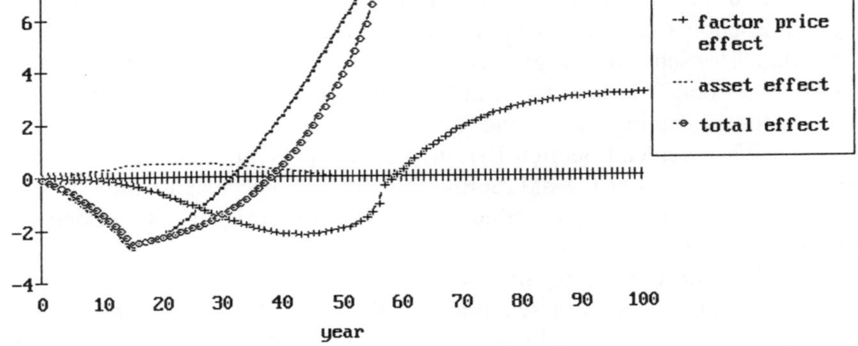

Fig. 4. Percentage change in lifetime resources after time-0 elimination of social security, $E/xK = 0.20$

years 30–31. Beyond year 31, the direct effect is also positive, surpassing the asset effect in magnitude by year 34.

In Figure 4, the "asset effect" reduces the maximal welfare loss by about 20 percent: the change in the lifetime equivalent variation from the "direct effect" for the cohort dying at year 15 is -2.736 percent, the "factor-price effect" is -0.287 percent, the "asset effect" is 0.495 percent, and the total effect is -2.528 percent.

V. Conclusion

This paper presents a general equilibrium framework in which national net worth exceeds the replacement cost of the aggregate stock of reproducible capital. Reductions in the scale of the social security system generate capital gains for owners of the inelastically supplied factor, and price appreciation on this factor crowds out part of the increase in reproducible capital which would otherwise occur.

We began by attempting to assess the empirical fraction of US net worth accounted for by inelastically supplied factors. The data arguably suggest one part in six (though the fraction seems to have moved higher very recently). According to numerical calculations in Section IV, reducing that share to zero would raise the percentage increase in reproducible capital following social security reform by slightly more than one-third. In the crucial early years after reform, unanticipated capital gains on stocks of inelastically supplied factors could mitigate the welfare losses of cohorts suffering social security benefit cuts after paying high taxes throughout their earning years. In the baseline simulation, this effect reduces maximal welfare losses by about 20 percent for retired cohorts. The analysis in Section III warns, however, that if in practice a government is slow to implement reforms which citizens have begun to anticipate, the delays may affect intergenerational equity during the transition to the new long-run equilibrium. The results suggest that proposals for phasing in social security changes, for example, should be carefully scrutinized.

Appendix

Below is a brief description of our calculations for the dynamic analysis in Section IV. Begin with a steady-state equilibrium for $\sigma = 0.0918$, and suppose reform consists of a permanent, surprise increase in σ and in corresponding social security benefits at time 0.

The economy has one household of each age 21, ..., 78. We construct a system of difference equations as follows. Line (21) provides one equation. Our households are liquidity constrained only at the beginning of life, say, ages 21, ..., S. Household budget constraint (16) provides an equation for $NW(t, s+1)$ each $s = S$,

…, 77; household first-order condition (24) provides an equation for $C(t, s+1)$ each $s = S, \ldots, 77$. There is no equation determining $NW(t, S)$, but its value is 0. There is no equation determining $C(t, S)$, but we can eliminate the need for that variable by using the last household first–order condition and the fact that a household consumes all of its remaining resources at age 78. Finally, we can drop the last consumption first–order condition since no other equation uses $C(t, 78)$. We are left with $2 \cdot (78 - S)$ equations taking the vector, say, $\vec{Z}_t$,

$$\vec{Z}_t \equiv (E(t-1), NW(t, S+1), \ldots, N(t, 78), C(t, S+1), \ldots, C(t, 77)),$$

into the next-period version of itself. We use Proposition 1 to detrend all variables, leaving a time-autonomous system. As in Laitner (1990), we differentiate the system with respect to σ, yielding a block of first-order difference equations for $\mathrm{d}\vec{Z}_t/\mathrm{d}\sigma$. These equations are linear—representing a linearization at the old steady state. We compute eigenvalues. As arguments $E(t-1)$ and $C(t, S+1), \ldots, C(t, 77)$ are "jump variables", we need $78 - S$ eigenvalues with absolute value greater than 1 (and the same number with eigenvalues less than 1) for saddle-point stability. In fact, the necessary configuration of eigenvalues emerges in each case.

References

Auerbach, A.J. and Kotlikoff, L. J. (1987), *Dynamic Fiscal Policy*, Cambridge University Press, Cambridge.

Blanchard, O., Rhee, C. and Summers, L. (1993)), The Stock Market, Profit and Investment, *Quarterly Journal of Economics 108* (1), 115–136.

Chamley, C. and Wright, B. (1987), Fiscal Incidence in an Overlapping Generations Model with a Fixed Asset, *Journal of Public Economics 32* (1), 3–24.

Economic Report of the President (1997), US Government Printing Office, Washington, DC.

Feldstein, M (1977), The Surprising Incidence of a Tax on Pure Rent: A New Answer to an Old Question, *Journal of Political Economy 83* (2), 349–360.

Feldstein, M. (1998), Introduction, in M. Feldstein (ed.), *Privatizing Social Security*, University of Chicago Press, Chicago, IL.

Feldstein, M. and Samwick, A. (1998), The Transition Path in Privatizing Social Security, in M. Feldstein (ed.), *Privatizing Social Security*, University of Chicago Press, Chicago, IL.

Faumeni, B. M. (1997), The Measurement of Depreciation in the US National Income and Products Accounts, *Survey of Current Business 77* (7), 7–23.

Hall, B. H. (1993), Industrial Research during the 1980s: Did the Rate of Return Fall? *Brookings Papers on Economic Activity: Microeconomics 2*, 289–330.

Hayashi, F. (1982), Tobin's Marginal *q* and Average *q*: A Neoclassical Interpretation, *Econometrica 50* (1), 213–224.

Hubbard, R. G. and Judd, K. L. (1987), Social Security and Individual Welfare, *American Economic Review 77* (4), 630–646.

Katz, A. J. and Herman, S. W. (1997), Improved Estimates of Fixed Reproducible Tangible Wealth, 1929–95, *Survey of Current Business 77* (5), 69–92.

Kotlikoff, L. J. (1988), Intergenerational Transfers and Savings, *Journal of Economic Perspectives 2* (2), 41–58.

Kotlikoff, L. J. (1998), Simulating the Privatization of Social Security in General

Equilibrium, in M. Feldstein (ed.), *Privatizing Social Security*, University of Chicago Press, Chicago, IL.

Kotlikoff, L. J. and Summers, L. H. (1981), The Role of Intergenerational Transfers in Aggregate Capital Accumulation, *Journal of Political Economy 89* (2), 372–391.

Kotlikoff, L. J., Smetters, K. A. and Walliser, J. (1998), Social Security: Privatization and Progressivity, *American Economic Review 88* (2), 137–141.

Laitner, J. (1990), Tax Changes and Phase Diagrams for an Overlapping Generations Model, *Journal of Political Economy 98* (1), 193–220.

Laitner, J. (1992), Random Earnings Differences, Lifetime Liquidity Constraints, and Altruistic Intergenerational Transfers, *Journal of Economic Theory 58* (2), 135–170.

Mariger, R. P. (1986), *Consumption Behavior and the Effects of Government Fiscal Policy*, Harvard University Press, Cambridge, MA.

McGrattan, E. R. (1998), A Defense of AK Growth Models, *Quarterly Review 22* (4), Federal Reserve Bank of Minneapolis, 13–27.

Modigliani, F. (1988), The Role of Intergenerational Transfers and Life Cycle Saving in the Accumulation of Wealth, *Journal of Economic Perspectives 2* (2), 15–24.

National Science Foundation (1996), *National Patterns of R&D Resources*, Arlington, VA.

Poterba, J. M. and Samwick, A. (1995), Stock Ownership Patterns, Stock Market Fluctuations, and Consumption, *Brookings Papers on Economic Activity 2*, 295–357.

US Department of Commerce (1997), Fixed Reproducible Tangible Wealth in the United States: Revised Estimates for 1993–95 and Summary Estimates for 1925–96, *Survey of Current Business 77* (9), 37–47.

US Department of Health and Human Services (1993), *Annual Statistical Supplement, 1993, to the Social Security Bulletin*, US Government Printing Office, Washington, DC.

Von Furstenberg, G. M. (1997), Corporate Investment: Does Market Valuation Matter in the Aggregate? *Brookings Papers on Economic Activity 2*, 347–408.

3

Adverse Selection in the Annuities Market and the Impact of Privatizing Social Security

*Jan Walliser**

"In life, one sometimes makes bad deals."

(Comment by 122-year-old Jeanne Louise Calment on the notary public who purchased her apartment for a monthly annuity of $500 in 1965 when Calment was 90 years old. He paid twice the market value for the apartment and died in December 1996 at age 77. His widow and children were obligated to continue the payments until Calment's death in 1997.)

I. Introduction

Few Americans purchase life annuities as protection against life span uncertainty. The weak demand for private annuities has been largely attributed to two effects: unfavorable annuity prices due to adverse selection, and crowding out of annuity demand by social security and private pensions. Adverse selection arises if the insurance company cannot distinguish among different risk types. In the case of annuity insurance, the insurance company may have less information about longevity prospects than the potential annuitant. Since consumers who expect to live longer—the high-risk type for an insurance company—buy larger annuities, the insurance company incurs a loss if it charges a premium based on average survival probabilities. Consequently, prices for annuities rise above those based on average population mortality, and higher prices may induce some consumers to drop out of the annuities market.

This study investigates the price of single-premium immediate life

---

*This paper draws on the first chapter of my Ph.D. dissertation. I thank my adviser Larry Kotlikoff for his suggestions and advice. I also received very helpful comments from an anonymous referee, Russell Cooper, Paul Cullinan, Robert Dennis, Simon Gilchrist, Douglas Hamilton, Joyce Manchester, Jim Poterba, Kent Smetters, Joachim Winter and participants of the August 1997 NBER Social Security meeting. The views expressed in this paper do not necessarily represent those of the International Monetary Fund.

annuities. Under this type of insurance contract, the insurance company converts a lump-sum payment into a constant income stream contingent on the survival of the annuitant. A fundamental question still unanswered in the literature is whether the observable cost of annuities can be endogenously generated in a life cycle model. In this chapter, the price of annuities is derived in a 75-period life cycle model with life span uncertainty. The model is calibrated to a cohort of the 1995 Current Population Survey and reflects the empirical variation of survival probabilities with family income and marital status. It also reflects the progressivity of the current US social security system.

A second and related question is how much of the lack of actuarial fairness can be blamed on the existence of social security benefits. Social security provides an annuity in old age and therefore crowds out private demand for annuities. Since social security induces individuals with shorter life expectancy to reduce their annuity demand disproportionately more than individuals with longer life expectancy, social security may exacerbate the adverse selection problem; see Abel (1986). The interaction between social security benefits and private annuity demand has recently received increasing attention due to the debate on reforming social security systems. Some reform proposals would force individuals to rely much more on private retirement planning. The cost of insurance against life span uncertainty is therefore a crucial criterion for evaluating those proposals.

It is shown in this chapter that a life cycle model can generate annuity prices that are 6.5–10.5 percent higher than actuarial fair prices for 65-year-old males. The model also reflects the empirical result that adverse selection raises prices in the annuities market for women to a lesser extent than for men and that the adverse selection problem rises with the age of the annuitant.

Privatization—here understood as the elimination—of social security may reduce the adverse selection-induced loading of annuity prices by 2–3 percentage points for individuals aged 65. However, privatization cannot reduce adverse selection to negligible proportions. Moreover, the simulations reveal that between 40 and 60 percent of the measured adverse selection is due to the positive correlation between income and mortality, and could not be removed by mandating annuitization of private accounts that are proportional to income.

The chapter is organized as follows. Previous theoretical and empirical findings concerning adverse selection are discussed in Section II. Section III develops a two-period model of annuity demand and derives insurance load factors. In Section IV, the simulation model is extended to 75 periods and calibrated to a cohort of 50-year-old agents using an empirically based spread in survival probabilities. Section V summarizes and concludes the chapter.

II. Annuity Insurance and Adverse Selection—Theory and Evidence

Ideally, insurance companies would have full information and each individual could purchase an annuity based on his or her specific survival probabilities. Under such a regime, the assets of each consumer would be converted into an income stream that is actuarially fair. However, insurance companies generally do not have enough information about survival prospects to calculate actuarially fair premia for individuals. Either information can be successfully hidden by prospective annuitants or regulatory constraints prevent insurers from making use of available data, for example by forcing them to offer the same contract to males and females. The resulting private information about survival probabilities can give rise to adverse selection.

Empirical Evidence for Adverse Selection

A number of papers by Friedman and Warshawsky (1988, 1990) and Warshawsky (1988) thoroughly analyze annuity prices in the United States.[1] They compile prices for single immediate life annuities charged by the 10 largest suppliers of these contracts between 1968 and 1983. According to their findings, annuity prices are between 24 and 39 percent higher than implied by the value of an actuarially fair annuity if the price of the latter is calculated with population average survival probabilities.[2] Only part of this so-called "loading" or "load factor" is due to adverse selection; the other part is attributable to overhead costs due to administration, taxes and profits.[3] Using the difference in survival probabilities between annuity purchasers and the average population, Friedman and Warshawsky find that about half of the load factor (13–15 percentage points) can be explained by adverse selection.

Annuity prices have recently been re-evaluated by Mitchell, Poterba and Warshawsky (1997). They conclude that, depending on the discount rate, the loading of annuity insurance prices in 1995 amounted to 17–25 percent for 65-year-old males. As summarized in Table 1, adverse selection accounted

---

[1] With the exception of a recently introduced CREF annuity based on US Treasury Inflation-protected Securities, annuities are nominal annuities and do not insure against inflation risk.

[2] I report the results which use the 20-year government bond rate for discounting. The results using the corporate bond rate tend to show similar load factors due to adverse selection but higher overall loading.

[3] According to Friedman and Warshawsky (1988) the loading due to overhead costs is comparable to other insurance markets. Since this paper focuses on adverse selection, overhead costs are not taken into account.

Table 1. *Percentage difference between US annuity prices and actuarially fair prices caused by adverse selection*

	Men		Women	
Age at purchase	Annuity discounted with treasury bond rate	Annuity discounted with corporate bond rate	Annuity discounted with treasury bond rate	Annuity discounted with corporate bond rate
55	6.6	5.1	4.6	3.5
65	10.0	8.3	6.4	5.2
75	12.5	10.8	6.9	5.9

Source: Mitchell *et al.* (1997, Tables 3 and 4).

for 8–10 percentage points of the measured loading. Moreover, Mitchell *et al.* find a significant increase in the effect of adverse selection with age and a significantly smaller effect of adverse selection on annuity prices for women.

Adverse Selection Equilibria

Most theoretical papers dealing with adverse selection have applied the Rothschild-Stiglitz (1976) or the Wilson (1977) equilibrium concept.[4] The existence of these equilibria requires that each insurance company can perfectly monitor the insurance purchases of all customers and prevent customers from buying more than one contract.[5] Whereas this assumption may be justifiable for some insurance markets, it seems difficult to apply to the annuity insurance market. Even if an annuity contract explicitly restricted further purchases of annuities, this might not suffice since monitoring would be very difficult. First, the receipt of annuity payments from different insurance companies would not be observable. Second, in contrast to other insurance markets, the catastrophe for (death of) the customer ends the liability of the insurance company rather than creating it. This fact precludes withholding payments and investigating compliance with the insurance contract as, for example, in fire insurance or car insurance markets. It also rules out market separation through insurance menus with different co-payments as for medical insurance.

If insurance companies cannot control the quantity of insurance purchased, it seems reasonable to use an equilibrium concept in which the

[4]See, for example, Eckstein, Eichenbaum and Peled (1985).

[5]Aside from this important assumption, the characteristics of insurance market equilibria have been found to be dependent on their specific assumptions about the order of "moves" in the contracting game, as pointed out by Hellwig (1987).

insurer can only choose the price of the annuity. This kind of equilibrium, previously considered by Abel (1986) and Pauly (1974), is also used in this chapter. Such an equilibrium could be alternatively interpreted as a Nash equilibrium in which any firm deviating from the zero profit price incurs losses.

III. A Two-period Model of Annuity Demand

The basic model used here to evaluate the effects of adverse selection on annuity prices, annuity demand and welfare combines features of Eckstein *et al.* (1985) and Abel (1986). In contrast to the previous literature, this study incorporates heterogeneity in income and explicitly derives load factors for annuities that can be compared with the empirical values of Mitchell *et al.* (1997). In Eckstein *et al.* (1985), insurers charge actuarially fair prices but impose quantity constraints. Abel (1986), whose equilibrium concept is applied in this chapter, focuses on the interaction between adverse selection in annuities markets and capital accumulation, and does not derive the load factor of annuity prices.

Adverse Selection and Load Factors in the Basic Model

Consider an economy with N types of consumers, $j \in \{1, N\}$, who live for a maximum of two periods. Survival at the end of the first period of life is uncertain and occurs with probability π^j, $0 < \pi^j < 1$. Agents exogenously supply one unit of labour during their first period of life and receive labour income w^j. Survivors retire in the second period of their lives. Note that each type j can hence be perfectly characterized by the pair $\{\pi^j, w^j\}$. Income and survival probabilities may be correlated. Each type represents a share ε^j of the population with $\sum_j \varepsilon^j = 1$.

Consumers choose consumption in both periods $\{c_1, c_2\}$ to maximize expected utility from a time-separable utility function. The utility function is assumed to be twice continuously differentiable with $U' > 0$ and $U'' < 0$. Future utility is discounted with the pure rate of time preference δ.

$$U(c_1^j) + \frac{\pi^j}{1+\delta} U(c_2^j) \tag{1}$$

In order to smooth consumption over the expected life span, agents can hold their wealth in the form of bonds that offer an exogenous rate of return r. The price of a bond is accordingly $1/R$ where $R = 1 + r$. Alternatively, individuals can buy an annuity a^j that is paid in year 2 conditional on the agent's survival. An annuity a^j can be purchased in period 1 for a price Z^j. Since the insurance company implicitly distributes the estate of a deceased annuity purchaser among all surviving annuitants, the annuity can always offer a higher rate of return than a bond, and hence $Z^j < 1/R$. Bonds are therefore a dominated asset and all agents in this economy would like to hold their wealth in annuities; see Yaari (1965).[6]

Social security may affect the intertemporal allocation of consumption. Social security benefits are assumed to be pay-as-you-go. A payroll tax with rate s finances benefits $SS^j(w^j)$, which are a function of w^j and assumed to be twice differentiable with $SS' \geqslant 0$ and $SS'' \leqslant 0$, i.e., social security benefits rise proportionally or less than proportionally with first-period income. Equations (2) and (3) represent the budget constraints for the consumer in both periods of his life, and equation (4) imposes a non-negativity constraint on annuity demand:

$$c_1^j = w^j(1-s) - a^j Z^j \tag{2}$$

$$c_2^j = a^j + SS^j \tag{3}$$

$$a^j \geqslant 0. \tag{4}$$

Equation (4) warrants some discussion. If the government provides social security benefits some agents may be overannuitized and would prefer to borrow against future annuity income by selling annuities. Equivalently, as shown by Yaari (1965), they may borrow and simultaneously buy life insurance. The life insurance guarantees the loan in case of death. The assumption therefore rules out the possibility that individuals can draw loans on future social security income and guarantee repayments through life insurance.[7]

Annuity demand has to satisfy the following first-order condition:

$$U'(c_1^j)Z^j \geqslant \frac{\pi^j}{1+\delta} U'(c_2^j). \tag{5}$$

This equation also represents the conventional Euler equation for consumption with the price Z^j replacing the discount factor $1/(1+r)$. Equation (5) may hold with inequality if agents are overannuitized by social security.

[6]This result depends on the assumption that agents do not have a bequest motive. Fischer (1973), Abel (1986) and Friedman and Warshawsky (1990) include a bequest motive in their respective models. Hurd (1989) does not find that a bequest motive is empirically relevant and asserts that people are in fact overannuitized by social annuities. Bernheim (1991), using the same data set as Hurd, finds that the data are consistent with bequest motives.

[7]Friedman and Warshawsky (1988, 1990) make the same assumption in their simulations. Abel (1986) restricts survival probabilities such that annuity demand is non-negative.

Everything else being equal, annuity demand needs to increase with survival probabilities and income in order to satisfy the first-order condition if the latter holds with equality. Moreover, if part of second-period consumption is provided by social security benefits, annuity demand must fall to satisfy equation (5). Solving the intertemporal maximization problem as specified by the utility functions, the budget constraints and the non-negativity constraints yield an annuity demand function $a^j = a(Z^j, \pi^j, (1-s)w^j, SS^j(w^j))$ for each type j.

To specify an equilibrium in the annuity insurance market, Assumption 1 is made.

Assumption 1. Insurance companies have no information about the type of a customer. They cannot efficiently monitor the overall amount of annuities purchased by their customers and can therefore not restrict the quantity purchased. Insurance companies can observe age and sex but not income.

This assumption generates adverse selection by eliminating the first-best outcome in which annuities can be purchased based on individual survival prospects. It also eliminates the Rothschild–Stiglitz and Wilson separating and pooling equilibria since these rely on the assumption that the quantity of insurance can be constrained. Insurance companies set the price of insurance only, they cannot control the quantity. Hence, the type superscript is dropped from the annuity price from now on.

Insurance companies charge a price Z per dollar of annuity payments in period 2, irrespective of the type. An annuity a^j sold to a type j customer will generate expected profits equivalent to the price charged net of the discounted value of the expected future annuity payment. Therefore, expected profits for the type j annuity contract are equal to $(Z - \pi^j/R)a^j$. In a competitive insurance market, the price will be sufficient to break even across all types of customers in equilibrium. Accordingly, the equilibrium price Z^* is implicitly defined by the zero profit condition,

$$P(Z^*) = \sum_{j=1}^{N} \varepsilon^j (Z^* - \pi^j/R) a(Z^*, \pi^j, w^j(1-s), SS^j(w^j)) \equiv 0. \quad (6)$$

By extending Abel's (1986) argument, it can be shown that there exists at least one annuity price that satisfies equation (6) if social security benefits are sufficiently small.[8] If social security benefits are large and all agents are

[8] This result relies on a straightforward continuity argument. Under given assumptions, the profit function is continuous in annuity prices and must cross the zero-profit line at least once for sufficiently small social security benefits; see Walliser (1998).

overannuitized, however, the only zero-profit equilibrium for the annuities market may be one in which nobody demands private annuities. In general, unless $P(Z)$ is strictly concave, the equilibrium is not unique and depends on the specifics of the utility function and the accordant behavior of annuity demand functions.

As can be shown formally by extending an argument by Abel (1986), equilibrium annuity prices are higher than a price based on population average survival due to adverse selection as long as income and longevity are not negatively correlated and social security benefits are not rising more than proportionally with income.[9] Empirically, both assumptions hold and the correlation between income and longevity exacerbates the problem of adverse selection.[10]

This result raises the issue of how to measure adverse selection in the presence of a positive correlation between income and longevity. The traditional approach followed in the empirical literature is to calculate a "load factor" that measures in percent by how much the asking price Z^* of an annuity insurance company exceeds the actuarially fair price. The latter is calculated simply as the price based on the average mortality of the population. For the two-period model, the load factor can be derived as

$$\frac{Z^*}{Z^F} = \frac{Z^* R}{\sum_{j=1}^{N} \varepsilon^j \pi^j} = \frac{Z^* R}{\bar{\pi}} \tag{7}$$

where Z^F denotes the price of an annuity based on average mortality.

Some portion of the load factor derived in equation (7) is due to the positive correlation between income and longevity. If all agents were identical in their survival probabilities, type j's annuity would differ from type k's by the ratio of their lifetime income in present values. Therefore, one way to eliminate the effect of the correlation between income and mortality from the load factor is to weigh survival probabilities with lifetime income in present values. This "corrected" load factor can be derived as follows:

$$\frac{Z^*}{Z^S} = \frac{Z^* R \sum_{j=1}^{N} \varepsilon^j w^j}{\sum_{j=1}^{N} \varepsilon^j \pi^j w^j}. \tag{8}$$

---

[9]See Walliser (1998) for the formal argument.

[10]For results from the PSID and an overview of the literature, see Lillard and Panis (1996). Similar findings for the National Longitudinal Survey have been reported by Menchik (1993). For evidence from the SIPP, see Attanasio and Hoynes (1995). A broad survey of the literature can be found in Feinstein (1993).

Equation (8) may be interpreted as the load factor arising from a comparison of the price of the market annuity Z^* with the price Z^S of a mandatory annuity that is proportional to lifetime income. If income and mortality are uncorrelated, equations (7) and (8) coincide because the price of an income-proportional mandatory annuity Z^S and the price of an annuity based on average survival probabilities Z^F are identical. Hence, all loading measured by (7) is due to differences in mortality. If Z^S exceeds Z^F, however, this indicates that some of the loading is due to the income–mortality correlation, and the value of the corrected load factor in (8) is less than the overall loading measured in (7). Equation (8) thus reflects the importance of mortality differences in explaining the overall load factor (7), with the remainder of overall loading reflecting the income–mortality correlation.

Analytical Results for the Log Utility Case

It is instructive to solve analytically for the annuity price in a private annuity market assuming logarithmic utility. Annuity demand can then be derived as follows from the first-order condition and the budget constraints provided above:

$$a^j = \frac{w^j \pi^j (1-s) - Z(1+\delta) SS^j}{(1+\pi^j+\delta)Z} \tag{9}$$

and $a^j = 0$ if (9) results in a negative value.

As discussed in the previous section, annuity demand increases with wage income and the survival probability and decreases with the price of annuities. Lifetime resources are divided according to a personal discount factor. This factor depends on the type-independent pure rate of time preference and the type-specific survival probability. With increasing survival probabilities, agents discount future consumption less and annuity demand increases.

Annuity demand according to equation (9) can be used to demonstrate that equilibrium prices rise when social security benefits are introduced. It is sufficient to show that a marginal increase in social security benefits decreases the annuity demand of the shorter-lived types disproportionately more to prove that introducing social security reduces profits below zero. The result follows because profits are a weighted average of gains and losses from different types, and the shorter-lived types are those who generate profits. Equation (10) derives the marginal relative change, which can be shown to fall with rising survival probabilities. Hence, profits would fall below zero after introducing social security and equilibrium prices must rise.

$$\left.\frac{\partial a^j/\partial SS^j}{a^j}\right|_{SS^j=0} = \frac{-(1+\delta)(1+\pi^j+\delta)(Z^*)^2}{w^j\pi^j(1-s)}. \tag{10}$$

Consider next the load factor for annuity insurance. Equation (11) displays the formula for a log utility case without social security:[11]

$$\frac{Z^*}{Z^F} = \frac{1}{\bar{\pi}}\frac{\sum_{j=1}^{N}\varepsilon^j w^j\left(\frac{(\pi^j)^2}{1+\pi^j+\delta}\right)}{\sum_{j=1}^{N}\varepsilon^j w^j\left(\frac{\pi^j}{1+\pi^j+\delta}\right)}. \tag{11}$$

According to equation (11), the load factor depends on the ratio of weighted squared survival probabilities and weighted survival probabilities. The variance of survival probabilities in combination with the correlation between longevity and income plays a crucial role in the size of the load factor. A mean-preserving spread in survival probabilities raises the load factor, as does a stronger correlation between longevity and income because both would raise the value of the denominator by more than the value of the numerator.

IV. Adverse Selection and Annuity Insurance in a 75-period Model

The model of annuity demand can now be extended to 75 years (ages 25 to 100). A type j consumer maximizes the following expected utility function:

$$\sum_{t=1}^{75} U(c_t^j)\prod_{s=1}^{t-1}\frac{\pi_s^j}{(1+\delta)} a \tag{12}$$

where π_t^j stands for the probability that type j lives from age t to age $t+1$. The maximization is subject to a sequence of budget constraints evolving as follows:

$$c_t^j = w_t^j(1-s) + a_t^j - a_{t+1}^j Z_t + SS_t^j \tag{13}$$

with social security benefits set to zero before retirement and wages set to zero after retirement. Annuity demand is zero in the last period of life. Note

[11] See Walliser (1998) for a derivation of load factors with social security benefits.

also that the weights of the different types now change over time according to the following equation:

$$\varepsilon_t^j = \varepsilon_{t-1}^j \frac{\pi_{t-1}^j}{\overline{\pi}_{t-1}}. \tag{14}$$

In extending the two-period model to 75 years of life, it is assumed that survival probabilities are strictly ranked across types. This assumption ensures that a type j with higher chances of living from age 50 to age 51 than type k, say, also has a higher probability of living from age 51 to 52 than type k and so on; i.e., survival probabilities do not cross.

The multiperiod equilibrium for annuities can then be defined as a sequence of single-period contracts satisfying equation (6). The existence of this multiperiod equilibrium can be inferred from the existence of zero-profit annuity prices for each period.

The price of an annuity spanning several time periods can then be calculated from the sequence of prices prevailing in each period. In particular, the price PR_t of a \$1 life annuity in time t generated by the model equals:

$$PR_t = Z_t^* + Z_t^* Z_{t+1}^* + Z_t^* Z_{t+1}^* Z_{t+2}^* + \dots \tag{15}$$

Accordingly, the actuarial fair price PR_t^F can be calculated as:

$$PR_t^F = Z_t^F + Z_t^F Z_{t+1}^F + Z_t^F Z_{t+1}^F Z_{t+2}^F + \dots \tag{16}$$

and the percentage deviation of annuity prices from actuarial fairness (load factor) is just the ratio of PR_t and PR_t^F. A similar derivation holds for the annuity price Z^S that uses an income-weighted population survival probability.

Model Calibration and Solution

In order to reproduce an observable degree of adverse selection in the annuities market, the model was calibrated to a cohort from the CPS. Empirical estimates of survival functions were applied to the socio-economic characteristics of individuals in this cohort. The estimates reflect the relationship between family income, gender, education, race and longevity. The calibration also uses a stylized approximation of income over the life cycle, and takes into consideration the tax code and social security benefit rules in the United States. The calibration is explained in more detail in the Appendix.

All numerical simulations assume that utility is additively separable and takes the standard constant relative risk-aversion form $U(c_t) = (1/1 - \gamma) c_t^{1-\gamma}$, with $\gamma > 0$. The analysis below considers how results change with the risk-aversion parameter ranging from 1 (log utility) to 4. The pure rate of time preference is set to 1 percent or 3 percent, and the fixed real rate of return on bonds r is set to 3 percent in all subsequent runs.

The 75-period model is solved using an iterative procedure. First, the optimal forward-looking consumption path for a given set of annuity prices is calculated for each type. Second, the annuity demand is used to derive expected profits according to equation (6). Third, for given annuity demand, zero-profit annuity prices are calculated and a weighted average of the old price and the new price is assigned as the annuity price for the next iteration. This procedure is repeated until profits reach zero, which usually does not take more than 20–30 iterations.[12] If the non-negativity constraint is violated, the algorithm assigns a positive value to a Kuhn–Tucker multiplier capturing the difference in marginal utility between the two periods, and the consumption path is subsequently recomputed.[13]

Results

Table 2 exhibits the load factors generated by the calibrated life cycle model for ages 55, 65 and 75, different risk-aversion parameters of the utility function and pure rates of time preference of 1 and 3 percent. If consumers receive social security benefits, the model predicts that adverse selection will raise annuity prices for 65-year-old males by 6.5–10.5 percent above those based on the average mortality of the population. These load factors are similar to those summarized in Table 1. However, the sources of adverse selection differ somewhat between the theoretical model and the empirical calculations, since the load factor in the model also reflects the heterogeneity of annuity purchasers. Mitchell *et al.* (1997) instead focus exclusively on the difference between annuity purchasers and the average population.

The deviation from prices that are actuarially fair depends on the degree of risk-aversion. If economic agents are not very averse to risk as in the log utility case, demand is more responsive to the difference between the individual discount factor and the market rate of return. The first figure combines the pure rate of time preference and individual survival probabilities, and the second figure reflects the price of annuities (the inverse of the

[12] As mentioned previously, the equilibrium may not be unique. However, for the combination of parameter values chosen for the simulations, the resulting equilibrium prices are stable and independent of starting values.

[13] Zeldes (1989) derives the first-order conditions of consumer choice with non-negativity constraints.

Table 2. *Percentage difference between the equilibrium price of a life annuity and the price of a life annuity based on average survival probabilities (load factor)*

Rate of risk aversion	Age at purchase	Men: With social security	Men: Without social security	Women: With social security	Women: Without social security
			$\delta = 0.01$		
$\gamma = 1$	55	6.3	5.3	4.4	3.7
	65	8.3	6.9	5.9	5.0
	75	10.0	8.4	7.5	6.4
$\gamma = 2$	55	5.6	4.4	4.2	3.4
	65	7.2	5.7	5.6	4.4
	75	8.6	6.7	6.9	5.5
$\gamma = 4$	55	5.1	3.9	4.1	3.1
	65	6.5	4.9	5.4	4.1
	75	7.6	5.7	6.6	5.0
			$\delta = 0.03$		
$\gamma = 1$	55	7.8	5.3	5.6	3.7
	65	10.3	6.9	7.7	5.0
	75	12.5	8.4	9.9	6.4
$\gamma = 2$	55	6.5	4.4	4.9	3.4
	65	8.5	5.7	6.6	4.4
	75	10.2	6.7	8.3	5.5
$\gamma = 4$	55	5.5	3.9	4.5	3.1
	65	7.1	4.9	5.9	4.1
	75	8.4	5.7	7.3	5.0

Source: Author's calculations.

rate of return). The higher the degree of risk aversion, the less annuity demand differs among agents and the smaller the adverse selection problem. In addition, the existence of social security benefits raises adverse selection more with a higher pure rate of time preference, as shown in the "with social security" columns in Table 2.

A second result of the model is that load factors vary with age. Under the current system an annuity purchased by a male at age 55 is predicted to be 6.5 percent more expensive than a fair annuity. The loading rises to 8.5 percent at age 65 and 10.2 percent at age 75. However, as shown in Figures 1 and 2, the load factor begins to fall between ages 85 and 90. The dependency of adverse selection on age is a consequence of the endogeneity of the population weights. The higher death rates of some types cause a fall in their population shares. Thus, types with longer life expectancy exert a larger influence on the market without initially raising the average life expectancy to the same degree. In other words, the variance of life

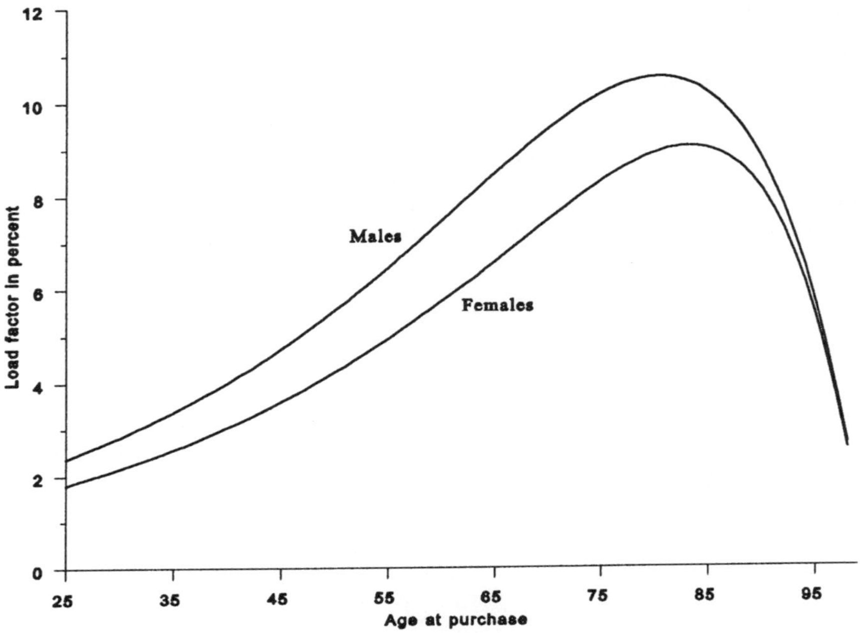

Fig. 1. Load factors for males and females (with social security benefits, $r = 0.03$, $\delta = 0.03$, $\gamma = 2$)

expectancies increases which, as shown in the two-period example, raises the load factor. In later years of life, there are almost no types with short life expectancy left. Therefore, the average agent is a long-lived agent and load factors fall with the variance in survival probabilities. As shown in Table 1, empirically measured loading induced by adverse selection increases significantly with age. Depending on their discount rate, prices are 5.1–6.6 percent higher for 55-year-old males and between 10.8 and 12.5 percent higher for 75-year-old males.

The results from the model as displayed in Table 2 and Figure 1 are also in line with the empirical finding that adverse selection affects annuity prices for females to a lesser extent. The life cycle model exhibits load factors for women that are about 20 percent smaller than those for males. Mitchell *et al.* (1997) find that the loading of annuities sold to women is around 35 percent smaller. Lower values for women can largely be attributed to lower variances in the factors determining survival. First, the variance of family income is smaller for women than for men. The variance in educational attainment is smaller as well, with higher concentration at high school degrees. Second, survival probabilities for women as estimated by Lillard and Panis (1996)

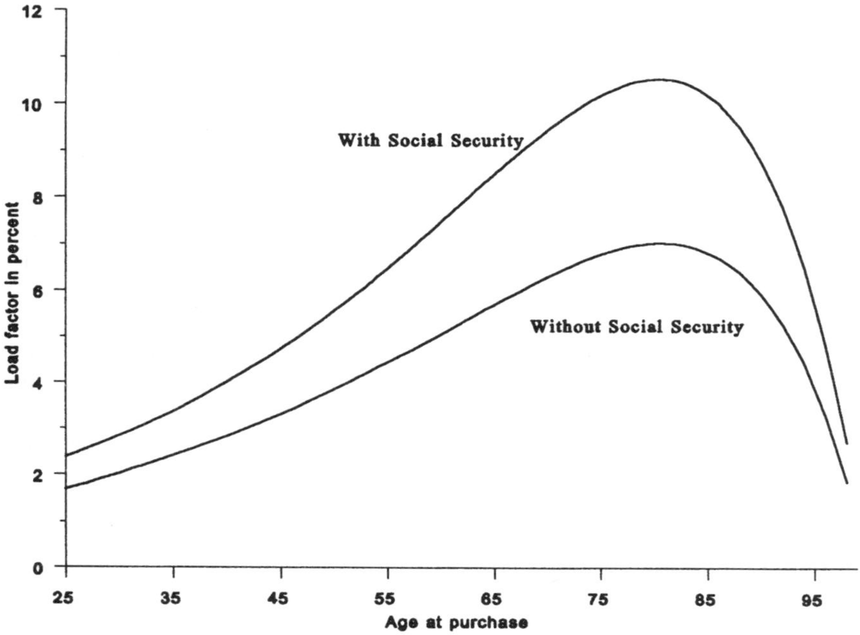

Fig. 2. Load factors for males with and without social security benefits ($r = 0.03$, $\delta = 0.03$, $\gamma = 2$)

vary to a much lesser degree with marital status than those for men. In fact, women who have never married or are widowed do not face a significantly different life expectancy than married women. Overall, the variance for female survival probabilities is therefore considerably smaller than the variance in survival probabilities for men.

According to the model, eliminating social security benefits may lead to a drop in the load factor by up to 3 percentage points. As shown by Figure 2, the drop occurs at all ages. Depending on the degree of risk aversion, the reduction of adverse selection implies a 12–30 percent fall in existing load factors. Generally speaking, the reduction is stronger for higher degrees of risk aversion and the higher rate of time preference.[14]

Results for the percent reduction in load factors are similar for males and

[14]Note, though, that the ultimate load factor in a system without social security is independent of the rate of time preference δ. Therefore, the top and bottom panels of columns 2 and 4 in Table 2 are identical. This result arises because load factors represent ratios of weighted annuity demand and the pure rate of time preference affects the numerator and denominator in an identical way. Equation (9) can be used to derive this result formally.

females. This finding follows from the increasing annuity demand of those with below-average survival probabilities. Indeed, the increasing demand of those with shorter lives has two driving forces: privatizing social security increases the demand of those with below-average survival probabilities more than proportionally. This alone reduces the adverse selection problem. However, a second feature of the model exacerbates this effect. Social security benefits are progressive, and longevity and income are positively correlated. Therefore, social security benefits replace a much larger proportion of wealth for the poor who also have shorter life expectancies. If those types enter the private market, the prices for annuities fall in response.

Another important feature of the model is that it captures the positive correlation between lifetime income and longevity. As outlined above, any empirically measured loading of annuity prices implicitly incorporates the effect of this correlation on annuity demand. In order to isolate the impact of the income–longevity correlation, Table 3 displays the "corrected" load factor for the case without social security benefits. It compares equilibrium annuity prices with prices based on lifetime-income-weighted survival probabilities. As explained earlier, the resulting load factor indicates how much of total loading can be attributed to mortality differences. A comparison of the "without social security" columns in Tables 2 and 3 reveals that a mandatory annuity proportional to income financed with proportional payroll taxes could only reduce the observed loading by 40–60 percent for a 65-year-old male. The higher the degree of risk aversion, the less important are mortality differences in explaining the loading of annuity prices and hence the more important the correlation between income and mortality.

An important resulting question for the design of a privatized retirement system is whether the government should subsidize the retirement savings of low-income workers to counterbalance the implicit redistribution through annuities to the advantage of longer-lived high-income workers. Some reform proposals call for explicitly subsidizing the retirement savings of low-income workers.[15] If designed appropriately, such subsidies could reverse the redistribution implied by pooling low-income and high-income workers in the annuities market.

V. Conclusion

A life cycle model that explicitly captures the heterogeneity of survival prospects can account for three stylized facts: the size of adverse selection, the increasing importance of adverse selection with age, and the smaller

[15]Subsidies introduce distortions. However, as shown by Kotlikoff, Smetters and Walliser (1998), the reduction in payroll tax rates and macroeconomic feedback effects of social security privatization outweigh these distortions.

Table 3. *Percentage difference between the equilibrium price of a life annuity and the price of a life annuity based on lifetime income weighted survival probabilities (corrected load factor)*

		Men	Women
Rate of risk aversion	Age at purchase	Without social security	Without social security
			$\delta = 0.01$
$\gamma = 1$	55	2.0	0.8
	65	2.8	1.3
	75	3.9	1.9
$\gamma = 2$	55	1.1	0.5
	65	1.6	0.7
	75	2.2	1.0
$\gamma = 4$	55	0.6	0.2
	65	0.9	0.4
	75	1.2	0.5
			$\delta = 0.03$
$\gamma = 1$	55	2.0	0.8
	65	2.8	1.3
	75	3.9	1.9
$\gamma = 2$	55	1.1	0.5
	65	1.6	0.7
	75	2.2	1.0
$\gamma = 4$	55	0.6	0.2
	65	0.9	0.4
	75	1.2	0.5

Source: Author's calculations.

adverse selection in the annuities market for women. However, the model still predicts higher annuity demand than empirically observed. At a minimum, 50 percent of the agents in the model purchase private annuities at any given age. By contrast, empirically fewer than 5 percent of the population purchase private annuities. Thus, adverse selection endogenously derived in a simple life cycle model cannot resolve the puzzle as to why people do not purchase more annuities. The model also predicts steeper asset profiles and more dissaving after retirement than are observable.

Extensions of the model in several directions might both better align savings profiles with observed patterns and reduce annuity demand. Such extensions include bequest motives and intra-family insurance, as in Kotlikoff and Spivak (1981), demand for housing, labor income uncertainty,

uncertainty regarding health and long-term care risks, uncertain capital income and inflation risk.[16]

The model shows that eliminating social security benefits can decrease the load factor by 2–3 percentage points, a reduction of 12–30 percent. The reduction in adverse selection is driven by the strong increase in annuity demand of shorter-lived poor agents who currently receive the most generous returns on their social security contributions. However, as a result of general equilibrium feedback effects, calibrated parameters such as income and interest rates might change after privatization (the Lucas critique). The exact results should therefore be interpreted with caution.

Finally, according to the model, a significant part of measured adverse selection can be attributed to the correlation between income and longevity. A mandate to annuitize retirement savings would therefore not be able to remove all measured adverse selection because people with more wealth demand larger annuities and also live longer. Moreover, it would implicitly redistribute resources from short-lived low-income workers to long-lived high-income workers. However, policy-makers could counterbalance this effect by subsidizing retirement savings of low-income people in a privatized system.

Appendix. Model Calibration

In order to reproduce an observable degree of adverse selection in the annuities market, calibration has to reflect the empirical distribution of survival probabilities. Vital statistics can only provide limited information on the socio-economic determinants of survival probabilities and do not reflect the downward trend in mortality rates. Survival probabilities were therefore estimated for a cohort of 50-year-old individuals in the 1995 Current Population Survey (CPS), a total of 1,458 individuals, 721 men and 737 women after excluding 180 individuals with family income below $5,000 or without labor income and a working spouse. Age 50 is convenient since there are few future changes in marital status outside of changes induced by the death of a spouse. Moreover, early retirement does not yet affect income measures.

To obtain survival probabilities for each individual in the CPS, a time-dependent baseline mortality hazard function estimated by Lillard and Panis (1996) from PSID data was applied to CPS variables. Variation in survival probabilities stems from characteristics such as lifetime family income, marital status, race and educational attainment.[17] Those variables shift the baseline survival function proportionally,

---

[16] For a survey of the different extensions to the simple model that could reduce annuity demand, see Walliser (1999).

[17] To apply the parameters estimated by Lillard and Panis, family income from the CPS cross-section is adjusted proportionally such that mean family income coincides with mean permanent income in the PSID sample.

ensuring that the assumption regarding strict ranking is always satisfied. For married agents, characteristics of the spouse play a role in survival probabilities since the potential death of spouse has negative effects on own survival prospects. This effect is incorporated into the survival probabilities after age 50.[18] Applying the empirical parameters to the CPS cohort results in average survival probabilities for 50-year-olds that are very close to the corresponding values in the 1991 life tables. Due to the time dependence built into Lillard and Panis's estimation, the probabilities derived for the CPS cohort imply a future increase in life expectancy of around three years for males and four years for females.

In order to specify agents' income paths, agents are assumed to retire at age 65 and—taking labour income at age 50 as a benchmark—wage profiles are assumed have the same curvature as the mean efficiency profile estimated by Altig *et al.* (1997). Since labour supply is exogenous, efficiency profiles are additionally adjusted for the change in hours worked to generate earnings profiles. Earnings are furthermore corrected for income tax payments.[19]

For couples, labour income of husband and wife are added and divided by two to approximate the spousal benefit rules and ownership rules of retirement accounts in a private retirement system.[20] Social security benefits are calculated according to the current benefit rules and take spousal benefit rules as well as the payroll tax ceiling into account. In line with the division of labour income, each spouse is assigned half of the joint social security benefits.

References

Abel, A. B. (1986), Capital Accumulation and Uncertain Lifetimes with Adverse Selection, *Econometrica 54*, 1079–1097.

Altig, D., Auerbach, A. J., Kotlikoff, L. J., Smetters, K. A. and Walliser, J. (1997), Simulating US Tax Reform, NBER Working Paper no. 6248, Cambridge, MA.

Attanasio, O. P. and Hoynes, H. W. (1995), Differential Mortality and Wealth Accumulation, NBER Working Paper no. 5126, Cambridge, MA.

Bernheim, B. D. (1991), How Strong Are Bequest Motives? Evidence Based on Estimates of the Demand for Life Insurance and Annuities, *Journal of Political Economy 99*, 899–927.

Brugiavini, A. (1993), Uncertainty Resolution and the Timing of Annuity Purchases, *Journal of Public Economics 50*, 31–62.

[18]See also Lillard, Brien and Panis (1996) for a derivation of survival probabilities when future events are unknown.

[19]Note that the assumption of exogenous retirement behavior excludes a possible interaction between retirement choices and the cost of private annuities; see Rust and Phelan (1997). However, by benchmarking income against the CPS, some of the endogenous labor supply choices are implicitly incorporated into the calibration and as long as the characterization of lifetime incomes is not biased to a major extent, the exogenous labor supply should not have a large effect on the results.

[20]Note that the sharing rule differs from joint maximization of annuity demand since couples may also share longevity risk within the family; see Kotlikoff and Spivak (1981). However, the focus of this paper is on single life annuities.

Eckstein, Z., Eichenbaum, M. and Peled, D. (1985), Uncertain Lifetimes and the Welfare Enhancing Properties of Annuity Markets and Social Security, *Journal of Public Economics 26*, 303–326.
Feinstein, J. S. (1993), The Relationship between Socioeconomic Status and Health: A Review of the Literature, *The Milbank Quarterly 71*, 279–309.
Fischer, S. (1973), A Life Cycle Model of Life Insurance Purchases, *International Economic Review 14*, 132–152.
Friedman, B. M. and Warshawsky, M. J. (1988), Annuity Prices and Saving Behavior in the United States, in Z. Bodie, J. Shoven and D. Wise (eds.), *Pensions in the U.S. Economy*, University of Chicago Press, Chicago, IL.
Friedman, B. M., and Warshawsky, M. J. (1990), The Cost of Annuities: Implications for Saving Behavior and Bequests, *Quarterly Journal of Economics 104*, 135–154.
Hellwig, M. (1987), Some Recent Developments in the Theory of Competition in Markets with Adverse Selection, *European Economic Review 31*, 319–325.
Hurd, M. D. (1989), Mortality Risks and Bequests, *Econometrica 57*, 779–813.
Kotlikoff, L. J., Smetters, K. A. and Walliser, J. (1998), Social Security: Privatization and Progressivity, *American Economic Review 88*, 137–141.
Kotlikoff, L. J. and Spivak, A. (1981), The Family as Incomplete Annuities Market, *Journal of Political Economy 89*, 372–91.
Lillard, L. A., Brien, M. J. and Panis, C. W. A. (1996), The Value of an Annuity. When Payments and Survival Probabilities Depend on Future Events, mimeo, RAND, Santa Monica, CA.
Lillard, L. A. and Panis, C. W. A. (1996), Income and Mortality, mimeo, RAND, Santa Monica, CA.
Menchik, P. L. (1993), Economic Status as a Determinant of Mortality Among Black and White Older Men: Does Poverty Kill? *Population Studies 47*, 427–436.
Mitchell, O. S., Poterba, J. M. and Warshawsky, M. J. (1997), New Evidence on the Money's Worth of Individual Annuities, NBER Working Paper no. 6002, Cambridge, MA.
Pauly, M. (1974), Overinsurance and Public Provision of Insurance: The Roles of Moral Hazard and Adverse Selection, *Quarterly Journal of Economics 88*, 44–62.
Rothschild, M. and Stiglitz, J. (1976), Equilibrium in Competitive Insurance Markets: An Essay on the Economics of Imperfect Information, *Quarterly Journal of Economics 90*, 629–649.
Rust, J. and Phelan, C. (1997), How Social Security and Medicare Affect Retirement Behavior in a World of Incomplete Markets, *Econometrica 65*, 781–831.
Walliser, J. (1998), Essays on Annuity Pricing and Social Security Privatization, Ph.D. dissertation, Boston University, Boston, MA.
Walliser, J. (1999), Regulation of Withdrawals in Individual Account Systems, Working Paper of the International Monetary Fund 99/153, Washington, DC.
Warshawsky, M. J. (1988), Private Annuity Markets in the United States: 1919–1984, *Journal of Risk and Insurance 55*, 518–528.
Wilson, C. (1977), A Model of Insurance Markets with Incomplete Information, *Journal of Economic Theory 16*, 167–207.
Yaari, M. E. (1965), Uncertain Lifetime, Life Insurance, and the Theory of the Consumer, *Review of Economic Studies 32*, 137–150.
Zeldes, S. P. (1989), Consumption and Liquidity Constraints: An Empirical Investigation, *Journal of Political Economy 97*, 305–346.

4

The Financial Stability of Notional Account Pensions

*Salvador Valdés-Prieto**

I. Introduction

A traditional pension system is financed using the pay-as-you-go (PAYG) method and determines benefits according to a salary-based formula. A notional account (NA) pension system is also financed using the PAYG method, but replaces the salary-based formula by an actuarial formula. It maintains individual accounts where contributions are recorded and interest is credited every year. These balances are imaginary, in the sense that they do not represent funds or investments held by the pension institution.[1] However, notional balances are real in another sense: they determine benefits, because the pension amount of each individual is calculated on the basis of the imaginary balance at pension age. NA systems combine an actuarial benefit formula with PAYG financing.

NA and points-based benefit formulas have been widespread in Western Europe since World War II. They are currently experiencing a revival—which motivates this chapter—in countries that have reformed their benefit formulas in the 1990s, such as Italy, Latvia, Poland and Sweden. The debate has centred on the advantages of NA benefit formulas as compared to traditional salary-based benefit formulas, where both systems are PAYG financed.

In the debate, it is argued that the actuarial benefit formulas of NA pension systems provide a better link between contributions and benefits at the individual level than the traditional salary-based benefit formulas. This, in turn, contributes to a reduction in the labour market distortions caused by

*This paper was written while receiving financial support from the World Bank and the Research Fund of the Faculty of Economics and Management of the Catholic University of Chile. The paper has benefited from the encouragement and extensive comments of Anita Schwarz and from information on the French points system provided by Florence Legros. Comments from two anonymous referees are gratefully acknowledged. I also thank seminar participants at the Catholic University of Chile, August 1997, and in Brasilia, December 1998.

[1] Even if the pension institution owns some funds, they are not allocated to individual accounts.

mandatory pensions; see Fox *et al*. (1996).[2] Although our chapter does not delve into this issue, it is clear that by retaining PAYG financing, the notional interest rate credited to the imaginary accounts is expected on average to be 2–4 percentage points per annum below market interest rates for similarly illiquid savings.[3] In present value, this difference creates not only a substantial tax component in contributions, which is higher in contributions made when young, but also reduces the actuarial factor. This tax component induces workers to avoid covered jobs, to reduce working hours and to prefer an earlier pension age (if allowed). Thus, the efficiency gains in this area appears limited.

Another advantage claimed in the debate is that NA benefit formulas are "fair"; see Palmer (1997). This claim should be disputed, in the senses that it appears inequitable (apart from distortionary) to tax more strongly the contributions made when young than those made closer to pension age. This distribution of taxes also hurts women who withdraw from the labour force to raise children. In addition, actual NA systems set a uniform actuarial factor, without reference to lifetime income or longevity risk classes. Given the established fact that the rich live longer, much of this redistribution is regressive.

To its promoters, the most attractive feature of NA systems is that they provide financial stability to the pension plan. For example, the goal of the Polish "first pillar" is to ensure a system that is "financially self-sufficient", "stable" and "financially sustainable"; see Office Report (1997, pp. 27–28). The reform approved by the Italian Parliament in August 1995 sought to "ensure financial equilibrium of the compulsory pension system"; see Reynaud and Hege (1996). The reform approved by Latvia's Parliament in November 1995 sought to modify the existing PAYG pension system to "assure affordability"; see Fox *et al.* (1996). The Swedish authorities adopted a new benefit formula for its earnings-related pension system because they regarded the current system as "too sensitive to changes in economic growth"; see Sundén (1998). This is the issue analysed here.

This chapter shows that NA systems cannot provide financial stability in the "short" run, i.e., when it matters, except in unlikely cases. In section II we define automatic financial balance and review the costs and benefits of financial stability in a pension plan. Section III reviews the basics of NA in a

---

[2]The main labour market distortions are financial disincentives to work in covered jobs, disincentives to work more covered hours, incentives to take early retirement and incentives to avoid paid work when pensioned.

[3]See evidence in Davis (1995). Note that the benchmark we propose is illiquid savings. Because of illiquidity, the benefit–contribution link is looser than in voluntary saving even in fully funded systems. A recent empirical study for the Chilean AFP system, which is fully funded, found that the perceived tax component in mandatory contributions was close to 50 percent; see Torche and Wagner (1997).

two-period model. Continuous time is introduced in Section IV and the general case where pensions are paid is analysed in Section V. Section VI shows that a particular NA benefit formula exhibits an automatic financial balance in a demographic and economic steady state.

II. Notional Accounts and Automatic Financial Stability

History of Thought about Notional Accounts

Notional accounts are an old concept, dating at least from the French points-based earnings-related pension introduced in 1945. The French mandatory "private" pension system, with complementary (ARRCO) and supplementary (AGIRC) pensions, became mandatory in 1972. Each year's contributions provide some "points" to the individual contributor, determined by the purchase price of a point at the time of purchase. At pension age, the sum of points is converted into a pension denominated in francs, which become indexed to price inflation. Each year, national boards adjust the following parameters in a discretionary way: (i) the purchase price of new points; (ii) the contribution rate;[4] and (iii) the value of points when they are sold to obtain a pension. However, these boards do not use long-term cash flow projections on a regular basis to adjust parameters in a time-consistent way.[5] Thus, the French point system seems to operate in the fashion of conventional defined-benefit plans, and not of NA.

Buchanan (1968) proposed replacing payroll taxes in the US by mandatory purchase of "social insurance bonds". Such bonds would carry no explicit rate of yield, but only the purchase amount and the date of purchase. The bonds would mature on the owner's retirement (at age 65) and "... on that date [an amount of interest will be credited] to the holder equal to the face value accumulated at the higher of the following two rates: (1) the rate of interest on long-term U.S. Treasury bonds, or (2) the rate of growth of Gross National Product" (p. 391).

Buchanan's proposal was not intended to achieve financial stability in the short run. On the contrary, he explicitly stated that "the attempted matching of the two sides of the separate account (revenue and expenditure) is not characteristic of the program suggested" (p. 391). Since he regarded PAYG

---

[4]The actual contribution rate is the product of the statutory contribution rate and the "call rate", which is currently 125 percent and can diverge from 100 percent for many years if necessary.

[5]For example, when a particular complementary pension scheme was reported to have a cash surplus, the board decided to reduce the contribution rate. A few years later the board was forced to re-raise the contribution rate, an event that could have been projected.

as having a higher return than financial investment,[6] PAYG financing appeared to be socially optimal.[7] However, he feared that political interference would prevent workers from obtaining access to this advantage.[8] His proposal tried to insulate benefits from politics while locking-in the rate of return of PAYG financing. To reduce political interference, he proposed backing benefit promises by contractual bonds rather than legislative promises. For the retirement period, Buchanan (1968, p. 394) proposed that retirees should be forced to use the proceeds from their social insurance bonds to purchase a variable annuity,[9] with payouts related to the actual rate of growth of GNP during the period in which benefits are received.

Boskin, Kotlikoff and Shoven proposed an NA scheme in 1982 (called Personal Security Accounts, PSA).[10] However, they did not propose automatic financial balance, but rather that "the real rate of return used to calculate each year's annuities be chosen each year by an independent board of actuaries to ensure . . . balance in present value between projected revenue and benefit payments over the succeeding 75 years . . ." (Boskin *et al.*, 1988, pp. 190-191).[11]

The German "personal point system" introduced in 1992 also has a flavour of NA. In this system, each contributor accumulates personal points, which are defined as the ratio between his taxable wage and the average taxable wage. At pension age the individual adds up the points earned over time (the average earner gets one per year) and the sum sets his entry pension as a proportion of the average wage at that date. After a reform in 1995, the average wage is calculated net of social security contributions.[12] Subsequent pensions are indexed to average net wages; see Queisser (1996). Contrary to the NA approach, the German government is expected to cover

---

[6]This belief may have been encouraged by the negative effects of Regulation Q on the real interest rate paid by American banks in the 1960s, by the assumption that equities were too risky to dominate a pension portfolio, and by the fast growth of the US economy and contribution revenue in those years.

[7]He accepted the economic arguments of Samuelson (1958), who believed that the growth rate of GNP could be above long-term interest rates. They were later shown by Tirole (1985) to be vulnerable to arbitrage.

[8]As of 1968, the US Congress had not yet legislated automatic CPI indexation of pensions in payment or indexation of past wages to wage growth before calculating the average wage on which the initial pension is based. Consequently, fears regarding benefit erosion through inflation and political inaction were reasonable.

[9]Variable annuities do not pay out a fixed dollar amount, but the current market value of a fixed number of units analogous to mutual fund shares.

[10]Their report, first presented in the US in 1982, was published in 1988.

[11]The real rate of return would be flat over time, unlike market yield curves. When determining the price of each deferred annuity, this flat interest rate would apply both before and after pension age.

[12]This seems to follow a proposal by Musgrave (1981).

the fluctuations in the deficit of the plan, and repeated legislation will be used as the financial stabilizer of last resort.

Summing up, NA were not seen as providers of automatic short-run financial stability in the past. This seems to be a new aspiration of European reformers of the 1990s, as cited in the Introduction.[13]

Benefits and Costs of Automatic Financial Stability

We define "automatic financial stability" as the ability of a pension plan to adjust to financial shocks without legislative intervention. This is valuable because when legislative intervention is required to regain financial balance, three dangers arise:

(i) Politicians may use their discretion to delay legislation needed to adjust parameters, thereby allowing a build-up of financial imbalance. This is rational for them when parametric adjustment may anger important groups of voters, provided they have to compete for re-election. The build-up of imbalances increases fiscal risk and member risk.

(ii) When they finally act, politicians may use their discretion to bias the mix of parameter adjustments against future generations of plan members, who do not vote. For example, when a trend of increased longevity appears, the chosen adjustment may rely too much on higher contribution rates and too little on increases in pension age.

(iii) Politicians may take the initiative to enhance benefit promises in an unsustainable way. The public-choice literature has shown that legislation to "compensate" the damage inflicted by increases in contribution rates on current workers with higher or earlier benefits attracts a winning coalition in a democracy; see Browning (1975) and Disney (1998).

Instead, an *automatic* rule avoids the need to initiate new legislation, as such a rule only requires application of the legislated adjustment rule, thereby pre-empting delay, bias and activist legislation.

Of course, achieving financial stability through automatic rules may also have social costs. To identify them, it is useful to keep in mind the distinction between the particular mix of parameter changes used to regain financial balance, and overall adjustment. For a given financial imbalance, there exists a particular mix of adjustments to parameters—such as contribution rates, pension ages, replacement rates and other qualifying conditions—that is optimal and restores balance. For example, to take into account the

[13] Musgrave (1981) advocated automatic financial stability in the short run, but did not propose a notional account system.

fact that pensioners may be more risk averse than contributors, pensions could be subject to modest adjustments in comparison to contribution rates.[14] The point is that automatic financial stability is compatible with optimal selection of the mix of parameter changes.

It is also necessary to make a distinction between short- and long-run financial stability. Short-run financial stability is defined by the fact that it avoids a different type of adjustment which would entail reducing assets (in partially funded plans) and running up debts. In contrast, long-run financial stability allows assets and debts to evolve over time, possibly over several decades, but achieves financial equilibrium after all shocks cease and have worked their way through the plan.

A reduction in net assets is not an independent method of adjustment, because any drop in net assets has to be faced in the long run by means of further adjustments to the main parameters (contribution rates, pension ages, replacement rates etc.). Net asset adjustment only indicates how much of the adjustment to parameters is foisted on the future.

One problem with long-run financial stability is that the division of any shock into transitory and permanent components is risky, especially in pension plans. Inevitable errors in projections may induce the formula to delay adjustment for decades, so that the pension plan may require very large loans or asset reductions that may be painful and slow to reverse.

More importantly, we submit that in mandatory pension plans subject to legislative initiative, the critical time unit is the period between elections. If adjustments are delayed any longer than that, while imbalances accumulate, the probability of reform of the automatic adjustment rule increases. The shape of such reform is unpredictable. Thus, the financial stability of a rule that provides long-term (decades-long) financial stability is irrelevant, because the rule itself will be modified unpredictably by the political process.

Therefore, we offer the principle that it may be desirable to ensure that most of the automatic adjustment to any shock is completed within the critical time unit stipulated by the political process. In this context, it seems natural to define the "short run" as one or two calendar years. We submit that short-run financial stability is credible, because it achieves adjustment before the political process finds itself compelled to intervene, pre-empting legislation designed under pressure, with all its uncertainties. Of course, automatic short-run financial stability does not prevent a parliament from reforming the plan anyway.

One social cost of restricting a pension plan so that it exhibits the

---

[14]This is why an optimal pension plan is likely to exhibit frequent changes in contribution rates.

property of automatic financial stability in the short run seems to be that the opportunities for benevolent intergenerational redistribution to future generations of plan members are lost. However, society can still attain those opportunities through fiscal policy, by raising or reducing the public debt.[15]

Another social cost of automatic financial stability in the short run seems to be that pensions are adjusted frequently and risk-averse pensioners suffer. However, in economies where most plan members have access to consumer financial markets or to family insurance (transfers), or where they own some liquid financial assets that can be disposed of, they can react to the transitory component in the shocks that beset the plan and are transmitted to them by automatic parameter adjustment, by borrowing and lending in the voluntary financial market. Provided that the authorities of the plan inform members and lenders about the likely permanence of each shock, the financial market can be expected to do a reasonably efficient job of consumption smoothing.[16]

Of course, the poor old usually do not have access to credit or family assistance. But in Europe they receive social assistance, i.e., state guaranteed pensions which do not fluctuate. Provided the NA plan is a second pillar supplemented by a first pillar that provides lifetime redistribution, the poor are not affected by NA adjustments either.

However, in economies where a substantial number of plan members do not have access to financial markets or family insurance, and provided those members are not covered by a first pillar, full short-run adjustment does impose economic costs on members. On the other hand, it is likely that the benefits to members of reducing political interference are highest in precisely those same economies, so that automatic short-run balance may still be the optimal policy for such economies.

III. The Basics of Notional Accounts

The aggregate revenue (R_t) and expenditure (E_t) of a pension plan that is financed by the PAYG method, (i.e., has no reserves or pension funds) are:

$$R_t \equiv \sum_i \theta_t^i \cdot Y_t^i \tag{1a}$$

---

[15]The need to use public debt for intergenerational redistribution could even generate social gains, because the public debt is more transparent, and thus subject to more democratic accountability, than the debt hidden in PAYG financing.

[16]Pensioners do suffer because of the permanent component in the aggregate shocks that hit the plan. But in the case of permanent shocks, it is socially desirable to adjust sooner rather than later. If intergenerational insurance is desired, the public debt can be adjusted accordingly.

$$E_t \equiv \sum_j P_t^j \tag{1b}$$

where: θ_t^i is the contribution rate levied on the covered labour earnings of member i; Y_t^i are covered labour earnings of member i; and P_t^j is the pension benefit to be paid to (pensioned) member j in period t.

Let us consider an economy in which individual plan members live for two periods, one in which the member works and contributes, and the other in which he or she receives pension benefits. Covered labour income and demography are stochastic. *Ex post*, the internal rate of return on pension contributions is defined by:

$$1 + \rho_t^i \equiv \frac{P_{t+1}^i}{\theta_t^i \cdot Y_t^i} \tag{2}$$

where: P_{t+1}^i is the pension received by member i in the next period $(t+1)$; ρ_t^i is the internal rate of return received by i on contributions made in t. The realized value of this rate of return is revealed only at time $t+1$.

The information structure is as follows: at the beginning of each period, covered labour income and demography for the period are revealed. The contribution rate for the period is also revealed by the political process. This allows determination of the aggregate revenue that will be collected during the period, the pensions that will be paid and the internal rate of return received by the current old on previous contributions.

We now consider pension plans where members are given an individual account, to which their contribution is recorded, and an interest rate is credited *ex post*, when the second period begins. The rule for setting the interest rate is fixed, but the actual interest rate is unknown *ex ante*, as it depends on aggregate conditions. The benefit is set equal to the account balance in the second period. We only consider plans that are uniform, in the sense that the contribution rate at a given date is the same for all members, and where the interest rate credited to individual accounts at a given date is also the same for all members:

$$\theta_t^i = \theta_t \quad \text{for all } t; \qquad \rho_t^i = \rho_t \quad \text{for all } t. \tag{3}$$

There are several possible choices of notional interest rate. In any choice, the notional interest rate is set to be the growth rate of some variable X: $1 + \rho_t = X_{t+1}/X_t$. We now consider several choices of the variable X. The first possible X is the covered wage bill, denoted by $WB_t = \sum_i Y_t^i$. This is the formula chosen by Italy, Latvia and Poland. It is also the closest analogue to Buchanan (1968), who proposed that X should be GNP. In this case ρ_t is the *ex-post* growth rate of the covered wage bill. Here, benefit expenditure is:

$$E_{t+1} = \sum_i (1+\rho_t) \cdot \theta_t \cdot Y_t^i = \left[\frac{\sum_k Y_{t+1}^k}{\sum_i Y_t^i} \right] \cdot \theta_t \cdot \sum_i Y_t^i = \left(\frac{\theta_t}{\theta_{t+1}} \right) \cdot R_{t+1}. \tag{4}$$

Equation (4) shows that when the notional interest rate is the *ex-post* growth rate of the covered wage bill, benefit expenditure at time $t+1$ is proportional to current revenue, R_{t+1}. However, the constant of proportionality is not 1. Note that the political process *does* adjust contribution rates significantly over time. In Latvia, for example, contribution rates were scheduled to fall from 38 to 33 percent from 1996 to 2000. The Polish contribution rate is expected to fall from 24 to 18 percent over an extended period.

A second possible X is the average covered wage, denoted by $AW_t = (\sum_i Y_t^i)/N_t$, where N_t is the number of covered contributors at date t. This is the formula recently chosen by Sweden; see Sundén (1998). It is also analogous to the widespread practice in traditional state-managed defined-benefit plans in the OECD, where benefits are based on the average of "indexed" past wages, and the indexing factor is the growth rate of average wages. In this case ρ_t is the growth rate of the average wage, and benefit expenditure is:

$$\begin{aligned} E_{t+1} &= \sum_i (1+\rho_t) \cdot \theta_t \cdot Y_t^i = \left[\frac{\frac{1}{N_{t+1}} \sum_k Y_{t+1}^k}{\frac{1}{N_t} \sum_i Y_t^i} \right] \cdot \theta_t \cdot \sum_i Y_t^i \\ &= \left(\frac{\theta_t}{\theta_{t+1}} \right) \cdot \left(\frac{N_t}{N_{t+1}} \right) \cdot R_{t+1}. \end{aligned} \tag{5}$$

Equation (5) shows that when the notional interest rate is the growth rate of average covered wages, benefit expenditure at time $t+1$ is proportional to current revenue, R_{t+1}. However, the constant of proportionality is not 1 and changes over time in response to demographic and coverage shocks (through changes in the number of contributors N_t and in the contribution rate). Thus, we have the well-known result:

Result 1. Notional account systems where the interest rate credited *ex post* is the growth rate of the average covered wage, or the growth rate of the covered wage bill, or the growth rate of GNP, do not exhibit automatic financial stability, except in hypothetical cases where the number of contributors and the contribution rate remain constant forever.

A third possible X is aggregate contribution revenue. To our knowledge, no country in Europe has legislated this method. In this case, ρ_t is the *ex-post* growth rate of contribution revenue, and benefit expenditure is:

$$E_{t+1} = \sum_i (1+\rho_t)\cdot\theta_t\cdot Y_t^i = \left[\frac{\sum_k \theta_{t+1}\cdot Y_{t+1}^k}{\sum_i \theta_t\cdot Y_t^i}\right]\cdot\theta_t\cdot\sum_i Y_t^i = R_{t+1}. \quad (6)$$

Equation (6) suggests that when the notional interest rate is the growth rate of contribution revenue, benefit expenditure at time $t+1$ is equal to current revenue, R_{t+1}, in any state of nature. Unfortunately, the result in equation (6) is flawed, as it relies on the artifice of a two-period lifetime, which embeds a number of strong demographic and economic assumptions, as will be shown in Sections IV and V.

The simple model of this section is also useful for evaluating composite NA plans where financial stability in the short run is achieved by varying the contribution rate θ_t at the beginning of each period. Equation (4) shows that when the notional interest rate is the growth rate of the wage bill, and the contribution rate θ_t is kept constant forever, automatic financial balance is assured. Equation (5) shows that when the notional interest rate is the growth rate of average wages, and the contribution rate θ_t is varied according to $\theta_{t+1} = \theta_t\cdot(N_t/N_{t+1})$, automatic financial balance is achieved.

When the notional interest rate is the growth rate of contribution revenue, the contribution rate may follow any path and financial balance obtains anyway. For example, any increase in θ_t that raises revenue, increases the *ex-post* notional interest rate and hence increases notional capital and benefit expenditure simultaneously, preventing any improvement in the net financial balance. Thus, in this case, the contribution rate is free to be used to attain other policy goals. Examples of such goals may be to keep constant the ratio of pensions to average wages. A related goal is to increase equity between generations by keeping expected ρ_t constant over time. For this goal choose:[17]

[17]Obtained from (2) and (3). θ_t must be set at the beginning of period t, but the realized value of R_{t+1} and P_{t+1}^{average} are known only at the beginning of period $t+1$. Thus, unlike the other formulas in this paper, (7) can be used only in expected value.

$$\theta_t \equiv \left(\frac{R_t}{R_{t+1}}\right) \cdot \frac{P_{t+1}^{\text{average}}}{Y_t^{\text{average}}}. \tag{7}$$

In fully funded defined-contribution plans, the path of θ_t may be adjusted to meet these same goals. However, seeking such goals may introduce instability into the path of the contribution rate, a topic which we do not explore. In addition, from the point of view of the generations not yet in the labour force, changes in θ_t can make net wages riskier.[18]

IV. Automatic Financial Balance in Unfunded Provident Funds

We now argue that the result in equation (6) is not general, in the sense that it depends on the strong demographic and economic assumptions embedded in the two-period model. From now on we use continuous time. In this section we assume that the pension plan pays a single lump sum at pension age, as in provident funds. We do not suggest that this is a desirable method of benefit payment. The assumption is adopted to postpone treating the issues of pension indexation, actuarial factors and longevity. We only consider the case where the notional interest rate is the growth rate of contribution revenue:

$$\rho(t) \equiv \frac{1}{R(t)} \frac{\mathrm{d}R(t)}{\mathrm{d}t} \quad \text{which implies} \quad \exp\left[\int_u^t \rho(z)\,\mathrm{d}z\right] \equiv R(t)/R(u). \tag{8}$$

Again, the instantaneous notional interest rate is determined *ex post* at the end of point in time t, according to the realization of revenue in t. Assuming that mortality is zero during active life (to simplify notation), each individual's account balance at pension age is:

$$K^i(x) \equiv \int_{x-(T_i-A_i)}^{x} \theta(w) \cdot Y^i(u, w) \cdot \exp\left[\int_w^x \rho(z)\,\mathrm{d}z\right] \mathrm{d}w \tag{9}$$

where: x is the current calendar date; K^i is the notional capital of each individual i who obtains a lump-sum benefit at date x; w is the calendar date when the contribution was made; A_i is the age at which individual i starts contributing; T_i is the pension age for individual i (age of exit from contributory phase); $\theta(w)$ is the contribution rate when the individual contributed; $Y^i(u, w)$ is the taxable labour earnings of individual i as of age

[18] There seems to be scope for partial risk sharing between pensioners and workers by adjusting θ_t.

u at calendar date w; and $u = T_i - (x - w)$ are the ages which each individual went through when contributing.

Substituting (8) in (9) we find that:

$$K^i(x) = R(x) \cdot \int_{x-T_i+A_i}^{x} \frac{\theta(w) \cdot Y^i(T_i + w - x, w)}{R(w)} \, \mathrm{d}w. \tag{10}$$

Equation (10) shows that the benefit of each individual, and thus aggregate expenditure, is proportional to the contribution revenue available when he is paid. To assess aggregate financial balance, we have to see whether the expression for aggregate expenditure simplifies to contribution revenue:

$$E(x) \equiv \sum_i K^i(x) = R(x) \cdot \left[\sum_i \int_{x-T_i+A_i}^{x} \frac{\theta(w) \cdot Y^i(T_i + w - x, w)}{R(w)} \, \mathrm{d}w \right]. \tag{11}$$

The question now is whether the expression in square brackets can be made to equal 1.

Result 2. Notional accounts do not provide automatic financial balance in the short run when the credited notional interest rate is the growth rate of contribution revenue, except for the steady-state growth case identified in the Appendix.

Proof: We prove this result by counterexample. In our example, $T_i = T$ and $A_i = A$ for all individuals i and cohorts x. This allows us to express expenditure as $E(x) = N(x) \cdot K(x)$, where $N(x)$ is the number of members who obtain a lump sum at date x. In addition, labour productivity growth among covered workers is assumed to be constant and zero. We also assume that individual taxable earnings vary by age only as indicated by a single age–earnings profile $h(u)$, which is constant over time. This proof has two parts:

(a) Show that the authorities cannot influence financial balance by modifying the path of the contribution rate $\theta(w)$. To prove this, recall that $R(w)$ is the contribution revenue received by the plan in year w in the past, when current beneficiaries were contributing:

$$R(w) \equiv \theta(w) \cdot \int_{A}^{T} N(w + T - u) \cdot Y(u, w) \, \mathrm{d}u \tag{12}$$

where $N(w + T - u)$ is the number of contributors of age u as of calendar year w (who will obtain a benefit in calendar year $w + T - u$), $Y(u, w) = h(u) \cdot Y(A)$ is the covered income of contributors of age u as of calendar year w, and $Y(A)$ is the covered income of workers just entering the covered labour force. In this simple case $Y(A)$ is a constant. For consistency with the other definitions, $Y(T + w - x, w) = h(w - x + T) \cdot Y(A)$. Inserting these expressions and (12) into (11), the ratio of current expenditure to current revenue becomes:

$$\frac{E(x)}{R(x)} = \int_{x-(T-A)}^{x} \frac{N(x) \cdot \theta(w) \cdot h(w - x + T)}{\theta(w) \cdot \int_{A}^{T} N(w + T - u) \cdot h(u)\,\mathrm{d}u}\,\mathrm{d}w. \qquad (13)$$

The fact that $\theta(w)$ simplifies in (13) completes the proof of part (a).

(b) We calculate financial balance when the realized path of the growth rate of new workers entering coverage is initially "n_1", and then rises permanently to "n_2" ($> n_1$) as of date D. This realized path implies:

$$N(x) = \begin{cases} N(D) \cdot e^{-n_1 \cdot (D-x)} & \text{for } x \leqslant D + T - A \\ N(D) \cdot e^{(n_1 - n_2)(T-A)} \cdot e^{n_2 \cdot (x-D)} & \text{for } x > D + T - A \end{cases}. \qquad (14)$$

Consider year $x = D + (T - A)$.[19] For that date, we integrate (13) numerically; the results are shown in Table 1. The ratio is different from 1 when $n_1 \neq n_2$. Q.E.D.

The intuition for the deviation from financial balance is as follows: when the growth rate of the number of new workers entering coverage rises to "n_2" ($> n_1$) at date D, the growth rate of contribution revenue rises. As this is the notional interest rate credited to the *stock of* notional capital of those members reaching age 65, the rise in expenditure is larger than the rise in revenue, generating a deficit. This deficit grows over time and reaches a maximum at date $D + T - A$. The next few generations of beneficiaries still earn part of their notional pension rights while previous generations are still contributing, so total contribution revenue does not yet grow at rate n_2. Thus the ratio is still above 1 after date $D + T - A$. Finally, $2 \cdot (T - A)$ years after date D, the ratio reaches 1 again.

---

[19]From (14) it is easy to show that in calendar year $x = D + T - A$, the ratio $E(D + T - A)/R(D + T - A)$ takes the value

$$\int_{A}^{T} h(q)\,\mathrm{d}q \Big/ \left[e^{n_1 q} \cdot \int_{A}^{q} h(u) e^{-n_1 u}\,\mathrm{d}u + e^{n_2 q} \cdot \int_{q}^{T} h(u) e^{-n_2 u}\,\mathrm{d}u \right]$$

by the change of variable $q = W - D + A$.

Table 1. *Ratio $E(x)/R(x)$ for date $x = D + T - A$*
(Case $h(u) = 1$, $A = 20$ years, $T = 65$ years)

Initial growth rate of covered workers (n_1)	0.0%	−0.5%
Final growth rate (n_2)		
0.0%	1.000	1.038
0.5%	1.038	1.077
1.0%	1.077	1.116
1.5%	1.116	1.156

Note: It can also be shown, for the case $h(u) = 1$, that $\partial(E/R)/\partial n_1 = -1/(T - A) \neq 0$ at $n_1 = 0$ and $n_2 = 0$.

Other reasons to expect imbalances, not explored in our example, are: (i) different cohorts start contributions at different ages and choose different pension ages; (ii) the taxable earnings of each generation do not grow at a constant rate; and (iii) the age–earnings profile $h(u)$ changes across cohorts.

V. The Dispersion Phase and Pensions

We now discuss schemes where notional capital is disbursed over time as pensions. In such plans, new controls become available to the authorities, but new goals also emerge. A new source of financial imbalance arises, i.e., shocks to longevity.

The first new control is the *actual* rate of indexation of pensions in real terms:

$$i^a(z) \equiv \frac{1}{P(z)} \cdot \frac{\mathrm{d}P(z)}{\mathrm{d}z} \quad \text{or equivalently} \quad P^i(t, x) = P^i(x) \cdot \exp\left[\int_x^t i^a(z)\,\mathrm{d}z\right] \tag{15}$$

where: $P(z)$ is the actual path of the real pension (adjusted by CPI inflation) as of time z; and $i^a(z)$ is the actual rate of indexation of pensions over and above the CPI, as of time z.

Let us review possible indexation rules. First, when pension disbursements are indexed to the CPI, $i^a(z) = 0$ for all z. By analogy to Result 1, benefit expenditure cannot track the shocks to contribution revenue when pensions are indexed with this rule. The same analogy applies in the case where pension disbursements are indexed to the *ex-post* growth rate of the average covered wage, i.e. $i^a(z) = \mathrm{d}\ln AW(z)/\mathrm{d}z$. Next, consider Buchanan's (1968, p. 394) proposal[20] that an NA benefit formula should pay a variable annuity

[20]Palmer (1997) made a similar proposal for Sweden, but it was not accepted by the authorities.

that yields the *ex-post* growth rate of GNP. In our framework, the closest analogue to GNP growth is the growth rate of the covered wage bill, so $i^a(z) = \mathrm{d}\ln WB(z)/\mathrm{d}z$. Again, the analogy to Result 1 shows this indexing rule to be incompatible with automatic financial balance in the short run.

The obvious next step is to consider indexing pensions to the growth rate of contribution revenue, i.e., $i^a(z) = \mathrm{d}\ln R(z)/\mathrm{d}z = \rho(z)$. This and equation (15) imply that pension disbursements evolve over time as $P^i(t, x) = P^i(x) \cdot [R(t)/R(x)]$. As each individual's pension benefit tracks current aggregate contribution revenue $R(t)$, this suggests that automatic financial balance *may* be reached with this indexing rule. The new control (the indexation rule) must be used in this way to achieve financial balance.

The second new control that becomes available to the authorities is the annuity conversion factor used by the plan. The entry pension is calculated as:

$$P^i(x) \equiv f^i(x) \cdot K^i(x) \tag{16}$$

where: $P^i(x)$ is the entry pension for individual i, who retires at time x; and $f^i(x)$ is the annuity conversion factor for individual i, as of time x.

The annuity conversion factor depends in turn on at least three parameters. First, the expected rate of pension indexation, which is:

$$i^e(z, x) \equiv \frac{1}{P^{ei}(z, x)} \cdot \frac{\mathrm{d}P^{ei}}{\mathrm{d}z} \quad \text{thus,} \quad P^{ei}(t, x) \equiv P^i(x) \cdot \exp\left[\int_x^t i^e(z, x)\,\mathrm{d}z\right] \tag{17}$$

where: $i^e(z, x)$ is the rate of indexation of pensions above the CPI, at time z, as expected at time x. We presume i^e is uniform across all pensioners as of time z.

Second, the annuity conversion factor depends on the notional interest rate credited to notional capital *after* pension age. We denote the path of the expected notional interest rate credited in passive life as $\rho^{ep}(z, x)$. We presume that this notional interest rate is uniform across all pensioners as of time z. Third, the annuity conversion factor depends on the mortality projection. To simplify the notation we assume that every member of a cohort dies at the same time. We define life expectancy at pension age as $G^{ei}(x)$, where the expectation reflects the fact that the actual duration of life after pension age for a cohort may differ from the life expectancy as of the pension age at date x for this same cohort.

The annuity conversion factor is defined to spread out pension payments in such a way that the individual's notional capital at pension age is exhausted in expected value:

$$K^i(x) = \int_{T_i}^{T_i+G^{ei}(x)} P_x^{ei}(t, x) \cdot \exp\left[-\int_x^t \rho^{ep}(z, x)\,\mathrm{d}z\right] \mathrm{d}t. \tag{18}$$

Combining definitions (16) and (17) with equation (18) we find that:

$$f^i(x) = 1 \Big/ \left[\int_0^{G_i^e(x)} \exp\left\{\int_0^w [i^{ex}(z, x) - \rho^{ep}(z, x)]\,\mathrm{d}z\right\} \mathrm{d}w\right]. \tag{19}$$

The pension phase brings forth new policy goals. To achieve horizontal equity, let us choose the notional interest rate credited *ex post* to pensioners in the dispersion phase $\rho^p(z)$ to be equal to that credited to active workers who are simultaneously alive. Thus:

$$i^e(z, x) - \rho^{ep}(z, x) = E_x\{i^a(z) - \rho^p(z)\} = E_x\{0\} = 0$$

$$\text{constant for all } z \text{ and } x. \tag{20}$$

Even though the future notional interest rate credited to passive account balances and the future pension indexation rate cannot be predicted at the pension-age date, the difference between their paths can be predicted, and our equity goal leads us to make it equal to zero. Inserting (20) in (19), the annuity conversion factor simplifies to:

$$f^i(x) = \frac{1}{G^{ei}(x)}. \tag{21}$$

Unless we consider cases where the authorities purposefully interfere with mortality projections to achieve other goals, this annuity conversion factor is *not* under the control of the authorities. Now we go back to financial balance. In the case where $i^a = \mathrm{d}\ln R(z)/\mathrm{d}z = \rho(z)$, equations (15), (16) and (9), together with (21), determine the size of pensions as:

$$P^i(t, x) = R(t) \cdot \frac{1}{G^{ei}(x)} \int_{x-(T_i-A_i)}^{x} \frac{\theta(w) \cdot Y^i(T_i + w - x, w)}{R(w)}\,\mathrm{d}w. \tag{22}$$

Equation (22) shows that with these particular controls, each individual's pension is proportional to aggregate contribution revenue available at the time when he or she receives the pension, $R(t)$. The remaining question is whether individual pensions aggregate to current revenue.

As in the previous section, we argue that the remaining tool under the authorities' control, which is the contribution rate, simplifies away when calculating the ratio of expenditure to revenue. To build an expression that measures expenditure, we revert to the demographic homogeneity assumptions: $T_i = T(x)$, $A_i(x) = A(x)$ and $G^{ei}(x) = G^e(x)$. To simplify notation we also assume $T(x) = T$ and $A(x) = A$ for all x. We use the notation:

$M(u, w)$ = number of contributors of age u as of calendar year w
$N(x)$ = number of members who start a pension in calendar year x
$u = T - (x - w)$ = age expressed in terms of calendar dates
$x - (T - A) = w - (u - A)$ = calendar date at which the individual starts contributions.

Because mortality is zero until every member of a generation dies simultaneously at age $T + G$, aggregate expenditure is:

$$E(t) \equiv \int_{\{x:G(x) \geqslant t-x\}} N(x) \cdot P(t, x)\,\mathrm{d}x. \tag{23}$$

Note that the integration region (which depends on t) is given by the actual longevity of those alive at date t, which may be different from expected longevity as of date x.

Result 3. Consider a notional account plan where: (i) the notional interest rate is the growth rate of contribution revenue; (ii) pensions are indexed to the growth rate of contribution revenue; (iii) pensioner balances are credited *ex post* the same notional interest rate as contemporaneous contributors; and (iv) the authorities do not interfere with mortality projections to achieve financial balance. This plan is not in automatic financial balance in the short run, except in the case identified in the Appendix.

Proof: First we show that the authorities cannot control the ratio of expenditure to revenue in this pension plan. To do this we introduce the expression for $R(w)$, the contribution revenue paid into the plan far in the past, when current pensioners were contributing:

$$R(w) \equiv \theta(w) \cdot \int_A^T M(u, w) \cdot Y(u, w)\,\mathrm{d}u. \tag{24}$$

Combining (24) with (23) and (22) we find that:

$$\frac{E(t)}{R(t)} = \int_{\{x:G(x) \geqslant t-x\}} \frac{N(x)}{G^e(x)} \cdot \int_{x-(T-A)}^{x} \frac{\theta(w) \cdot Y(T + w - x, w)}{\theta(w) \cdot \int_A^T M(u, w) \cdot Y(u, w)\,\mathrm{d}u}\,\mathrm{d}w\,\mathrm{d}x. \tag{25}$$

As $\theta(w)$ simplifies away inside the second integral in (25), we have shown the desired result. An exception arises when the authorities purposefully interfere with mortality projections $G^e(x)$ to achieve financial balance. However, such interference is equivalent to discretionary parameter setting in traditional benefit formulas, which is precisely what advocates expect to avoid by adopting fixed-benefit formulas such as those in NA that operate automatically.

Second, we have to provide a counterexample where the RHS of (25) is not 1 for a fairly common realized path. The example in Section IV shows that the second integral is above 1 at date $[D+T-A]$. By continuity it is also above 1 for all dates in $(D+T-A, D+2[T-A])$. Provided $G(x) = G^e(x) = G$, then the outside integral of a function that is above $1/G$ for all x, between $x = t - G$ and $x = t$, is also above 1. Q.E.D.

VI. Requirements for Financial Balance

We now show that the specific benefit formula identified in Section V exhibits a tendency towards financial equilibrium in the *long* run, in the limited sense that financial equilibrium obtains in a scenario where both demography and the economy are in a growing steady state. This is of interest if demographic and economic ratios are believed to exhibit mean reversion, because in that case demography and the economy exhibit a trend towards such a steady state. To prove this result, we need seven assumptions. As shown before, we reached (25) by assuming:

(A) The population of a given cohort is demographically homogeneous, in the sense that $T_i = T(x)$, $A_i(x) = A(x)$, $G^i(x) = G(x)$ (actual mortality) and $G^{ei}(x) = G^e(x)$ (expected mortality) for all individuals i in each date x.

(B) The pension age and the age at which contributions start are the same for all generations, so $T(x) = T$ and $A(x) = A$ for all x. This is to simplify notation.

Consider now a growing steady state where the following assumptions obtain:

(C1) the number of covered workers increases at a constant rate "n";

(C2) labour productivity among covered workers increases at a constant rate λ;

(C3) individual taxable earnings vary only as indicated by the product of an age–earnings profile $h(u)$, which is constant over time, and a labour productivity factor linked solely to the date at which each worker joined the labour force.

Inserting assumptions (C1)–(C3) into (25), the expression for current expenditure simplifies to (see Appendix):

$$\frac{E(t)}{R(t)} = \int_{\{x:G(x)\geqslant t-x\}} \frac{\mathrm{d}x}{G^e(x)}. \tag{26}$$

Equation (26) acknowledges the difference between expected longevity $G^e(x)$ and actual longevity $G(x)$. Actual mortality changes over time in at least two ways. First, it improves according to a predicted trend, which may be non-linear. Second, it deviates from the trend in unpredictable ways. To gauge the size of fluctuations, note that in the US (a large country, where mortality fluctuations are more diversified), the average annual rate of mortality improvement for men was −0.19 percent 1954–1968, but shifted to 1.58 percent in 1968–1988, see Diamond (1997), citing the Social Security Technical Panel (1991). These deviations may accumulate into sizeable amounts.

To ensure that the RHS of (26) is 1, we need further assumptions:[21]

(D1) $G^e(x) = G(x)$. This assumption allows us to define $x_0(t)$, which is the solution z to the equation $G(z) = t - z$, where $G(z)$ is the actual longevity of the generation that started its pension at age z. This in turn allows us to replace the integration set $\{x\colon G(x) \geqslant t - x\}$ with the integration limits $[x_0(t) \leqslant x \leqslant t]$, while still allowing longevity to change over time.

What happens to the RHS of (26) as time passes? Using Leibniz's rule:

$$\frac{\mathrm{d}}{\mathrm{d}t}\left(\frac{E(t)}{R(t)}\right) = \frac{1}{G(t)} - \frac{1}{G(x_0(t))} \cdot \frac{\mathrm{d}x_0(t)}{\mathrm{d}t}. \tag{27}$$

The definition of $x_0(t)$ also implies that $\mathrm{d}x_0/\mathrm{d}t = 1/[1 + G'(x_0(t))]$. Thus, the RHS of (27) is not zero for a general path of longevity $G(x)$, implying that financial balance does not obtain yet. The reason is as follows. When longevity increases, a forward-looking annuity conversion factor reduces pensions immediately to take future improvements into account. As contribution revenue has not yet fallen, this triggers a financial surplus. By the same token, however, there will be a financial deficit when longevity falls, as in the US in 1954–1968 and Russia in the 1990s. Thus we make the further assumption:

---

[21] Indexing pensions in the same way as CREF annuities (accounting for mortality deviations), rather than to the growth rate of contribution revenue, may allow us to avoid assumption (D1). See footnote 24 below for a brief description of CREF annuities.

(D2) $G(x) = G$ for all x, i.e. there are no longevity trends.

In this case the RHS of (27) is equal to 0 and the RHS of (26) is equal to 1. Thus, we have proven:

Result 4. Under assumptions (A)–(D), the particular notional account plan described in Result 3 achieves automatic financial stability in the short run and the long run.

Remarks:

(a) This financial stabilizer is fully integrated into *this particular* benefit formula, and only this formula.
(b) Its weakness, as argued in Section II, is that it operates solely in a growing steady state, which we have made analogous to the long run. However, the long run seems too late when confronted with political interference that operates in the short run.
(c) The strategy of raising the pension age in response to an increase in longevity has mixed financial effects. In the short run, it increases revenue. But the increase in longevity already induces a surplus (provided a forward-looking life table is used). Later, the actuarial factor increases, raising expenditure to meet the higher revenue. In addition, the increase in revenue raises the notional interest rate, raising the benefits of all members. Moreover, as they contribute for more years, they claim larger pensions a few decades later.
(d) It might be claimed that the financial stability of this particular NA plan could be enhanced by adding a reserve fund; i.e., by engaging in partial funding. Such a conclusion is unwarranted, however, because if the reserve fund is always positive, then the notional interest rate credited to members must be raised to incorporate interest earnings. But if this is done, Result 4 becomes invalid. If the plan runs into debt, and market interest rates rise, the plan may be unable to return to financial equilibrium.

VII. Concluding Comments

We have argued that automatic financial balance in the short run is a desirable property. However, it has been shown that even with the most favourable formula, NA benefit formulas can achieve this property only in an unrealistic steady state. Thus, NA systems always need to have other financial adjustment mechanisms, such as government guarantees and repeated legislation, superimposed on them, just as traditional defined benefit plans.[22]

Some schemes do achieve automatic financial balance in the short run.[23] A fully funded defined-contribution plan that pays CREF annuities,[24] as used by TIAA–CREF in the US since 1952[25], provides pensions with automatic financial stability in the short run and does not require guarantors.[26] Within PAYG financing, the plan proposed by Musgrave (1981) achieves financial stability in the short run.[27]

We conclude with a question about the economic interpretation of the expression "defined contribution": it surely does not mean that contribution rates never change. Does it mean that the plan formula ensures automatic financial stability in the short run (as in Musgrave's plan), or that the benefit formula is actuarial (as in notional accounts)? Funded defined-contribution plans satisfy both definitions, but notional-account plans fulfil only the latter.

Appendix. Proof of Equation (26)

Assumptions (C1)–(C3) imply that:

$$N(x) = N(t) \cdot e^{-n(t-x)} \tag{A1}$$

$$M(u, w) = N(w + T - u) = N(t) \cdot e^{-n(t-[w+(T-u)])} \tag{A2}$$

$$Y(u, w) = h(u) \cdot Y(A, t) \cdot e^{-\lambda(t-[w-(u-A)])} \tag{A3a}$$

$$Y(w - x + T, w) = h(w - x + T) \cdot Y(A, t) \cdot e^{-\lambda(t-w+(w-x+T)-A)}. \tag{A3b}$$

---

[22] A reserve fund, i.e. to increase the degree of funding, also requires repeated intervention because of the vagaries of market interest rates.

[23] Defined-benefit plans do not, because they require a guarantor to absorb the non-diversifiable risk. Life insurance companies also guarantee investment and mortality risk in annuities.

[24] The CREF annuity, introduced by Duncan (1952), pays a monthly pension $P_{it} = V_t \cdot N_i$, where N_i is the number of "annuity units" owned by pensioner i and V_t is the price of each annuity unit in date t. The price is adjusted periodically to ensure automatic financial balance. The CREF annuity formula adjusts pensions over time not only according to investment experience, as normal variable annuities do, but also according to mortality experience and changes in mortality projections; see Valdés-Prieto (1998) for more details.

[25] A mandatory CREF annuity was legislated by Bolivia in 1996. Detailed rules were introduced in 1999.

[26] Traditional provident funds that pay a lump sum also achieve automatic financial balance in the short run. Although they fail to provide longevity insurance, they provide more liquidity than annuities, and may thus be preferable.

[27] This proposal keeps the ratio of average pensions to net average wages constant over time.

Inserting these assumptions into (25), and using (D1), the expression for current expenditure simplifies to:

$$\frac{E(t)}{R(t)} = \int_{\{x:G(x)\geqslant t-x\}} \frac{e^{-n(t-x)}}{G(x)} \cdot \int_{x-T+A}^{x} \frac{h(T+w-x)\cdot e^{-\lambda(t-x+T-A)}}{\int_{A}^{T} h(u)\cdot e^{-n(t-w-T+u)}\cdot e^{-\lambda(t-w+u-A)}\,\mathrm{d}u}\,\mathrm{d}w\,\mathrm{d}x. \tag{A4}$$

Next, take the exponentials in t, w, T and A outside of the innermost integral to find that this integral does not depend on w. Thus, this integral can be taken outside of the second integral, leaving $\exp(-(n+\lambda)w)$ inside the second integral:

$$\frac{E(t)}{R(t)} = \int_{\{x:G(x)\geqslant t-x\}} \frac{e^{(n+\lambda)(x-T)}}{G(x)} \cdot \left[\frac{\int_{x-T+A}^{x} h(T+w-x)\cdot e^{-(n+\lambda)w}\,\mathrm{d}w}{\int_{A}^{T} h(u)\cdot e^{-(n+\lambda)u}\,\mathrm{d}u}\right]\mathrm{d}x. \tag{A5}$$

Changing variables in the second integral to $q = w - x + T$, the second and third integrals cancel out for any shape $h(u)$ of the age–earnings profile. From this, (26) obtains. Q.E.D.

References

Boskin, M., Kotlikoff, L. and Shoven, J. (1988), Personal Security Accounts: A Proposal for Fundamental Social Security Reform, Chapter 7 in S. Wachter (ed.), *Social Security and Private Pensions*, 179–206, Lexington Books, Lexington, KY.

Browning, E. K. (1975), Why the Social Insurance Budget is Too Large in a Democracy, *Economic Inquiry 13*, 373–388.

Buchanan, J. (1968), Social Insurance in a Growing Economy: A Proposal for Radical Reform, *National Tax Journal 21* (4), 386–395.

Davis, E. P. (1995), *Pension Funds*, Clarendon Press/Oxford University Press, Oxford.

Diamond, P. A. (1997), Insulation of Pensions from Political Risk, Chapter 2 in S. Valdés-Prieto (ed.), *The Economics of Pensions*, Cambridge University Press, Cambridge.

Disney, R. (1998), *Can We Afford to Grow Older?,* MIT Press, Cambridge, MA.

Duncan, R. (1952), A Retirement System Granting Unit Annuities and Investing in Equities, *Transactions of the Society of Actuaries 4*, 317–344 and 770–788, Chicago, IL.

Fox, L., Palmer, E. and McIsaac, D. (1996), Latvian Pension Reform, mimeo, World Bank, Washington, DC.

Hamann, J. (1997), The Reform of the Pension System in Italy, IMF Working Paper no. 97/18, International Monetary Fund, Washington, DC.

Munnell, A. (1988), Comment in S. Wachter (ed.), *Social Security and Private Pensions*, 207–208, Lexington Books, Lexington, KY.

Musgrave, R. A. (1981), A Reappraisal of Social Security Financing, Chapter 3 in F. Skidmore (ed.), *Social Security Financing*, MIT Press, Cambridge, MA.

Office of the Government Plenipotentiary for Social Security Reform (1997), *Security through Diversity: Reform of the Pension System in Poland*, Warsaw.

Palmer, E. (1997), The Swedish Pension Reform Model—Framework and Issues, mimeo, National Social Insurance Board, Stockholm.

Queisser, M. (1996), Pensions in Germany, Policy Research Working Paper no. 1664, World Bank, Washington, DC.

Reynaud, E. and Hege, A. (1996), Italy: A Fundamental Transformation of the Pension System, *International Social Security Review 49* (3/9), 65–74.

Samuelson, P. (1958), An Exact Consumption–Loan Model of Interest without the Social Contrivance of Money, *Journal of Political Economy 66*, 467–482.

Sundén, A. (1998), The Swedish NDC Pension Reform, *Annals of Public and Cooperative Economics 4*; E. James (ed.), Special Issue on Comparative Analysis of Old Age Security Arrangements.

Tirole, J. (1985), Asset Bubbles and Overlapping Generations, *Econometrica 53* (6), 1499–1527.

Torche, A. and Wagner, G. (1997), Previsión social: Valoración individual de un beneficio mandatado, *Cuadernos de Economía* No. 103, 363–390, Santiago, Chile.

Valdés-Prieto, S. (1998), Risks in Pensions and Annuities: Efficient Designs, Social Protection Discussion Paper Series no. 9804, World Bank, Washington, DC.

5

Pension Reform during the Demographic Transition

*Hans Fehr**

I. Introduction

As in many other industrialized countries, declining fertility and rising life expectancy will enormously alter the future demographic structure of the German population. While pensioners currently constitute about 40 percent of the working population, their share is projected to double in the next 50 years. This will undermine the sustainability of pay-as-you-go financed social insurance arrangements such as the statutory pension system. If current benefit levels and labour force participation rates are maintained, the contribution rate of the pension system is projected to increase from 20 percent today to 31 percent in 2035 (Bundesministerium für Wirtschaft, 1998). In combination with income taxes and mandatory contributions to health and long-term care insurance, the resulting payroll tax burdens would further distort individual labour supply decisions, erode the tax base and thereby exaggerate the strains on the social security system. Consequently, in order to achieve long-run financial flexibility and reduce the fiscal pressure from population ageing, a reform of the current system seems necessary.

The recent pension reform debate in Germany has focused mainly on two alternative options. The first direction, outlined by the previous conservative government, was to reduce the benefit level by raising the retirement age, tightening eligibility criteria and lowering indexation. In addition, the federal grant would have been increased gradually. Although such a reform package would reduce future contribution rates significantly, the main characteristics of the current pension scheme would still be preserved. A growing number of analysts, however, argue that such measures only provide some short- and medium-run relief, especially if future economic conditions are less favourable than expected. In order to promote national savings and economic growth, they propose a fundamental policy reform towards a partially funded pension system. The resulting (mandatory) pension scheme would consist of

*I wish to thank Stefan Homburg and two anonymous referees for helpful and detailed comments on an earlier version of this paper.

an unfunded tier that provides a minimum pension and a fully funded tier for saving.[1] The unfunded tier could be designed as a tax-financed flat-rate pension which provides an unconditional minimum income after retirement or as an obligatory minimum old-age insurance where the benefits are still linked to former contributions.[2]

Various studies have already analysed the effects of different reform strategies on specific generations. For example, Börsch-Supan (1998) computes the changes in tax burdens for different generations if the current unfunded system would be completely replaced by a funded system within the next 50 years. Besendorfer *et al.* (1998) apply the generational accounting approach to compare the intergenerational redistribution effects of the moderate reform package proposed by the government and two variants of a minimum pension. However, both studies share two central shortcomings. First, since they do not incorporate behavioural reactions and macroeconomic repercussion effects, it is not possible to quantify any efficiency consequences. Second, since both studies do not disaggregate within generations, they could not compare the intra-generational redistribution effects of different reforms. The purpose of the present paper is to address these issues and analyse various pension reform strategies within a full general equilibrium model. This entails quantifying the impact of each reform on the macroeconomy as well as the efficiency and equity effects on different generations and households.

The numerical analysis is based on an overlapping generations model in the Auerbach–Kotlikoff (1987) tradition. It extends earlier work—see Fehr (1999)—in two directions which are particularly important in the present context. First, the model is able to replicate the demographic transition by allowing for rising life span and time-dependent fertility rates. Second, the model incorporates the strong linkage between contributions and benefits in Germany. The quantitative results show that a comprehensive evaluation of a pension reform strategy has to include intra-generational equity and efficiency considerations. Although the welfare calculations refer only to the German institutional setting, this message also applies to many other OECD countries which are currently attempting to reform their pension systems.

In the next section, I briefly describe the German pension system. Section III sketches the basic structure of the simulation model, while Section IV explains the calibration and simulation approach. Finally, Section V reports the simulation results and Section VI offers some concluding remarks.

---

[1] Similar reforms are currently under discussion or have been applied in a number of other countries; see the papers in Feldstein (1998) or Siebert (1998).

[2] Proposals for a flat-rate pension date back to the 1980s; see Miegel and Wahl (1985). For a recent discussion, see Breyer (1998). A switch to minimum old-age insurance has recently been proposed by the Sachverständigenrat (1996).

II. An Introduction to the German Pension System[3]

In 1998, total expenditures of the statutory pension scheme amounted to DM 400 billion or about 11.5 percent of GDP. Except for civil servants, whose pensions are paid directly from the budget, all dependent employees are compulsorily insured. In 1998, the contribution rate was 20.3 percent, which was applicable up to a monthly contribution ceiling of DM 8,400 or about 1.8 times the average gross earnings of all insured persons. In addition to these contributions, the federal government provides a grant which is intended to cover benefits that are not directly related to old-age insurance. In Germany, normal retirement with full benefits can begin at age 63, after a contribution record of at least 35 years. However, the average retirement age is much lower, at about 60 years, due to generous early retirement options.

In the case of early retirement, a strict earnings test has to be passed by those who work in addition to receiving an old-age pension. Since pensions are reduced quite dramatically if earnings exceed certain limits, partial retirement is relatively rare in Germany.

Pension benefits are computed by multiplying the number of "earning points" (EP) and the "actual pension amount" (APA). For each year of service, a worker receives an earning point which reflects his relative income position in that year. If he receives the average wage, then he gets exactly one earning point. If he receives more or less than average earnings, he receives points on a pro-rata basis. Owing to the contribution ceiling, there is an upper limit of about 1.8 points per year of service. Various credits are given for non-contributory periods such as child-rearing and military service. If an insured worker has contributed for 35 years, earning points below 0.75 are raised by 50 percent to a maximum of 0.75. This increase predominantly benefits female pensioners who made very low contributions during their working years. When a worker retires, the sum of his EP is multiplied by the APA; i.e., the (monthly) payment in a certain year for one EP. The APA is adjusted annually according to the growth of net wages. Currently, the so-called standard pension received after a 45-year contribution history by a worker who always earned the average wage amounts to 70 percent of average net earnings.

Summing up, although the system comprises some redistributive elements, pensions in Germany are strongly linked to former contributions. Due to this tax–benefit linkage, the marginal contribution rate for most households is much lower than the respective average contribution rate. Furthermore, households that earn an income above the contribution ceiling face a

[3]For a detailed description of the German pension system, see Börsch-Supan and Schnabel (1999).

zero marginal contribution rate. The simulation model which is described in the next section tries to take these important features into account.

III. The Structure of the Simulation Model

The model used in this paper is a modified version of the numerical general equilibrium model described in detail in Fehr (1999). This section contains a brief review of the general structure and concentrates on the new features which have been introduced to capture the demographic dynamics and the functioning of the pension system.

Demographic Structure

The households in the model are distinguished by their dates of birth and their lifetime labour productivity endowments. Each generation is split into five lifetime income quintiles $j = 1, \ldots, 5$. All agents within one cohort live for the same number of periods with certainty. However, in order to account for rising life expectancy, economic lifetime a^d increases from 58 years in the initial year 1998 to 64 years in 2060. After 2060 it is kept constant at this level. Since each adult enters the labour force at age 21, this corresponds to an increase in the "natural" age from 78 to 84 years. Hence, in each period, the model distinguishes between 290 and 320 types of households according to age and income class. In each period, a new generation enters economic life. Since population growth rates n_t differ across periods, cohorts grow according to

$$N^j_{t+1} = (1 + n_t)N^j_t, \tag{1}$$

where N^j_t denotes the number of the j-type cohort in period t. Note that the population growth rates are independent of household type; i.e., the structure of lifetime incomes remains constant throughout the transition. Adding up all cohorts living in a specific year t gives the total population POP_t living in that year:

$$POP_t = \sum_{j=1}^{5}\left(\sum_{s=1}^{a^d_t} N^j_{t+1-s} + \sum_{s=1}^{20} N^j_{t+s}\right). \tag{2}$$

The first term in parentheses sums the economic active generations in year t, while the second term takes into account the cohorts younger than 21 that enter the labour force in future years.

Household Preferences and Budget Constraints

Each household decides how much to consume and how many hours to work in each period, and when to withdraw from the workforce. As in the original Auerbach–Kotlikoff (1987) model, the preference structure is represented by a time-separable, nested CES utility function. Lifetime utility of a representative household of income class j takes the form[4]

$$U^j = \frac{1}{1-1/\gamma}\sum_{s=1}^{a^d}\left(\frac{1}{1+\theta}\right)^{s-1}[(c_s^j)^{1-1/\rho} + \xi_s(l_s^j)^{1-1/\rho}]^{\frac{1-1/\gamma}{1-1/\rho}}, \qquad (3)$$

where c and l denote consumption and leisure, respectively. The parameters θ, ρ, γ and ξ_s represent the "pure" rate of time preference, the intra- and intertemporal elasticity of substitution, and the leisure preference, respectively. The last parameter is assumed to be constant until age 55 and then increases slightly until the age of death. Note that preferences are identical for all lifetime income classes. This reflects the belief that poor households would behave as rich ones, provided they had the same (higher) income.

Households maximize (3) subject to the budget constraints given by

$$\sum_{s=1}^{a^d}[\underbrace{(1-l_s^j)w_s^j}_{y_s^j} - c_s^j - \Gamma_s^j - p_s^j](1+r)^{1-s} = 0, \qquad (4)$$

where the time endowment is normalized to unity, r denotes the pre-tax return on savings and Γ_s^j and p_s^j represent the individual tax liabilities and payments to or from the pension system, respectively. All taxes in the model are collected at the household level. The tax system includes progressive taxes on labour and capital income as well as consumption taxes. An individual's earning ability is an exogenous function of her age and her type. These skill differences by age and type are captured by the efficiency parameter ϵ_s^j, which increases with age to reflect the accumulation of human capital. Thus, the wage rate for an agent of type j at age s is $w_s^j = \epsilon_s^j w$. For corner solutions ($l_s^j = 1$) where the time constraint bites, a shadow price of labour is computed to make the corner solution satisfy the first-order condition.

---

[4]For the sake of notational simplicity, I omit the time index here and assume a long-run equilibrium.

Production Technology

The production technology of the economy is represented by a CES production function. Capital formation is subject to convex installation costs. However, due to the specific normalization, there are no installation costs in the long-run equilibrium. Investment decisions follow the Q-theory of investment, according to which firms will invest whenever the stock market value of their assets exceeds the cost of replacement.

The Government Sector

To capture the interaction between the tax system and the pension system in Germany, the goverment is represented by two budget constraints. Tax revenues are used to finance a stream of exogenous public consumption G_t and a fraction ϑ_t of aggregate pension benefits PB_t, i.e.

$$\sum_{j=1}^{5}\sum_{s=1}^{a_t^d}\Gamma_{st}^j N_{t+1-s}^j = \underbrace{gPOP_t}_{G_t} + \vartheta_t \underbrace{\sum_{j=1}^{5}\sum_{s=a_t^r}^{a_t^d} p_{st}^j N_{t+1-s}^j}_{PB_t}, \tag{5}$$

where a_t^r is the retirement age in year t. Note that the per capita supply of public goods remains constant. Since, by assumption, public goods enter the utility function in an additively separate manner, it is possible to omit them from the utility function (3). To concentrate on ageing and the pension system, I abstract from corporate taxes and government debt. In order to balance the budget each period, the consumption tax rate is adjusted.

The pension system pays old-age benefits and collects payroll contributions in each year. Individual pension benefits of a retiree in year t, $p_{a_t^r t}^j$ are computed from the sum of the earning points EP_{sk}^j the retiree has received during his past working life, multiplied by the actual pension amount of the respective year APA_t:

$$p_{a_t^r t}^j = \sum_{s=1}^{a_t^r - 1} EP_{sk}^j APA_t, \tag{6}$$

where $k = t - a_t^r + s$. The earning point received in working year k for her annual gross labour income y_{sk}^j is calculated according to the formula

$$EP^j_{sk} = \begin{cases} \min(1.5y^j_{sk}/\bar{y}_k;\ 0.75) & \text{if } y^j_{sk} \leqslant 0.75\bar{y}_k, \\ y^j_{sk}/\bar{y}_k & \text{if } 0.75\bar{y}_k < y^j_{sk} < 1.8\bar{y}_k, \\ 1.8 & \text{if } 1.8\bar{y}_k \leqslant y^j_{sk}. \end{cases} \quad (7)$$

This formulation reflects some of the redistributional features of the German pension system mentioned above. If individual income in year k is below 75 percent of average income $\bar{y}_k$, then the accounted earning point is increased up to 50 percent. If annual individual income is above the contribution ceiling, which exceeds average income by 80 percent, then a maximum earning point of 1.8 is credited. Below the contribution ceiling and above the minimum threshold, earning points are computed from the ratio of individual income to the average income in the respective year. The actual pension amount in the second part of equation (6) is set by the government. In the benchmark simulation, I assume that all individuals retire after 40 working years at age 61. APA_t is then computed so that the standard pension (i.e., where the sum of earning points is 40) amounts to a given percentage Θ_t of net average earnings $\overline{y^n_{t-1}}$ in the previous year, i.e.

$$40APA_t = \Theta_t\overline{y^n_{t-1}}. \quad (8)$$

The budget of the pension system must be balanced in each period. Therefore, the aggregate contribution rate, τ_t, has to be adjusted to fulfil the period budget constraint

$$\sum_{j=1}^{5}\sum_{s=1}^{a^r_t-1} p^j_{st}N^j_{t+1-s} = \tau_t PY_t = (1-\vartheta_t)PB_t, \quad (9)$$

where $PY_t = \sum_{j=1}^{5}\sum_{s=1}^{a^r_t-1}\min(y^j_{st}, 1.8\bar{y}_t)N^j_{t+1-s}$ defines the aggregate compulsory earnings base. In principle, households could still choose to work after receiving pension payments. However, since the representative household retires early in the model, I assume that individuals face a labour income tax surcharge of 50 percent if they work after passing the retirement age. This assumption should capture the above-mentioned earnings test applied to early retirement.

The aggregate social security contribution rate τ_t which is calculated from (9) is not necessarily identical to the individual contribution rates. Owing to the contribution ceiling, marginal and average contribution rates of a type-j individual of age s in year t are given by

$$\tau_{st}^{j} = \begin{cases} \tau_t(1-\varphi_{st}) & \text{if } y_{st}^{j} \leqslant 1.8\bar{y}_t, \\ 0 & \text{if } y_{st}^{j} > 1.8\bar{y}_t, \end{cases} \tag{10}$$

and

$$\bar{\tau}_{st}^{j} = \begin{cases} \tau_t & \text{if } y_{st}^{j} \leqslant 1.8\bar{y}_t, \\ \tau_t 1.8\bar{y}_t / y_{st}^{j} & \text{if } y_{st}^{j} > 1.8\bar{y}_t. \end{cases} \tag{11}$$

Above the contribution ceiling, the marginal social security tax is zero and the average social security tax falls with increasing income for an individual. Of course, since the marginal contribution rate falls abruptly with small changes in the agent's behaviour, the contribution ceiling creates a non-convexity in the budget constraint. In order to bridge this discontinuity, the model solves for so-called "virtual" marginal contribution rates which place the optimizing agent exactly at the kink of the budget constraint if he wishes to be there.[5] This procedure allows us to solve the optimization problem of the household despite the non-convexities in the budget constraint. The tax benefit linkage φ_s reflects the extent of redistributive elements within the pension system. If pensions were perfectly proportional to former contributions, households would only perceive a proportion of their contributions as taxes, which depends on the difference between the rate of return on the capital market and the implicit rate of return of the pension system. This proportion falls when the household approaches retirement age. In order to take this into account, I model the tax–benefit linkage as

$$\varphi_{st} = e^{\mu(s-a_t^r)}. \tag{12}$$

If pensions are exactly proportional to former contributions, μ reflects the difference between the rates of return on the capital market and in the pension system. If pensions are completely independent of former contributions, μ approaches infinity (i.e., $\varphi_{st} = 0$).

IV. Dynamic Calibration and Baseline Simulation

Given a set of demographic, preference, technology and fiscal parameters, the above model can be solved numerically. In the traditional model of Auerbach and Kotlikoff (1987), the initial equilibrium is a steady state due

[5] Similarly, the model also solves for "virtual" marginal income tax rates to bridge discontinuities in the marginal income tax rate function.

to the time-invariant population growth rate. With demographic dynamics, however, the problem is more complicated, since the initial year is not a long-run equilibrium and the reference simulation for the policy reforms is a baseline path of the economy under the existing fiscal system. Here, households of the initial year are endowed with a profile of assets and pension claims. Given such a profile it is possible to compute the initial equilibrium and the subsequent baseline path of the economy. In the short and medium run, the baseline path of the economy depends mainly on the dynamics of the population structure. In the long run, the model returns to a stable population structure and the economy, therefore, converges to a steady state. The chosen population structure of the model is reported in Table 1 and compared with some official population projections.

The base year of the model is chosen to be 1998. In this year, people die at age 78. In the following years, the life span of households increases up to 84 years in 2060 and remains constant thereafter. As shown in the second and third columns, the chosen population growth rates allow us to replicate the demographic structure of the base year quite well. Although households do not die before the given life expectancy and no immigration is taken into account, the model also matches the official forecasts of future dependency ratios. In the long run, population size approaches 62.3 million, since I assume zero population growth after 2020. I will not report all of the other

Table 1. *Official and simulated population dynamics*

Year	1996	1998	2000	2010	2020	2030	2040	2050	2100
Life expectancy									
$a^d + 20$	–	78	78	78	79	80	80	82	84
Population (million)									
Model	–	83.1	82.7	80.1	77.1	74.5	70.9	67.4	62.3
Official[a]	82.8	–	82.2	81.0	78.4	74.3	68.8	–	–
Age groups	Official[b]					Model			
1–20	22.6	19.5	19.0	18.6	19.2	19.9	20.9	22.0	23.8
21–40	29.2	31.2	30.8	24.9	20.4	19.9	20.9	22.0	23.8
41–60	26.6	26.9	26.9	31.0	33.1	26.8	22.2	22.0	23.8
61–84	21.4	22.4	23.2	25.5	27.3	33.4	36.0	33.9	28.6
Dependency ratios[c]									
Model	–	38.5	40.1	45.6	51.0	71.4	83.5	77.1	60.0
Official[a]	37.0	–	40.8	44.8	53.1	73.2	76.4	80.2	–

[a]Bundesministerium für Wirtschaft (1998, p. 6).
[b]Statistisches Bundesamt (1998, p. 58).
[c]Population aged 61–84 as percentage of population aged 21–60.

exogenously chosen parameters explicitly.[6] The preference and technology parameters are mainly in accordance with other numerical and econometric studies and generate—given the other fiscal parameters—a realistic economic structure in the initial year (see below). On the government side, I fix the initial consumption tax rate at 16.4 percent. Labour and capital income is subject to a progressive tax. For the labour income tax, the model exactly reproduces the step function of the tax rate schedule of 1998. Taxable labour income in the base year is derived after deducting a personal allowance of DM 13,000 from gross labour earnings. In addition to personal allowances, a basic allowance of DM 12,000 is also untaxed. The marginal tax rate then jumps to 26 percent and rises linearly to 53 percent at an annual taxable income of DM 120,000. The marginal capital income tax rate is set at 35 percent. For capital income, a uniform allowance of DM 6,000 is assumed for all households.

Households retire in the baseline simulation after 40 working years. The pension level of a standard pensioner is set at 70 percent of net average labour earnings (i.e., $\Theta = 0.7$) and the government grant is set at zero (i.e., $\vartheta = 0$). As explained above, the tax–benefit linkage μ depends mainly on the difference between the rate of return in a funded system and the implicit rate of return of the unfunded system. Börsch-Supan (1998, p. 412) reports rates of return of between 4.2 and 8 percent (depending on the type of investment) from investing in the German capital market. Schnabel (1998) calculates the implicit rates of return of the German pension system for various cohorts and demographic groups. The rates of return fall significantly for cohorts born between 1930 and 1980; for the youngest cohort they will be between 0 and 1 percent. This suggests a difference in the rates of return of 4–6 percent. Since, in addition, pension benefits are not completely proportional to contributions, I fix the parameter for the tax–benefit linkage in the baseline at $\mu = 0.06$.

Table 2 reports the structure of the model's initial equilibrium and compares it with the respective actual figures for 1998. All in all, the model represents the basic economic and fiscal structure of Germany quite well. Since the model is simulated as a closed economy, the interest rate is endogenous and the trade balance is zero. Of course, since the model neglects important features such as government debt and corporate taxes, the government sector is not represented very well. On the other hand, the model captures the central interaction between the pension system and the remaining tax system, which is mostly important in the present context. While the pension benefits are slightly above the actual figures, the aggregate average contribution rate seems to be too low. Note, however, that this is mainly due

[6]Of course, they are available on request from the author.

Table 2. *The benchmark equilibrium*

	Model benchmark	Germany 1998[a]
Expenditures on GDP (% of GDP)		
Private consumption	63.7	57.5
Government consumption	21.0	18.9
Gross fixed investment	15.3	21.9
Export–import	0.0	1.7
General government indicators		
Aggregate pension benefits (% of GDP)	13.3	11.5
Aggregate contribution rates		
Average	18.8	20.3
Marginal	10.2	–
Tax revenues (% of GDP)	21.0	22.9
Labour income tax	9.1	7.7
Capital income tax	1.4	1.8
Tax on goods and services	10.5	9.0
Interest rate (in %)	4.1	5.6
Capital–output ratio	2.5	2.9

[a]Deutsche Bundesbank (1999)

to the overrepresentation of households with an income above the contribution ceiling. The aggregate marginal contribution rate is in line with some recent estimates of Schnabel (1998).

Figures 1a and 1b show the effects of the tax–benefit linkage and the contribution ceiling on the average and marginal contribution rates across the life cycle in the initial year for the five income quintiles. Households in the first four income quintiles never reach the contribution ceiling with their annual income. Therefore, they all face an average contribution rate of 19.9 percent in the base year, which almost exactly matches the actual figure of 20.3 percent. The marginal contribution rate is slightly below the average rate at the beginning of working life but falls continuously with age. Households that are just about to retire regard only a small share of their contributions as taxes.[7] Now consider the contribution rates of households in the top income quintile. At age 35 their annual income passes the contribution ceiling. While their marginal contribution rate immediately drops to zero, their average contribution rate declines to about 15 percent until age 50 where they reach the peak in their annual income. Then it increases again, because of their falling annual income. In the last year before retirement, annual income falls below the contribution ceiling so that the average contribution rate is again 19.9 percent.

[7]For similar modelling see Kotlikoff *et al.* (1999).

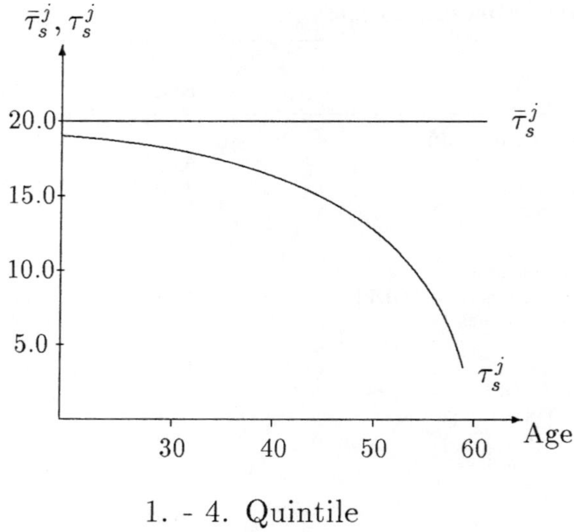

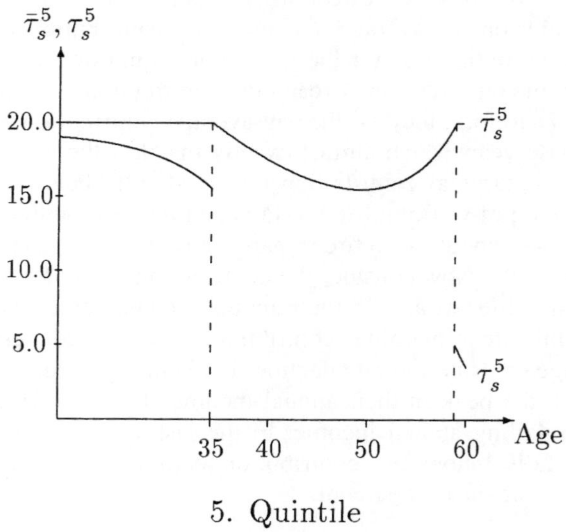

Figs. 1a and 1b. Average and marginal contribution rates in 1998

Table 3 reports the changes in some important macroeconomic variables after the base year 1998. Employment, capital stock and consumption are expressed per capita of the cohort which enters the labour force. Since the absolute number of this cohort falls in the first phase of the transition, the per capita values of the macro aggregates increase. In addition, the change in the age structure of the population also increases the labour force initially, since households work more in middle age when their human capital endowment reaches a peak. After year 2020 it is assumed that the same number of households enter the labour force each year. Consequently, employment per capita starts falling again due to the now falling share of older people (between ages 40 and 60) in the labour force. In the long run, employment per capita declines by almost 7 percent. The pattern of changes in the capital stock is quite similar to that of the labour force. Since consumption propensity rises with age, the observed changes in consumption per capita reflect the profound change in the age structure during the transition. The path of wages and interest rates results directly from the changes in employment and the capital stock. Rising pre-tax wages also increase labour income tax revenues. In addition, consumption per capita also rises and, consequently, the consumption tax rate falls in the first phase of the transition in order to balance the budget. Finally, the change in the age structure has a dramatic impact on the pension system. Owing to the rising share of pensioners, the contribution rate rises in the baseline simulation from 20 percent today to almost 32 percent in 2040. This is consistent with the currently discussed projections mentioned above.

V. Simulation Findings

Next, I compare the macroeconomic and welfare consequences of alternative pension reform strategies. After explaining the specific policy reforms and

Table 3. *Baseline path of the economy*[a]

Year	2000	2010	2020	2030	2040	2050	2100
Employment[b]	6.5	33.7	32.5	16.5	3.1	−2.0	−6.7
Capital[b]	5.1	26.6	40.0	43.9	28.3	8.6	1.7
Consumption[b]	5.4	27.6	27.5	18.5	6.5	−0.7	−9.1
Wage	−0.3	−1.6	1.6	6.5	6.7	3.1	2.6
Interest rate	2.4	3.8	3.3	0.8	2.5	5.3	3.1
Consumption tax	18.5	15.5	13.2	13.1	14.4	14.4	16.0
Average wage tax	12.5	13.9	15.3	17.2	17.4	16.3	15.1
Average contribution rate	19.4	21.0	22.6	28.8	31.7	30.0	25.7

[a]All changes are expressed as percentage differences to the base year, except for interest rates as well as tax and contribution rates, which are already expressed in percentage points.
[b]Variables are expressed per capita of the cohort which enters the labour force.

the computation of welfare changes, the numerical results of the simulations are reported.

Experimental Design and Welfare Decomposition

In the following I distinguish between a moderate reform package and two radical reform strategies. The moderate reform package consists of three measures: an increase in the retirement age, a gradual decline of the pension level and a phased-in increase in the tax-financed proportion of pension expenditures. In order to separate the effects of the different measures, they are introduced successively. In the first simulation, the retirement age (a^r) is increased in year 1999 and year 2009 to 62 and 63, respectively, and kept on this level in the future. In the second simulation, the benefit level (Θ) is reduced in years 2008, 2018 and 2028 by 2 percentage points, respectively. Therefore, 30 years after the announcement, the pension level of a standard pensioner will be reduced from 70 percent to 64 percent of average net earnings. The third simulation includes the whole reform package. In addition to the other two measures, the tax-financed proportion of pension expenditures (ϑ) is increased between 1999 and 2009 from 0 to 0.2. Since such a measure is intended to improve the tax–benefit linkage, I also reduce μ from 0.06 to 0.04 in and after year 2005.

As regards the two radical reform strategies, I maintain the increase in the retirement age. However, while the moderate reform measures reduce the future pension level by about 10 percent, the future pension level is now decreased by about 40 percent. Since such a dramatic switch requires a smooth transition, I directly alter the earning point formula (7) and assume that the reforms are implemented with a time lag of seven years. In the first scenario, public pensions are still contribution related—the "variable benefit" scenario. However, the intra-generational redistribution towards low-income households is eliminated and therefore the earning point formula in and after year 2005 changes to

$$EP^j_{sk} = \begin{cases} 0.6y^j_{sk}/\bar{y}_k & \text{if } y^j_{sk} \leqslant 1.8\bar{y}_k, \\ 1.08 & \text{if } y^j_{sk} > 1.8\bar{y}_k. \end{cases} \tag{13}$$

As in the previous simulation, the new system features an improved tax–benefit linkage. Consequently, I reduce μ again from 0.06 to 0.04 in and after year 2005. The second radical scenario differs from the first in two respects. First, when the unfunded tier is fully implemented, benefits will be uniform across all households. Therefore, under the "flat benefit" scenario, the earning point formula in and after year 2005 changes to $EP^j_{sk} = 0.6$. Second, since the tax–benefit linkage is now completely lost, φ is set at zero in year

2005. Of course, both reforms also include a fully funded tier provided by the government through forced savings. However, since the model features a perfect capital market, forcing individuals to have private pensions accounts would make no difference, since they only crowd out voluntary private savings. Hence, there is no need for an explicit funded pension system in the model.

Given a baseline path of the economy as described in Table 3, all experiments start at the beginning of year 1999. As in the baseline, the consumption tax rate is adjusted in each year to balance the government budget (5) and the contribution rate adjusts to balance the pension budget (9). Given a new transition path of the economy and a new long-run equilibrium, I computed the macroeconomic impact of a reform and the resulting changes in economic welfare or utility for the different generations and households. The welfare changes must be due either to (re)distributional effects or otherwise to efficiency effects. Redistributionally determined welfare effects may work through two different channels. First, any pension reform will change the net tax burdens (i.e., contributions plus taxes minus benefits received) of specific households. While public sector budgets remain balanced in each year, net tax burdens will increase for some households and decrease for others. Second, pension reforms will typically affect gross-of-tax prices; this effect redistributes between agents on different sides of the market. For example, if wages increase and the interest rate falls, then workers will gain at the expense of owners of firms. Fehr (1999) shows in detail how these income effects are computed for each individual household and demonstrates that they add up to zero in each period. The latter allows to design a compensation mechanism which neutralizes all individual income gains and losses via countervailing lump-sum transfers. The individual welfare changes calculated from this simulation reflect the efficiency effects of the pension reform which are reported in the following tables.

Numerical Results

Let us now turn to the numerical results. Table 4 shows the macroeconomic adjustment for the five reform scenarios described above. The table reports the changes in employment, capital stock, wages, interest rates, consumption tax rates and contribution rates for five different years during the transition and in the long-run equilibrium.

Consider first the increase in the retirement age in the left column. Since the cohort aged 61 is not allowed to retire, the contribution rate falls and the labour force increases immediately. On the labour market, wages fall slightly and employment rises. Higher employment also increases capital productivity which, in turn, induces a higher investment demand and a slowly rising

Table 4. *Macroeconomic effects of pension reforms*[a]

Variable	Increase in retirement age	Moderate reforms		Radical reforms	
		Benefit reduction	Increase in gov. grant	Variable benefit	Flat benefit
Employment					
2000	0.8	1.0	0.5	1.1	1.9
2010	0.6	0.8	0.8	2.3	−1.8
2020	0.5	0.8	0.5	2.4	−1.9
2030	0.6	1.0	0.4	3.2	−1.5
2040	0.0	0.2	−0.2	3.0	−1.3
Long run	0.4	0.5	0.2	2.1	−0.6
Capital stock					
2000	0.0	0.1	0.0	0.1	0.3
2010	0.5	1.1	1.2	1.9	2.2
2020	1.1	2.4	3.3	4.9	3.5
2030	1.6	3.5	4.7	8.6	5.7
2040	1.8	4.7	6.3	13.8	9.5
Long run	1.1	5.7	8.0	30.6	23.7
Wage rate					
2000	−0.2	−0.2	−0.1	−0.3	−0.4
2010	0.0	0.0	0.1	−0.1	1.2
2020	0.1	0.4	0.8	0.7	1.6
2030	0.2	0.7	1.2	1.5	2.1
2040	0.5	1.2	1.8	2.9	3.1
Long run	0.2	1.4	2.2	7.5	6.7
Interest rate					
2000	−0.1	−0.1	0.0	−0.1	0.0
2010	−0.2	−0.2	−0.3	−0.2	−0.4
2020	−0.1	−0.2	−0.3	−0.2	−0.4
2030	−0.2	−0.3	−0.4	−0.4	−0.6
2040	−0.3	−0.5	−0.7	−1.0	−1.0
Long run	−0.1	−0.4	−0.6	−1.9	−1.7
Consumption tax rate					
2000	0.0	0.0	0.8	0.0	−0.4
2010	0.5	0.4	5.1	−0.2	1.0
2020	0.9	0.6	5.7	−0.2	1.1
2030	1.7	1.3	7.4	−0.1	1.2
2040	1.6	1.1	8.2	−1.0	0.4
Long run	0.9	0.3	6.1	−2.6	−1.5
Contribution rate					
2000	−1.2	−1.2	−1.9	−1.2	−1.3
2010	−1.8	−2.3	−5.4	−2.0	−1.8
2020	−2.2	−3.1	−6.3	−3.4	−3.0
2030	−2.9	−4.5	−8.3	−6.7	−6.2
2040	−1.6	−3.4	−7.5	−8.2	−7.9
Long run	−1.4	−3.0	−6.5	−10.4	−9.1

[a]All changes reported are in percentage over baseline simulation, except for changes in interest, consumption tax and contribution rates, which are already expressed as changes in percentage points.

capital stock. Of course, the reduction in the contribution rates is especially strong in 30 years, when the current baby-boom generations retire. Note that the consumption tax rate increases during the transition although employment and consumption are higher than before. This is mainly due to intertemporal labour supply substitution. Households reduce their labour supply during their middle years when they pay high taxes. Consequently, labour income tax revenues fall and consumption taxes have to be increased.

The next column displays the macroeconomic adjustment if, in addition to the increase in the retirement age, benefits are also reduced to 64 percent. In the short run this has only negligible effects; in the medium and long run, however, consumption tax and contribution rates fall significantly. While the reduced pension claims decrease the human wealth of older households, younger and future households experience an increase of their human wealth endowment. Owing to lower contribution rates and the negative human wealth effect, labour supply and employment rise in the short and medium run above the level of the first simulation. In addition, households save more in order to balance the reduced pension wealth. Therefore, the capital stock increases much more strongly than before.

Next consider the column where the government grant is increased gradually. Although their tax bases are quite similar, the increase in the consumption tax rate during the transition is significantly stronger than the fall in the contribution rate. Since labour supply and employment fall compared to the previous simulation, labour income tax revenues are now significantly lower than before. The reduction in labour supply is mainly due to households that are above the contribution ceiling and, consequently, face a zero marginal contribution rate. For these households, a switch towards consumption tax financing increases labour supply distortions and reduces employment. At the same time, consumption tax financing redistributes towards younger and future generations, which in turn increases savings. Therefore, capital accumulation accelerates during the transition, inducing a rise in wages and a fall in interest rates. Since labour income tax revenues and consumption rise again, the long-run increase in the consumption tax rate is dampened in the second phase of the transition.

The last two columns of Table 4 report the macroeconomic impact of the two radical reform options. Due to the policy preannouncement, economic activity rises only slightly in the short run if the variable benefit strategy is implemented. However, as soon as the contribution rate starts to fall after about 10 years, labour supply, investment and wages rise much more strongly than under the moderate reform scenario. This allows a steady reduction in the contribution rates and the consumption tax rates during the transition. In contrast, if the flat benefit option is implemented, economic activity will only increase in the short run due to intertemporal labour supply substitution effects. As soon as the tax–benefit linkage is eliminated, labour supply is reduced significantly. Consequently, employment falls although capital stock and wages rise. While the contribution rate falls as in the previous simulation, the consumption tax rate now has to be increased in order to balance the lower revenues from labour income taxation.

So far we have seen that alternative pension reforms may have quite different impacts on the macroeconomy. Although these effects are important, we are nevertheless mainly interested in the welfare consequences of the different reform options. Can we expect any efficiency gains from pension reforms and, if so, what is their magnitude and how are they distributed across generations and income classes? Who are the winners and losers in the different reform scenarios? Before turning to the details of the simulation results, I report the aggregate efficiency effects in Table 5.

In the first row of Table 5 the aggregate efficiency effects were computed as a percentage of the present value of the pension payments in the baseline simulation. In order to get some idea of their magnitude, I then calculated the implied average annual efficiency effects in billion DM. The latter figures were computed from the aggregate pension benefits in the base year (i.e., DM400 billion); they are even understated, since pension outlays increase due to population ageing in the future. Despite these quantitative shortcomings, Table 5 reports three qualitative results. First, the efficiency gains of the moderate reform package are mainly due to the increase in the retirement age. The benefit reduction and the rising share of tax financing have only a minor impact on efficiency, even though the tax benefit linkage is increased slightly in the latter simulation. Second, variable benefits yield a significant efficiency gain by combining a strong future reduction in the highly distortive contribution rates with an increase in the tax–benefit linkage. As a result, intertemporal and intra-temporal distortions are reduced. Finally, flat benefits yield considerable efficiency losses. Although future contribution rates are reduced, intra-temporal distortions increase due to the elimination of the tax–benefit linkage. Of course, these numbers just give a preliminary idea of the magnitude of the estimated effects. A valuable

Table 5. *Aggregate efficiency effects of pension reforms*

		Moderate reforms		Radical reforms	
	Increase in retirement age	Benefit reduction	Increase in gov. grant	Variable benefit	Flat benefit
In % of baseline benefits	1.03	1.64	1.58	6.08	−4.03
In billion DM annually[a]	4.12	6.56	6.32	24.32	−16.12

[a]Computed from aggregate pensions benefits of base year.

economic interpretation cannot be made without considering the welfare and efficiency effects of the different experiments for specific households and generations.

The head columns in Tables 6 and 7 list the different income quintiles and representative generations for which the welfare effects are reported. I have selected only the lowest, the middle and the top income quintiles. In addition, I report the aggregate effect for the entire generation. The numbers in the head column refer to the birth year of a household or generation. Households born in 1930 are already retired, while households born in the

Table 6. *Welfare effects of moderate pension reforms*[a]

	Increase in retirement age		Reduction in benefits		Increase in government grant	
Birth year	Welfare	Efficiency	Welfare	Efficiency	Welfare	Efficiency
Lowest quintile						
1930	0.08	0.00	0.12	0.00	−0.17	0.00
1950	−0.93	0.28	−1.34	0.29	−1.68	0.25
1970	−0.02	0.11	−0.22	0.12	−0.21	0.05
1990	0.27	0.12	0.62	0.16	0.75	0.13
2010	0.22	0.10	1.01	0.19	1.27	0.27
2030	0.05	0.09	0.89	0.17	1.18	0.24
Long run	0.15	0.12	1.04	0.20	1.25	0.26
Third quintile						
1930	0.08	0.00	0.12	0.00	−0.18	0.00
1950	−0.51	0.18	−0.85	0.19	−1.23	0.11
1970	0.16	0.04	−0.02	0.07	−0.05	0.13
1990	0.41	0.01	0.73	0.12	0.93	0.35
2010	0.29	−0.03	0.93	0.15	1.15	0.54
2030	0.18	0.02	0.88	0.17	1.11	0.43
Long run	0.26	0.05	0.95	0.19	1.11	0.44
Top quintile						
1930	0.05	0.00	0.08	0.00	−0.14	0.00
1950	−0.41	0.12	−0.70	0.13	−1.01	−0.05
1970	0.23	0.08	0.11	0.08	0.22	−0.18
1990	0.49	0.07	0.78	0.11	0.98	−0.07
2010	0.40	0.09	1.03	0.25	1.47	0.37
2030	0.24	0.05	0.83	0.19	1.21	0.23
Long run	0.20	0.15	0.81	0.27	1.12	0.25
Aggregate						
1930	0.06	0.00	0.10	0.00	−0.15	0.00
1950	−0.53	0.17	−0.86	0.18	−1.20	0.07
1970	0.17	0.05	0.01	0.07	0.06	0.01
1990	0.43	0.04	0.75	0.12	0.98	0.17
2010	0.33	0.03	1.00	0.21	1.36	0.47
2030	0.19	0.03	0.86	0.17	1.18	0.33
Long run	0.23	0.08	0.92	0.21	1.18	0.35

[a]Changes expressed as a percentage of the present value of remaining lifetime resources.

Table 7. *Welfare effects of radical pension reforms*[a]

	Variable benefits		Flat benefits	
Birth year	Welfare	Efficiency	Welfare	Efficiency
Lowest quintile				
1930	0.33	−0.01	0.15	0.00
1950	−1.32	0.30	−1.43	−0.04
1970	−1.71	0.19	−0.27	−0.19
1990	−1.14	0.32	2.04	−0.13
2010	1.62	0.54	4.43	0.06
2030	2.90	0.57	5.60	0.17
Long run	3.53	0.61	6.59	0.24
Third quintile				
1930	0.31	0.00	0.15	0.00
1950	−0.75	0.21	−1.43	−0.19
1970	−0.62	0.30	−0.79	−0.73
1990	0.12	0.67	0.88	−0.88
2010	2.15	1.08	2.56	−0.21
2030	3.47	1.05	3.54	0.00
Long run	3.83	1.06	3.91	0.05
Top quintile				
1930	0.20	0.00	0.08	0.00
1950	−0.51	0.17	−1.77	−0.45
1970	−0.55	0.13	−2.31	−0.27
1990	0.57	0.28	−0.83	−0.30
2010	3.02	0.91	0.86	0.08
2030	3.86	0.89	1.20	0.24
Long run	4.22	0.91	1.34	0.31
Aggregate				
1930	0.24	0.00	0.11	0.00
1950	−0.70	0.21	−1.60	−0.31
1970	−0.77	0.22	−1.54	−0.54
1990	0.22	0.50	0.13	−0.63
2010	2.55	1.00	2.01	−0.10
2030	3.56	0.94	2.64	0.09
Long run	4.01	0.97	3.02	0.14

[a]Changes expressed as a percentage of the present value of remaining lifetime resources.

"long run" live in the new steady-state equilibrium. The following columns report the individual welfare changes without and with compensation. All welfare changes are expressed as a percentage of the remaining lifetime resources of the respective generation in the benchmark equilibrium.

Consider now the increase in the retirement age in the left part of Table 6. Assume for a moment that the model does not distinguish among different lifetime income classes. In this case only the aggregate, generation-specific welfare measures would be reported. Note first that all generations who are not retired receive efficiency gains, especially generations born in 1950 who are close to retirement around 1999. Of course, the elderly mainly experience efficiency gains since the high marginal tax rate due to the income tax surcharge is reduced considerably for ages 61 and 62. Younger and future generations, on the other hand, benefit from the future decline in consumption tax and contribution rates. However, the rising retirement age also increases the marginal contribution rates for households that are below the contribution ceiling—see equation (12). Consequently, the efficiency gains are relatively low for middle-aged generations. The difference between the efficiency column and the welfare column is mainly due to changes in tax burdens. Of course, those generations who are close to retirement now face a higher tax burden since they have to pay into the pension system for a longer period of time and receive fewer benefits than before. Since the increase in the tax burden overcompensates the efficiency gain, older generations who are close to retirement experience a reduction in welfare. Younger and future generations now face a lower tax burden, since the reduced contributions occur earlier in their lives than the reduced benefits. Therefore, the welfare gain is higher than the respective efficiency gain of these generations.

Turning now to the different income quintiles, we note that the welfare effects are fairly similar across income classes. However, two observations deserve some comment. First, households that are close to retirement experience the highest efficiency gains in the lowest income quintile. As it seems, the labour income tax surcharge is more distortive for low-income households than for high-income households.[8] Despite the higher efficiency gains, low-income households close to retirement experience stronger welfare losses than households in the other quintiles. This probably reflects the reduced intra-generational redistribution towards low-income households which is implied by the reduced retirement phase. Finally, note that due to the rise in marginal contribution rates, some middle-aged households in the third quintile even realize some slight efficiency losses.

The middle part of Table 6 reports the welfare changes of the benefit reduction under consideration. While the efficiency gains of older generations are hardly affected, efficiency gains of younger and future generations rise significantly due to the lower future tax and contribution rates. Of course, the intergenerational redistribution works in favour of younger generations too, since their tax burdens fall further while the tax burden of the elderly now increases considerably. Note that the reform is intragenerationally neutral; i.e., the benefit reduction produces no significant differences between lifetime income classes.

The right part of Table 6, finally, reports the welfare effects of the

[8]Note that in the baseline simulation, households in the middle and top quintiles were still working during the first years after retirement despite the income tax surcharge.

complete reform package. The increase in consumption tax financing of pension outlays mainly hurts the elderly generations, since they do not benefit from the simultaneous reduction in pension contributions. While they experience efficiency losses due to the higher consumption tax rates and income losses due to increases in tax burdens, younger and future generations experience exactly the opposite. The reason is, of course, that consumption taxes are paid later in life than social security contributions. Consequently, tax burdens and distortions fall for younger cohorts. However, the efficiency gains are not equally distributed across income classes. Households in the top income quintile born between 1950 and 1990 now even realize efficiency losses. Owing to the contribution ceiling, these households face a zero marginal contribution rate. Consequently, their marginal contribution rate is not affected by the reform measure, while their consumption tax rate increases.

Next we turn to the welfare results of the more radical reform proposals, which are reported in Table 7. First, compare the aggregate efficiency effects of the variable benefit scenario and the moderate reform in the right part of Table 6. The efficiency gains for all working generations increase strongly, especially for those generations who are born in the future. Compared to the previous simulation, tax burdens increase mainly for middle-aged generations born around 1970 since the reform is now phased-in very smoothly. On the other hand, future generations now gain much more strongly than under the moderate reform. This is due to both intergenerational redistribution and efficiency gains. Note that households of the lowest income quintile realize less than proportional efficiency gains in the long run. Since gross-of-tax wages now increase strongly, taxable labour income of some low-income households rises above the basic exemption level. Consequently, their marginal labour income tax rates rise sharply which dampens the efficiency gain.

Finally, consider the welfare changes in the last simulation where a flat benefit is provided in the long run. During the pre-announcement phase, households increase their labour supply. As soon as the tax–benefit linkage is eliminated, working households experience a sharp rise in their marginal contribution rates. The resulting efficiency loss is very dramatic for households born around 1970 since they will not benefit from the lower tax rates in the future. Younger households and households born after the year 2000 experience a lower efficiency loss, since they also face much lower contribution rates (see Table 4). The intergenerational redistribution again favours the future generations. However, now the welfare losses of the elderly are much more pronounced. This is due to the fact that consumption taxes are now higher than in the variable-benefit simulation. Since the consumption propensity is higher for the elderly, tax burdens are shifted from younger towards older generations. Owing to the contribution ceiling, households in the top quintile experience less than proportional efficiency losses. Of course, their marginal contribution rate does not increase over the whole life cycle. Nevertheless, the flat-benefit pension system strongly favours low-income classes. Consequently, the last simulation shows considerable intra-generational redistribution from rich towards poor households.

VI. Conclusions

The above analysis highlights some important insights. First, since the reduction in future contribution rates might come at the cost of a rise in other taxes, pension reform options have to be evaluated within the context of the whole tax–benefit system. In the case of Germany, this implies modelling the indexation of benefits to net wages and the progressivity schedule of the labour income tax. Second, the reduction of the unfunded pension level alone might be a poor indicator for the implied intergenerational effects. Although the contribution rate is reduced quite similarly in the two radical reform scenarios, the respective intergenerational welfare consequences differ substantially. Third, the simulations reveal that pension reforms should not be motivated solely by considerations of intergenerational equity. They might also differ significantly in their intra-generational effects as well as in their efficiency consequences. As a result, models that do not allow for intra-generational redistribution and behavioural reactions are only of limited use for a comprehensive evaluation.

The specific policy results of this paper can be summarized as follows. First, from an efficiency point of view, the variable-benefit strategy is preferable to the moderate reform and to the flat-benefit reform. The latter even yields efficiency losses. Second, all reforms redistribute towards future generations at the cost of currently living older generations. While this is hardly surprising, the extent of the intergenerational redistribution differs quite significantly. The future gains are strongest under the variable-benefit strategy, they are slightly lower under the flat-benefit system and considerably lower under the moderate reform. At the same time, the losses of the current elderly are highest under the flat-benefit proposal. In terms of intra-generational redistribution, the flat-benefit reform redistributes strongly in favour of low-income classes, whereas the variable-benefit proposal redistributes slightly from poor to rich households. Since none of the proposed reforms yields a Pareto improvement, a ranking has to be based on some value judgements. In my view, the flat-benefit proposal cancels out because of the significant efficiency losses and high burdens placed on the current elderly. As regards the two remaining proposals, the variable-benefit option seems to be preferable since this scenario yields the highest efficiency gains and distributes the burden of the reform more evenly among current elderly.

Of course, although the simulation model incorporates many complex real-world details, it also abstracts—as does any model—in important ways from reality. The quantitative numerical results, therefore, have to be interpreted cautiously. Two important extensions of this model would be relatively straightforward to incorporate. First, the tax–benefit linkage should be modelled endogenously along the lines of Hirte and Weber (1997). In the present model this would imply that changes in the population growth rates directly affect the tax–benefit linkage. A second extension would be to introduce liquidity constraints, especially for households in the lowest income quintile. In the presence of liquidity-constrained households it makes a difference whether people are forced by the government into private saving accounts or whether they contribute voluntarily. In future work I plan to incorporate these extensions.

References

Auerbach, A. J. and Kotlikoff, L. J. (1987), *Dynamic Fiscal Policy*, Cambridge University Press, Cambridge.

Besendorfer, D., Borgman, C. and Raffelhüschen, B. (1998), Ein Plädoyer für intergenerative Ausgewogenheit: Rentenreformvorschläge auf dem Prüfstand, *ifo Studien 44*, 209-231.

Börsch-Supan, A. (1998), Zur deutschen Diskussion eines Übergangs vom Umlage- zum Kapitaldeckungsverfahren in der gesetzlichen Rentenversicherung, *Finanzarchiv 55*, 400–428.

Börsch-Supan, A. and Schnabel, G. (1999), Social Security and Retirement in Germany in J. Gruber and D. Wise (eds.), *Social Security and Retirement around the World*, 135–180, University of Chicago Press, Chicago.

Breyer, F. (1998), The Economics of Minimum Pensions, in H. Siebert (ed.), *Redesigning Social Security*, 129–159, Mohr Siebeck, Tübingen.

Bundesministerium für Wirtschaft (1998), Grundlegende Reform der gesetzlichen Rentenversicherung, Gutachten des Wissenschaftlichen Beirats beim Bundesministration für Wirtschaft, Studienreihe No. 99, Bonn.

Deutsche Bundesbank (1999), Statistical Section, Monthly Report, March, Frankfurt.

Fehr, H. (1999), *Welfare Effects of Dynamic Tax Policies*, Mohr Siebeck, Tübingen.

Feldstein, M. (1998), *Privatizing Social Security*, University of Chicago Press, Chicago.

Hirte, G. and Weber, R. (1997), Pareto Improving Transition from Pay-as-you-go to a Fully Funded System—Is It Politically Feasible? *Finanzarchiv 54*, 303–330.

Kotlikoff, L. J., Smetters, K. and Walliser, J. (1999), Privatization of Social Security in the United States—Comparing the Options, *Review of Economic Dynamics 2*, 532–574.

Miegel, M. and Wahl, S. (1985), *Gesetzliche Grundsicherung, private Vorsorge—der Weg aus der Rentenkrise*, Verlag Bonn Aktuell, Stuttgart.

Sachverständigenrat (1996), Reformen voranbringen, Jahresgutachten 1996/97, Metzler-Poeschel, Stuttgart.

Schnabel, R. (1998), Rates of Return of the German Pay-as-you-go Pension System, *Finanzarchiv 55*, 374–399.

Siebert, H. (1998), *Redesigning Social Security*, Mohr Siebeck, Tübingen.

Statistisches Bundesamt (1998), Statistisches Jahrbuch für die Bundesrepublik Deutschland 1998, Metzler-Poeschel, Stuttgart.

6

The Welfare State, Budgetary Pressure and Labour Market Shifts

*Anthony B. Atkinson**

I. Introduction

There is a widespread belief that the welfare state in OECD countries needs to be reformed to meet changing economic and social circumstances. Demographic changes have, it is argued, led to rising public expenditure, with the ageing of the population, coupled with the fragmentation of households. Slower growth of the economy, together with the maturing of state pension commitments, has increased the tax rates necessary to finance a given rate of replacement of past earnings. The resulting budgetary pressure has coincided with a shift in the labour market of industrialized countries, in the form of a tilt in the wage/skill nexus, penalizing low-skilled workers and benefiting those in the upper part of the distribution. According to the conventional wisdom, see e.g. Krugman (1994), in Anglo-Saxon countries such as the United States and the United Kingdom, this labour market shift has led to widening wage dispersion; in Continental Europe, it has led to sustained increases in unemployment as minimum wages and social protection have prevented wages from falling at the lower end of the scale. This interpretation may be questioned, as in Atkinson (2000a and 2000b), but the standard view is that the welfare state has to cope with both budgetary and labour market shocks. The dilemma is well captured in the title of the article by Buti, Franco and Pench (1997): "Reconciling the Welfare State with Sound Public Finances and High Employment".

How should the welfare state respond to this twofold set of shocks? In considering this, we need to incorporate explicitly the objectives of social transfers (indeed, transfers are the aspect of the welfare state on which this paper concentrates). Much of the economic literature considers only the costs of the welfare state, without considering its rationale. However, any decision about welfare state policy requires us to look at both sides of the

*I am grateful to two referees for their comments, which have been most useful in revising this paper.

balance: the economic costs are relevant, but so too are the benefits in terms of social objectives. Of course, the objectives differ from one society to another, and from one government to another, and an important part of the analysis is to consider the implications of different attitudes towards distributive justice.

The aim of this paper is to set out a simple framework which allows us to examine the implications of budgetary and labour market shocks for the optimal size and structure of social transfers, financed by a payroll tax on earnings. It might seem that the answers are obvious: the adverse shocks experienced by industrialized countries can only be expected to lead to a scaling back of the optimal welfare state. Analysis of the optimal linear income tax/basic income shows how a rise in the size of the dependent population implies a fall in the optimal basic income chosen by a Rawlsian government (maximizing the welfare of the least advantaged) as a proportion of the average net income for workers; see Atkinson (1995). In one special case, the burden of adjustment to increased dependency should be borne fully by the replacement rate, with the average tax per worker remaining unchanged. However, this conclusion is not robust to changes in the specification of the labour supply function and does not carry over to other forms of the government's objective function. Moreover, the labour market shift disadvantaging low-skilled workers might be expected to produce a policy response which *increases* the redistributive role of the government budget. In originating the literature on optimal income taxation, Mirrlees (1971) concluded that:

> "The results seem to say that, in an economy where there is more intrinsic inequality in economic skill, the income tax is a more important weapon of public control than it is in an economy where the dispersion of innate skills is less" (p. 207).

The same conclusion was reached by Stern (1976) in the case of the linear income tax.[1]

There is, therefore, a question to be answered. What is more, we are interested here in a "double difference". We are concerned not only with policy before and after a shift in the external circumstances, but also with how *different societies* respond to the same shift. It is striking that a number of OECD countries have in common a rise in the inequality of market incomes (incomes from earnings and investments) between 1980 and the mid-1990s, but that the outcomes in terms of disposable incomes (after direct taxes and social transfers) differed; see Gottschalk and Smeeding (1997) and Atkinson (1999b). In some countries, such as the United States

[1] See also Tuomala (1990) and Zee (1999).

and the United Kingdom, there was an increase in the inequality of disposable incomes, but in others, such as Canada, there was no such increase. The difference "before and after" a budgetary shock, or a labour market shift, differs according to the existing redistributive policy, which is itself the product of circumstances and objectives. To this end, I give particular attention to two cases. The first is a welfare state limited by the constraint that there is no inducement to leave the labour force, a case which I label—for purposes of reference, but not necessarily accurately—the "United States" case. In the second case, labelled "Continental Europe", redistributive objectives lead to a more extensive welfare state at the cost of causing some people to leave the labour force. How can the differing societies be expected to accommodate their welfare states to shocks to market incomes?

II. A Model of Social Transfers under Different Redistributive Objectives

Choice of an appropriate model is open to debate. Here I take a model which, from the outset, imposes strong assumptions but which has the merits of being directly related to the "labour market shift" explanation of rising market inequality and of being relatively simple. People of working age differ in their earning power, denoted by a wage rate, w. There is by assumption a perfectly elastic demand for their labour valued at w. It is assumed that there are no other differences between them: they have the same preferences and endowment of time. There are no other sources of income apart from earnings. The cumulative distribution is assumed to be linear in the logarithm of w:

$$F(w) = [\log_e w - \alpha]/\beta \quad (0 \leqslant F \leqslant 1). \tag{1}$$

This means that the log wage rises linearly with a person's rank in the skill distribution, with a slope β. The parameter β is an index of the extent of dispersion in gross wages.[2] The impact of a labour market shift is to tilt this relationship around the mean: β rises and α falls. This is illustrated in Figure 1. The mean wage is assumed to remain unchanged, and is given by

[2] An idea of the possible values of β may be obtained from the observed 10th and 90th percentiles, w_{10} and w_{90} (the assumed linear in logarithms cumulative distribution cannot be expected to fit outside this range), since $0.8\beta = \log_e(w_{90}/w_{10})$. The values in Table 1 of Gottschalk and Smeeding (1997) for full-year full-time male workers give values for β of 1.1 for the Netherlands, 1.6 for Sweden and 2.2 for the United States. It should be borne in mind that these figures relate to the *actual*, not the *potential*, working population.

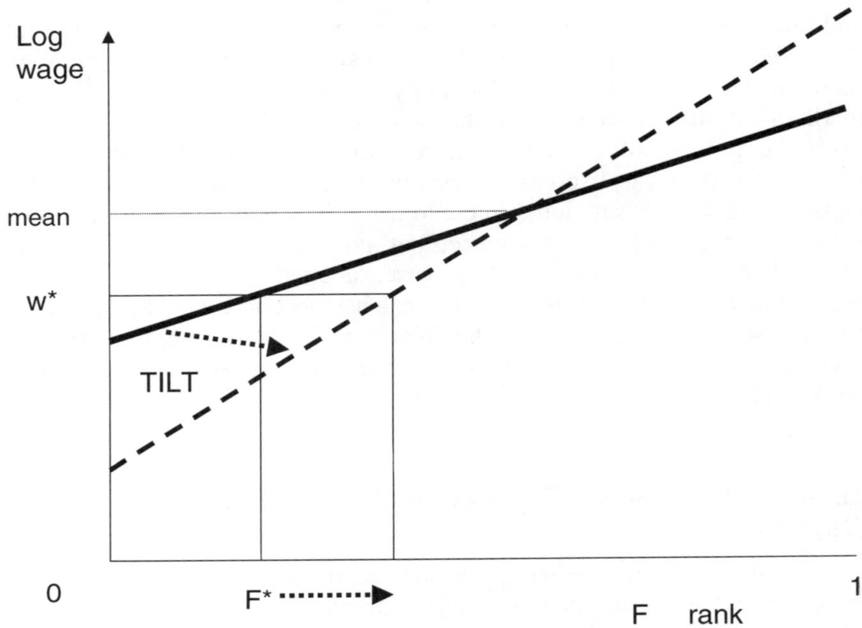

Fig. 1. Tilt in wage/skill nexus

$$\mu = e^{\alpha}[e^{\beta} - 1]/\beta. \tag{2a}$$

There is a lowest demand-wage, e^{α}, written as $w_{\min}$, and one may define as an alternative index of dispersion

$$\omega \equiv \mu/w_{\min} = [e^{\beta} - 1]/\beta, \tag{2b}$$

which is an increasing function of β.

Policy Frontier

The government is assumed to finance the welfare state by levying an employee payroll tax at rate t. The assumptions made above mean that the incidence of the tax falls entirely on workers.[3] The payroll tax finances a uniform benefit, b, paid to two groups: a proportion, p, of the population who are retired, and the unemployed. Unemployment is here modelled in the

[3] In this highly simplified model, no issues of competitiveness of different welfare states arise, since wage levels, or exchange rates, adjust to ensure that the burden of financing the welfare state falls on the country's workers.

way that has become commonplace in economics (although I have argued elsewhere, in Atkinson (1999a), that it ignores important institutional features), with workers assumed to have a reservation wage, w^*, which net of tax is equal to the benefit:

$$(1 - t)w^* = b, \tag{3}$$

where $w^* > w_{\min}$, a fraction $F(w^*)$, written F^* for short, of the potential labour force are unemployed (see Figure 1) and receive b. Since the potential labour force are $(1 - p)$ of the population, the unemployed constitute $(1 - p)F^*$.

The government budget constraint means that the revenue from the population at work must cover the benefits paid to the two groups. Writing the net revenue as R,

$$R \equiv (1 - p)t\int_{F^*}^{1} w(F)\,\mathrm{d}F - b[p + F^*(1 - p)] = 0. \tag{4}$$

From (3), and the fact that $\partial F/\partial w = 1/(\beta w)$, the proportion of unemployed rises with b and t:

$$\partial F^*/\partial b = 1/(b\beta); \quad \partial F^*/\partial t = 1/[(1 - t)\beta]. \tag{5}$$

Where $F^* > 0$, the derivatives of net revenue are

$$-\partial R/\partial b = [p + (1 - p)F^*] + (1 - p)(b + tw^*)/(b\beta), \tag{6a}$$

where the first term on the RHS is the extra cost of the benefit; the second term is the marginal benefit cost plus loss of revenue from people leaving the labour force:

$$\partial R/\partial t = (1 - p)\int_{F^*}^{1} w(F)\,\mathrm{d}F - (1 - p)(b + tw^*)/[(1 - t)\beta], \tag{6b}$$

where the first term on the RHS is the extra revenue from those working; the second term is the marginal benefit cost plus loss of revenue from people leaving the labour force. Evaluated at $F^* = 0$, these give the right-hand derivatives at this point.

A key issue is whether the government sets the level of b such that $F^* = 0$: i.e., a *limited* welfare state which avoids inducing any of the potential working population to opt out of working. It is possible that this "no dependency" condition may be imposed as a separate side constraint;

see Atkinson (1995). Here we ask whether it emerges unprompted from welfare maximization. The maximum benefit consistent with $F^* = 0$ is given by $b = (1 - t)w_{\min}$, and, from (4),

$$b = t\mu/\delta, \tag{7}$$

where $\delta \equiv p/(1 - p)$ is the old-age dependency ratio. Solving, using (2b), gives

$$t/(1 - t) = \delta/\omega; \quad b = \mu/[\omega + \delta]. \tag{8}$$

As a foretaste of results to come (in Section III), we may note that a rise in the old-age dependency ratio is associated with a fall in the benefit level but a rise in the tax rate. Adjustments are made on both sides of the account. A tilt in the earnings distribution such that ω rises is associated with a fall in both the tax rate and in b. The two types of shock have therefore different effects.

The policy "possibility frontier" in (t, b) space is shown in Figure 2.[4] The frontier is linear up to the point given by (8), since the tax at this level has no impact on economic behaviour. The slope is μ/δ. Beyond this point, a rise in t causes F^* to rise and hence reduces the tax base. From (6a) and (6b), evaluated at $F^* = 0$, we can see that, dividing by $(1 - p)$, $(\partial R/\partial t)$ is less than μ and that $(-\partial R/\partial b)$ is greater than δ, so that there is a kink in the possibility frontier: the slope beyond $F^* = 0$ is less steep than μ/δ. The reduction in the tax base could indeed be sufficient to mean that revenue falls, and hence that the feasible value of b turns down, as shown by the dashed curve. The condition for this not to happen is that the derivative of R with respect to t is positive at $F^* = 0$. From (6b), and using (2b) and (8), we can see that revenue can be increased where

$$\delta < \omega[\beta\omega - 1] = [e^\beta - 1][e^\beta - 2]/\beta. \tag{9}$$

This condition will *not* hold (i.e., there is no scope for increasing b beyond $F^* = 0$) where the dependent population is sufficiently large or where there is little inequality in wage income (the RHS is increasing in β). In fact it seems likely that the condition holds. Suppose that we take $\beta = 1$, which is a reasonably low value. This implies $\omega = 1.718$ (the lowest wage is 58 percent of the mean); the retired population would have to exceed 123 percent of the potential workforce for this condition not to be satisfied.

[4]I am most grateful to one of the referees for suggesting the use of this diagram, and even plotting it in Maple for sample values of the parameters.

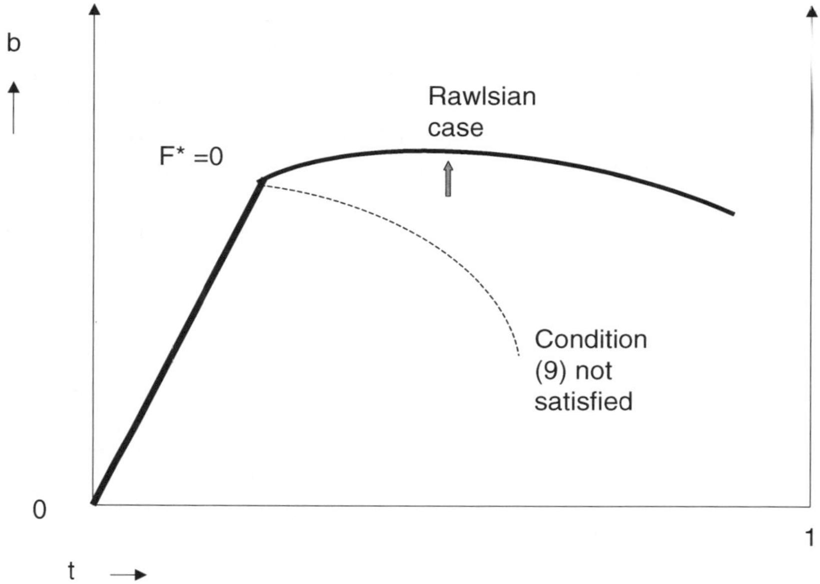

Fig. 2. Policy possibility frontier

If we compare the United States and Continental Europe, then it does not seem reasonable to suppose that the United States has either a lower value of earnings dispersion or a sufficiently larger dependent elderly population, which is what would be required for (9) to hold in Continental Europe but not in the United States. A situation where the United States chooses a limited welfare state, while Continental Europe chooses a *more extensive* welfare state with $F^* > 0$, has to be explained by differing social objectives, to which I now turn, or by considerations not covered by the model. In what follows, I assume that condition (9) holds.

Different Distributional Objectives

The level of social welfare is assumed to be an additive function of net incomes:

$$\Omega \equiv pV\{b\} + F^*(1-p)V\{b\} + (1-p)\int_{F^*}^{1} V\{w(1-t)\}\mathrm{d}F, \qquad (10)$$

where $V\{\cdot\}$ denotes the social valuation of individual net incomes, and we are adding in turn the welfare of the retired, of the unemployed and of the working population. I consider five variations on this social welfare function. Five variations may be considered excessive, but one of the main purposes of the paper is to illuminate the implications of different redistributive objectives, and there can be little doubt that in the real world there is considerable diversity of views regarding the appropriate degree of redistribution.

Three of the five variations may be considered as special cases of the isoelastic version of $V\{\cdot\}$:

$$V\{x\} = (x^{1-\epsilon} - 1)/(1 - \epsilon). \tag{11}$$

The social marginal valuation of income is equal to $x^{-\epsilon}$ which declines with x where ϵ is positive. The first case, however, is that of *distributional indifference*, where $\epsilon = 0$: i.e., a euro of income counts the same irrespective of the recipient. Maximizing social welfare then reduces to maximizing the sum of net incomes, which by the government budget constraint is equal to the sum of gross incomes. In (t, b) space, there is a social indifference curve which, where $F^* = 0$, coincides with the straight-line segment of the possibility frontier. Beyond $F^* = 0$, the slope of the social indifference curve changes continuously (there is no kink), so that a distributionally indifferent government would not wish to expand the welfare state beyond F^*. It is indeed indifferent about its scale below this point, unlike any government with concern about inequality.

Even the most conservative of governments typically has some degree of concern for the poor. Suppose that we consider as a second case what may be called the *charitable conservative* objective, where distributional concern is restricted to the dependent elderly population. According to this set of values, there is a higher social marginal valuation of income by a multiple θ for the retired population (not the voluntarily unemployed), but otherwise the government attaches a weight of 1 to all incomes. On this view, the slope of the social indifference curve is given by

$$(1/D) \equiv (-\partial\Omega/\partial t)/(\partial\Omega/\partial b) = M(F^*)/(\delta\theta + F^*), \tag{12}$$

where

$$M(F^*) \equiv \int_{F^*}^{1} w \, \mathrm{d}F \tag{13}$$

is the incomplete integral: i.e., the actual, as opposed to the potential, tax base. The slope is written as $(1/D)$ since the social indifference curve captures the *demand* side of the policy choice, and the less steep the indifference curve, the greater the willingness to pay higher taxes to secure a given increase in benefits. The *supply* side is given by the budget constraint in terms of the necessary increase in the tax rate (where $\partial R/\partial t$ is positive):

$$(1/S) \equiv (\partial R/\partial t)/(-\partial R/\partial b). \tag{14}$$

From (6a) and (6b), this is equal to

$$(1/S) = [M(F^*) - (1 + t/(1 - t))w^*/\beta]/[\delta + F^* + (1 + t/(1 - t))/\beta]. \tag{15}$$

Evaluated at $F^* = 0$, using (8), we have

$$\mu S(F^* = 0) = [\delta + (1 + \delta/\omega)/\beta]/[1 - (1 + \delta/\omega)/(\beta\omega)] \equiv K(\beta, \delta), \tag{16}$$

where it should be noted that ω is an increasing function of β, and hence that K is a declining function of β (greater than δ for all finite β).

The charitable conservative government would not want to set the benefit below the maximum level consistent with $F^* = 0$, but would it want to expand the welfare state beyond $F^* = 0$? On the demand side, $\mu D(F^* = 0) = \delta\theta$. The condition for the solution not to be constrained at $F^* = 0$ is then that

$$\delta\theta > K(\beta, \delta). \tag{17}$$

The RHS is greater than δ, so that for θ close to 1 the welfare state remains at its restricted scale, but where there is a sufficient degree of concern for the elderly relative to the working population, the welfare state is not limited to $F^* = 0$. Suppose that we take $\beta = 2$, which implies $\omega = 3.19$ (the lowest wage is 31 percent of the mean) and $\delta = 0.5$, then the critical value of θ is 2.6.

A more thoroughgoing approach to redistribution is where the marginal valuation of income declines steadily with income, as in the third case considered, which is the *logarithmic social welfare function*, where $\epsilon = 1$. The possibility frontier is unchanged, but the demand term is now given by

$$D = (\delta + F^*)/[w^*(1 - F^*)]. \tag{18}$$

Evaluating at $F^* = 0$, the condition for going beyond a limited welfare state is that

$$\delta\omega > K(\beta, \delta) \tag{19}$$

(i.e., ω replaces θ in (17)). Where this condition is satisfied, and there is an interior solution, the first-order conditions require the equation of D and S. From (15) and (18), this requires

$$t/(1-t) = \beta[M(F^*)/w^* - (1-F^*)](F^* + \delta)/(1+\delta) - 1. \tag{20}$$

Together, (20) and the budget constraint provide the solution in terms of F^* and $t/(1-t)$. These curves are sketched in Figure 3. The budget constraint may be written using (3) as

$$t/(1-t) = [\delta + F^*]w^*/M(F^*). \tag{21}$$

The condition (19) means that the RHS of (20) is greater than that of (21) at $F^* = 0$, and it may be shown that there is an interior value of F^* such that the RHS of (20) is zero. It follows that there is a solution as shown in Figure 3.

The logarithmic social welfare function implies that the social marginal valuation of income falls with the reciprocal of income; an alternative is to

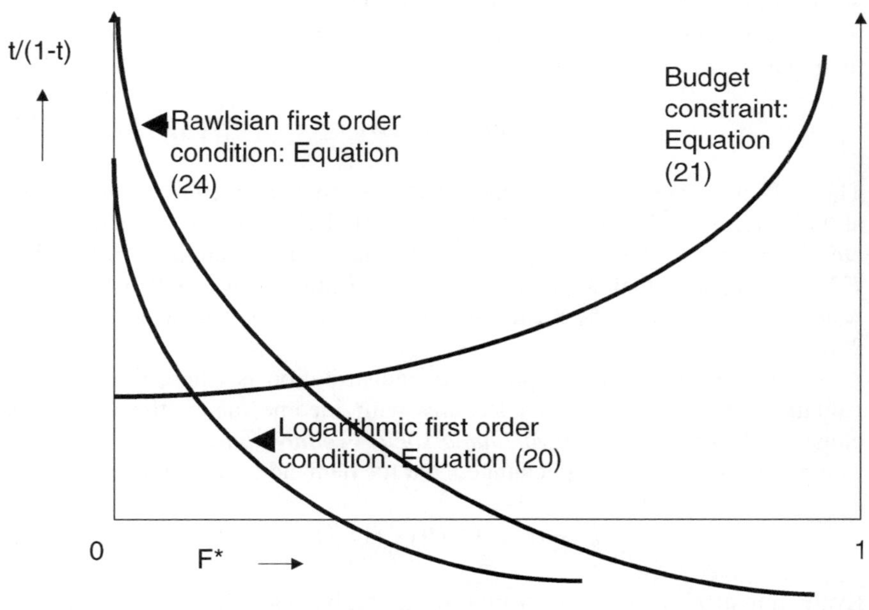

Fig. 3. Determination of policy in "more extensive" welfare state

attach a weight which depends on the rank order of the person concerned. Such a *rank order social welfare function* is implicitly used by the many people who consider mean income and the Gini coefficient as welfare indicators. In this case, the social weight attached to the income of a person at the point P in the cumulative distribution ($0 \leqslant P \leqslant 1$) is $2(1-P)$, so that the weights are greatest for the least advantaged person but decline smoothly to zero for the person at the top of the distribution. With this social welfare function, the level of social welfare is given by

$$\Omega = [1-(1-p)^2(1-F^*)^2]b + 2(1-p)^2\int_{F^*}^{1}(1-F)[w(1-t)]\mathrm{d}F. \quad (22)$$

Evaluating at $F^* = 0$, we obtain the condition for the solution not to be constrained at $F^* = 0$:

$$\delta(2+\delta)/(1-G) > K(\beta, \delta), \quad (23)$$

where G denotes the Gini coefficient for earnings among the potentially employed population. The cost of raising revenue from the working population is less, the greater the inequality. In the limiting case where all earnings are received by the top person, then the cost is zero since the social valuation of his (or her) weight is zero. Comparing (23) with (17) and (19), we may see that δ does not enter the LHS simply as a weighting factor. The existence of the dependent population affects the weight attached to the incomes of the working population: a person at a specified point F in the skill distribution moves up the overall distribution P as δ increases and therefore gets less weight in the social welfare function.

The working population get zero weight in the final objective considered here, which is the *Rawlsian* case where the government is concerned solely with the level of income, b, received by the least advantaged. This may be seen as the limit of the (transformed) isoelastic social welfare function V as ϵ goes to infinity. Where condition (9) holds, it is clear that a Rawlsian government would not limit the benefit level such that $F^* = 0$ (see Figure 2). The choice of a Rawlsian government is determined by $\partial R/\partial t = 0$, which may be written (from (6b))

$$t/(1-t) = \beta M(F^*)/w^* - 1 \quad (24)$$

and by the budget constraint. Comparing (24) with (20), we can see that this lies above the corresponding curve for the logarithmic social welfare function, as shown in Figure 3. The earlier assumption (9) means that the RHS of (24) is greater than that of (21) at $F^* = 0$, and there is a value of F^* such that the RHS of (24) is zero. There is therefore a solution as shown in Figure 3.

Conclusion

The framework set out here ignores many important factors. It takes no account of other economic decisions, such as savings, which are affected by the welfare state. No allowance is made for the differential treatment of different groups: for example, payment of lower benefits to the unemployed. The payroll tax is proportional and does not allow for the exemption of lower-paid workers. It does not allow for the administrative conditions under which social transfers are administered. Nevertheless, it provides a simple laboratory in which to examine how different arguments for the welfare state are affected by changes in the economic environment. It does so allowing for five different formulations of social objectives, summarized in Table 1. The expressions determining the size of the welfare state are complex, but there is considerable intuitive content. Countries with identical "supply" conditions will differ in their policies according to differences in objectives (different rows in Table 1) and according to the factors which enter the "demand" side for each objective. The latter include the relative marginal valuation of income (charitable conservative objective), the dispersion of wage income (logarithmic social welfare function and rank order weights), and the size of the dependent population (in all three of these cases). Contrasting the United States and Continental Europe, it is unlikely, as already noted, that intrinsic wage inequality is less in the United States, so that if the United States has only a limited welfare state ($F^* = 0$), then this may well reflect a weaker preference for redistribution.

III. Response to Budgetary Pressures, Labour Market Shifts and Changing Policy Objectives

How are arguments for the welfare state affected by increased budgetary

Table 1. *Different objectives*

Objective (relation to isoelastic social welfare function)	Condition for $F^* > 0$
Distributional indifference ($\epsilon = 0$)	Not possible
Charitable conservatism	$\delta\theta > K(\beta, \delta)$ (17)
Logarithmic social welfare function ($\epsilon = 1$)	$\delta\omega > K(\beta, \delta)$ (19)
Rank order social welfare function	$\delta(2+\delta)/(1-G) > K(\beta, \delta)$ (23)
Rawlsian objective ($\epsilon \rightarrow \infty$)	If (9) holds then $F^* > 0$

pressure, represented here by the dependency ratio δ, and by the tilt in the wage/skill nexus (rise in β and fall in α)? As already explained, it is of particular interest to examine the impact on two different situations: a limited welfare state, where benefit levels are constrained not to be sufficient to induce people to leave the labour force, and a more extensive welfare state where some cost in terms of reduced total income is accepted in order to make more generous provision for those without market income.

Budgetary Pressure

A rise in the old-age dependency ratio—a demographic shock—means, in a limited welfare state, that the proportion of benefit recipients rises, and the proportion of contributors falls, leading in the absence of policy change to budgetary pressure. For example, for a country which maintains the maximum benefit consistent with $F^* = 0$, we have seen from (8) that a rise in the dependency ratio is accommodated by both a reduction in the benefit level and a rise in the tax rate. The adjustment is not all borne by benefit recipients. Mean per capita income, $\mu/(1+\delta)$, is reduced by the demographic shift, and the benefit level is reduced less than proportionately: b divided by the overall mean is equal to $(1+\delta)/(\omega+\delta)$, which increases with δ.

Will there, however, be a shift in policy? Let us begin with the last of the five objectives considered in Section II: the Rawlsian case. From (21), we can see that a rise in δ shifts the budget constraint upwards at any F^*, leading to a fall in F^*, and a rise in t, at the interior solution. There is a fall in the fraction of the working population who do not work (although the combined total of $\delta + F^*$ may rise). A country which had previously chosen a more extensive welfare state may be forced to set benefits at a lower level. Indeed, it is possible that a rise in δ shifts the budget constraint above the intersection of (24) with the vertical axis. Fiscal discipline, as implied by the assumption that the government budget constraint is satisfied (there is no borrowing) means that "Europe" may be compelled to move to a "United States"-style limited welfare state.

In the Rawlsian case, this is the end of the story. However, this reveals a special feature of the Rawlsian objective as treated by economists: it is focused on the least advantaged to the complete exclusion of any concern for the *number of people* constituting this class. A society with 10 percent receiving the lowest income is ranked in the same way as a society where 20 percent receive this income. In the terminology introduced in Section II, δ does not enter the demand side. If we take the charitable conservative welfare function, for example, the size of the target population becomes a concern: the demand side in (17) is $\delta\theta$. A doubling of the dependency ratio doubles the desirability of a more extensive transfer. Of course, it also affects the supply side, and the overall effect may go either way. Calculation shows that (17) may be more or less likely to be satisfied after a rise in δ, depending on its initial value, on θ, and on the extent of labour market dispersion. The last of these means that the impacts of the two shocks considered here are interrelated. If technological change has led to a disequalizing tilt in the earnings relationship, then it may be more likely that a rise in the dependency ratio increases the pressure to extend the welfare state. In the case of the rank order objective, a doubling of δ more than doubles the LHS of (23). With this objective, the demand side is more sensitive to increases in the dependency ratio, since the relative welfare weights are affected by additions to the population.

Where, with objectives other than the Rawlsian, there is initially a more extensive welfare state (an interior solution), there are again conflicting effects of a rise in dependency. In the case of the logarithmic social welfare function illustrated in Figure 3, the rise in δ shifts the budget constraint upwards, raising the tax rate chosen, but reducing F^*. This effect is the same as in the Rawlsian case. In contrast, the balance between supply and demand in the first-order conditions also shifts upwards. The RHS of (20) is an increasing function of δ, which may lead to F^* rising overall. The tax rate will certainly rise.

Labour Market Tilt

The second change in external circumstances is the rise in wage dispersion. Suppose that the demand for unskilled workers has shifted down, causing the tilt shown in Figure 1. How does this affect the welfare state policy?

The RHS of condition (9) increases with β, so that the labour market tilt makes it more likely that $\partial R/\partial t$ is positive at $F^* = 0$. Equally, if we look at (17), the RHS is a declining function of β, so that it is less likely that a charitable conservative government will choose a limited welfare state. If, with a specified distributional preference and dependency ratio, the US had decided that the welfare state would not be increased beyond the point where disincentives start, then this decision might be revised if earnings dispersion increases. Falling wages at the bottom end mean that benefits have to be cut in order to maintain work incentives, and a point is reached where the level of benefit is no longer acceptable. In the logarithmic and rank order cases, this is reinforced by the appearance of distributional terms on the LHS. In (19), a rise in ω means that the case for an extensive welfare state is increased; in (23) the rise in the Gini coefficient for potential earnings has the same effect.

What is the effect where there is initially an interior solution with $F^* > 0$? The labour market tilt reduces the revenue cost from the unskilled leaving the labour force. It increases the revenue from a specified tax rate (since the incomplete integral above F^* increases). The revenue effect may be seen in the Rawlsian case, where the budget line (21) moves downwards at all points, and the first-order condition (24) moves upwards. The result is a rise in F^*. The tax rate may either rise or fall. The latter may happen if the rise in taxable capacity in the upper part of the distribution allows the tax rate to be reduced. The labour market tilt has, therefore, in this case an unambiguous effect on the level of F^*. This result should be interpreted carefully, however. The shift in itself reduces the level of benefit which corresponds to any given values of t and F^* if, as is to be expected, F^* is below the cross-over point in Figure 1. Put differently, constant b and t would imply a rise in F^*. The government may choose to react to the labour market tilt by cutting benefits, but by less than the amount which would reduce F^* below its previous level. The optimal response may be accommodating, but not to the extent of maintained benefit generosity. The logarithmic case is affected similarly, but we may note that a more general social welfare function would weight differently the "gain" from an increased tax base at the top and the "loss" from the extra welfare cost of charging payroll taxes on low-paid workers who have lost out from the labour market shift.

Changing Objectives

The implications of different formulations of the social welfare function have already been considered. It is possible that the policy responses in recent decades have also been affected by a shift in objectives. Just to give one example, with the charitable conservative position, it is possible that a perception that the elderly are on average better off has led to a fall in the weight θ attached to their incomes. This shift in objectives may offset the opposite pressure to give more weight to this group as it has become a larger fraction of the population.

The change in values may be within a class of objective functions, with a decline in the parameter measuring "aversion" to inequality (if we take the more general isoelastic social welfare function). Or, a shift in objectives may be represented by a discrete change. It is possible that earlier governments had more extensive redistributive ambitions, such as those embodied in the logarithmic social welfare function, where there is concern not just with the least advantaged but also with the relative distribution among those higher up on the scale. The switch may have been to the less ambitious charitable conservative position, or to complete distributional indifference. As we have just seen, the implications of abandoning these wider concerns are not immediately obvious. With the wider objective, greater earnings dispersion increases the tax base among the top earners, but makes us more concerned about the burden of the payroll tax on the lower paid.

Changed objectives may also take the form of increased weight attached to reducing the size of the government budget. The fiscal criteria adopted by European governments at Maastricht are an example. This could be represented in the present model by a revenue requirement tighter than break-even. In terms of the earlier analysis, a tighter revenue requirement would shift up the budget line in Figure 3. This could be expected to lead to both reduced F^* and increased taxation. Adjustments would be made on both sides of the account. Fiscal discipline on its own cannot explain a cut in benefits and a *cut* in taxation. Such an outcome would require a simultaneous shift in the welfare function.

IV. Conclusions

The aim of this paper has been to set out a framework within which we can explore the implications of budgetary pressure and the labour market tilt for the choice of welfare state policy by countries with different redistributive objectives. As scarcely needs to be pointed out, this does not explain the actual choices made by governments, which is a matter for public choice theory. No account has been taken, for example, of the increased political weight of the elderly or of any link between increased earnings at the top and political influence. Rather, it is intended to illuminate the arguments which can be made for and against policy reforms.

While the model is highly simplified, it serves to bring out points which have been underemphasized in the current debate. Whereas attention tends to concentrate on the cost side, the demand side is also important. A rise in the dependent population certainly increases the cost, but it also increases the value attached to providing adequate benefits. Taking both sides into account, it is possible that a rise in the dependency ratio would lead a country to extend its welfare state. Whether it would do so depends on the nature of social objectives. The analysis shows that in this respect the Rawlsian objective differs from the others considered, in that it attaches no weight to the size of the target population.

Two different changes in the external context have been distinguished. The results show that the impacts of demographic pressure and of labour market tilt are potentially different. While on balance a rise in dependency may point to a scaling back of welfare state generosity, a rise in earnings dispersion may have the reverse effect. Moreover, there may be interactions between the two kinds of shift. Widening dispersion of earnings may make it more likely that a rise in dependency is associated with an expansion of the welfare state.

A particular concern of the paper has been with the "double difference": the effect of a difference in external environment on countries pursuing different policies. We have seen that the effect of the dependency ratio on the demand side is absent in the case of the Rawlsian welfare function (and with distributional indifference), is proportional for the logarithmic and charitable conservative objective functions, and more than proportional with the rank order objective. On the other hand, with all redistributional objectives it may be necessary to make adjustments in policy in response to external shocks. This is rather different from the common assertion that it is Continental Europe which has to make all the adjustments.

Finally, the framework serves to separate those arguments which are concerned with the response to changes in the external environment from those based on changes in policy objectives. Objectives may indeed have changed, but this needs to be made explicit.

References

Atkinson, A. B. (1995), *Public Economics in Action: The Basic Income/Flat Tax Proposal*, Oxford University Press, Oxford.

Atkinson, A. B. (1999a), *The Economic Consequences of Rolling-back the Welfare State*, MIT Press, Cambridge, MA.

Atkinson, A. B. (1999b), Increased Income Inequality and the Redistributive Impact of the Government Budget, Paper prepared for WIDER study of "Inequality under the Washington Consensus", Helsinki.

Atkinson, A. B. (2000a), The Changing Distribution of Income: Evidence and Explanations, *German Economic Review 1*, 3–18.

Atkinson, A. B. (2000b), Is Rising Income Inequality Inevitable? A Critique of the Transatlantic Consensus, 1999 WIDER Lecture, Helsinki.

Buti, M., Franco, D. and Pench, L. R. (1997), Reconciling the Welfare State with Sound Public Finances and High Employment, *European Economy 4*, 7–42.

Gottschalk, P. and Smeeding, T. M. (1997), Cross-national Comparisons of Earnings and Income Inequality, *Journal of Economic Literature 35*, 633–687.

Krugman, P. (1994), Past and Prospective Causes of High Unemployment, in Federal Reserve Bank of Kansas City, *Reducing Unemployment: Current Issues and Policy Options*, Kansas City.

Mirrlees, J. A. (1971), An exploration in the Theory of Optimum Income Taxation, *Review of Economic Studies 38*, 175–208.

Stern, N. H. (1976), On the Specification of Models of Optimum Income Taxation, *Journal of Public Economics 6*, 123–162.

Tuomala, M. (1990), *Optimal Income Tax and Redistribution*, Clarendon Press, Oxford.

Zee, H. H. (1999), Inequality and Optimal Redistributive Tax and Transfer Policies, mimeo, International Monetary Fund, Washington, DC.

7

Unskilled Migration: A Burden or a Boon for the Welfare State?*

Assaf Razin and Efraim Sadka

I. Introduction

The flow of unskilled, low-earning migrants to developed nations with a comprehensive social security system, including retirement benefits, has attracted both public and academic attention in recent years. As relatively low earners, migrants are typically net beneficiaries of the welfare state in the short run.[1] Therefore, an almost unanimous opposition to migration may arise in the potential host countries. This host-country resistance phenomenon has been modelled by Wildasin (1994), Razin and Sadka (1995), and others.

An important pillar of the welfare state that has increasingly become the focus of attention is the pension system. It is commonly agreed that this system is heavily burdened in most countries and is in need of reform.[2] For instance, Gruber and Wise (1999, p. 34), state that

> "the population in all industrialized countries are aging rapidly, and individual life expectancies are increasing. Yet older workers are leaving the labour force at younger and younger ages. ... Together, these trends have put enormous pressure on the financial solvency of social security systems around the world."

In many countries, the theoretical tax (contribution) rates, i.e., the rates that would balance the system, are significantly higher than the statutory rates. For example, Brugiavini (1999) reports that this theoretical rate could reach 44 percent for Italy in 1991.

Migration may have important implications for the financial soundness of the pension system. As the *Economist* succinctly put it:

---

*Research on this topic was begun while we were visiting the International Monetary Fund, the first author at the Research Department and the second author at the Fiscal Affairs Department. Competent research assistance was provided by Evgeny Agronin. We also acknowledge comments and suggestions made by two anonymous referees.

[1] See, for instance, Lalonde and Topel (1997), Borjas (1994) and Borjas and Trejos (1991).

[2] For a survey of various reform proposals, see Heller (1998).

> "Demography and economics together suggest that Europe might do better to open its doors wider. Europeans now live longer and have fewer babies than they used to. The burden of a growing host of elderly people is shifting on to a dwindling number of young shoulders" (February 15, 1992).

While it is common sense to expect that young migrants, even if low-skilled, can help society pay the benefits to the current elderly, it may nevertheless be reasonable to argue that these migrants would adversely affect the current young, if the migrants are net beneficiaries of the welfare state. But this brings into play the ingenuity of Paul Samuelson's (1958) concept of the economy as everlasting machinery, even though each of its human components is finitely lived. Here we adopt this concept in a dynamic model of a welfare state with an old-age social security system, which is also inherently redistributive.

We first show that even though the migrants may be low-skilled and net beneficiaries of a pension system, all the existing income (low and high) and age (young and old) groups living at the time of the migrants' arrival, would still be better off when the economy is relatively small and has good access to international capital markets. Therefore, on these grounds, the political economy equilibrium will be overwhelmingly pro-migration in this case. Furthermore, this migration need not place any burden on future generations. If the migration episode repeats itself, or if the social security trust generates a surplus which is used to finance future benefits, all generations are made better off. This unambiguous result for a small open economy obtains regardless of whether or not the low-skilled migrants are net beneficiaries of or net contributors to the old-age social security system. That is, the result obtains when the contributions of the migrants to the pension system both fall short of, or exceed, the present value of the pension benefits. Indeed, when the market rate of interest exceeds the biological rate of interest (i.e., the population growth rate), which is typically the case, and the percentage of skilled in the native-born population is relatively small, then low-skilled migrants may well be net contributors to the pension system.[3]

Next we drop the open trade and capital accounts economy assumption which serves to fix factor prices in the wake of migration through either capital mobility or factor-price-equalizing trade in goods. We show that when migration affects factor prices,[4] particularly by depressing wages of

---

[3]This intertemporal aspect of the net contribution of low-skilled migrants to the welfare state seems to be absent from the static measures of the fiscal burden imposed by migrants, provided in much of the empirical literature cited earlier. Our finding that the social security fiscal burden is not necessarily a good welfare indicator is another drawback of this literature.

[4]This factor price effect of migration arises either when there is an inadequate inflow of capital in conjunction with the influx of labour or when the economy is large enough so as not to be a price taker in the global economy.

unskilled labour,[5] it might create some anti-migration elements that may counterbalance the initial positive effect on the pension system. Indeed, with a sufficiently small substitution between capital and labour, the factor price effect may well inflict losses on some income groups of the current generations and some future generations.

The organization of the chapter is as follows. The analytical framework is developed in Section II, where we also examine the effect of migration on a pay-as-you-go pension system in a fixed factor price environment. In Section III we re-examine this effect with variable factor prices. Section IV concludes.

II. Pension and Migration: Fixed Factor Prices

Consider an overlapping-generations model, where each generation lives for two periods. In each period a new generation with a continuum of individuals is born. Each individual possesses a time endowment of one unit in the first period (when young), but no labour endowment in the second period (when old). There is a pay-as-you-go, defined-benefit (PAYG-DB) pension system.

Innate Ability and Schooling

There are two levels of work skill, denoted by "low" and "high". A low-skill individual is also referred to as unskilled and a high-skill individual as skilled. Born unskilled, she can nevertheless acquire skills and become a skilled worker by investing e units of time in schooling. The remainder of her time is spent at work as a skilled worker.

The individual-specific parameter e reflects the innate ability of the individual in acquiring a work skill. The lower is e, that is, the less time she needs to acquire a work skill, the greater the ability of the individual. The parameter e ranges between 0 and 1 and its cumulative distribution function (c.d.f.) is denoted by $G(\cdot)$; that is, $G(e)$ is the number of individuals with an innate ability parameter below or equal to e. For the sake of simplicity, we normalize the number of individuals born in period zero (when we begin our analysis of the economy) to one, that is:

$$G(1) = 1. \tag{1}$$

Again for simplicity, we model the difference between skilled and unskilled workers by assuming that a skilled worker provides an effective

[5] For instance, Altonji and Card (1991) find that a 1 percent increase in a country's labour force due to immigration lowers wages by 1.2 percent.

labour supply of one unit per each unit of her working time, while an unskilled worker provides only $q < 1$ units of effective labour per each unit of her working time.

In the first period of her life, the individual decides whether to acquire skill, works, bears $1 + n$ children, consumes a single all-purpose good, and saves for retirement, which takes place in the second period. In the latter period she only consumes her retirement savings and her pension benefit.

Consider the schooling decision of the individual. If she acquires a skill by investing e units of her time, she will earn an after-tax income of $(1 - e)w(1 - \tau)$, where w is the wage rate per unit of effective labour and $\tau > 0$ is a flat social security contribution (tax) rate. If she does not acquire a skill, that is, spends all of her time endowment at work, she earns an after-tax income of $qw(1 - \tau)$. Thus, there will be a cut-off level of e, denoted by e^* and given by:

$$(1 - e^*)w(1 - \tau) = qw(1 - \tau), \qquad (2')$$

so that every individual with an innate ability parameter below e^* will acquire skill and become a skilled worker, while all individuals with innate ability parameters above e^* will not acquire education and remain unskilled. Rewriting (2′), we explicitly define e^* by:

$$e^* = 1 - q. \qquad (2)$$

Consumption and Saving

Denoting first-period and second-period consumption by c_1 and c_2, respectively, an individual born in period zero and onward faces the following intertemporal budget constraint:

$$c_1 + \frac{c_2}{1 + r} = W(e)(1 - \tau) + \frac{b_1}{1 + r}, \qquad (3)$$

where r is the interest rate,[6] $W(e)$ is the before-tax wage income for an individual with an innate ability parameter of e, and b_1 is the social security demogrant benefit (DB) paid to retirees at period one.[7] Note that:

---

[6]In addition to the social security tax, an income tax could also have been introduced, whereby interest income would be taxed too without affecting the results.

[7]Strictly speaking, a DB programme links benefits to wages before retirement. However, the link is very loose and there is a clear redistributive element in most publicly funded DB plans. In order to highlight the distributive nature of the DB programme, we simply assume that the benefit is in the form of a demogrant.

$$W(e) = \begin{cases} w(1-e) & \textit{for } e \leqslant e^* \\ qw & \textit{for } e \geqslant e^* \end{cases}. \tag{4}$$

We assume that preferences over first-period and second-period consumption are identical for all individuals and given by a Cobb–Douglas, log-linear utility function:

$$u(c_1, c_2) = \log c_1 + \delta \log c_2, \tag{5}$$

where $\delta < 1$ is the subjective intertemporal discount factor. These preferences give rise to the following saving and second-period consumption functions for a young individual of type e:

$$S(e) = \frac{\delta}{1+\delta} W(e)(1-\tau) - \frac{b_1}{(1+\delta)(1+r)} \tag{6}$$

and

$$c_2(e) = \frac{\delta}{1+\delta}\left[W(e)(1-\tau) + \frac{b_1}{1+r}\right](1+r). \tag{7}$$

The Current Old

In period zero there are also $1/(1+n)$ old (retired) individuals who were born in period -1. The consumption of each of them is equal to her savings from the first period, plus the social security benefit, denoted by b_0. In each period the aggregate savings of the old (retired) generation constitutes the aggregate stock of capital. Denote the aggregate stock of capital at period zero by K_0.

Migrants

In period zero, m migrants are allowed in. It is assumed that these migrants are all young and unskilled workers and they possess no capital. Once they enter the country, they adopt the domestic norms of the native-born population. Specifically, they grow up at the same rate (n), they have the same preferences (as given by (5)), and the ability index of their offspring is similarly distributed (according to the c.d.f. G).

Labour Supply

The aggregate supply of effective labour in period zero is given by:

$$L_0 = \int_0^{e^*} (1-e)\, \mathrm{d}G + q[1 - G(e^*)] + qm. \tag{8}$$

The first term on the RHS of equation (8) is the effective labour supply of the native-born skilled workers. The second term is the effective labour supply of the native-born unskilled workers (note that there are $1 - G(e^*)$ of them), and the last term is the effective labour supply of the unskilled migrants.

The aggregate supply of effective labour in period one is given by:

$$L_1 = (1+m)(1+n)\left\{\int_0^{e^*}(1-e)\,\mathrm{d}G + q[1 - G(e^*)]\right\}. \tag{9}$$

(Note that due to migration and natural growth there are altogether $(1+m)(1+n)$ young individuals born in period one.)

The Stock of Capital

The aggregate stock of capital in period zero was denoted by K_0. The aggregate stock of capital in period one consists of the savings of both the native-born young generation of period zero and the migrants. Thus, it is equal to:

$$\begin{aligned} K_1 = {} & \int_0^{e^*}\left[\frac{\delta}{1+\delta}w(1-e)(1-\tau) - \frac{b_1}{(1+\delta)(1+r)}\right]\mathrm{d}G \\ & + \left[\frac{\delta}{1+\delta}qw(1-\tau) - \frac{b_1}{(1+\delta)(1+r)}\right][1 - G(e^*) + m], \end{aligned} \tag{10$'$}$$

where use is made of the saving and earned income equations (6) and equation (4). (Note again that due to migrations there are $1 - G^*(e) + m$ unskilled individuals in period zero.) After some rewriting (10′) becomes:

$$\begin{aligned} K_1 = {} & \frac{\delta}{1+\delta}w(1-\tau)\left\{\int_0^{e^*}(1-e)\,\mathrm{d}G + q[1 - G(e^*) + m]\right\} \\ & - \frac{b_1(1+m)}{(1+\delta)(1+r)}. \end{aligned} \tag{10}$$

Output

In a small economy with free access to world capital markets, the domestic return to capital will converge to the world rate of interest. Thus, migration has no effect on the domestic rate of interest. Furthermore, when the technology exhibits constant returns to scale, migration will have no effect on wages as well. Thus, gross national output (denoted by $F(K, L)$) is given by:

$$F(K, L) = wL + (1 + r)K. \tag{11}$$

We assume, with no loss of generality, that capital fully depreciates at the end of the production process. In this setup, w is the (fixed) marginal product of labour and r is the (fixed) net-of-depreciation marginal product of capital.

The Pension System

As already mentioned, we consider a pay-as-you-go, defined benefit (PAYG-DB) pension system. The pensions to retirees are paid entirely from current contributions made by workers and the benefit takes the form of a demogrant. In period zero, total contributions amount to:

$$T_0 = \tau w \left\{ \int_0^{e^*} (1 - e)\, \mathrm{d}G + q[1 - G(e^*) + m] \right\}. \tag{12}$$

Thus, the demogrant benefit b_0 is equal to:

$$b_0 = (1 + n)\tau w \left\{ \int_0^{e^*} (1 - e)\, \mathrm{d}G + q[1 - G(e^*) + m] \right\}, \tag{13}$$

because there are $1/(1 + n)$ retirees at period zero. Total contributions in period one are equal to

$$T_1 = \tau w \left\{ \int_0^{e^*} (1 - e)\, \mathrm{d}G + q[1 - G(e^*)] \right\} (1 + m)(1 + n), \tag{14}$$

so that the demogrant benefit in period one is equal to:

$$b_1 = \tau w \left\{ \int_0^{e^*} (1 - e)\, \mathrm{d}G + q[1 - G(e^*)] \right\} (1 + n), \tag{15}$$

because there are $1 + m$ retirees in period one.

Dynamics

The dynamics of this economy is quite simple. Owing to the linearity of the technology, the economy converges to a steady state within two periods. The pension benefit in period two is going to be equal to b_1, the pension benefit in period one, because the characteristics of the offspring of the migrants and of the offspring of the native-born population of period zero are stationary. Thus, the pension benefits will equal b_1 from period one onward. The stock of capital will stabilize from period two onward because in period one it is still affected by the contribution to savings of the migrants who arrived in period zero.

In this stylized model, the impact of migration on the economy is manifested through the pension benefit only. This is because factor prices are constant and, consequently, schooling decisions are unaffected by migration.

The Benefits from Migration

Upon inspection of equation (13), it can be observed that b_0, the pension benefit to retirees at period zero in which the migrants arrive, increases in the number of migrants. Thus, as expected, the old generation at period zero is clearly better-off with migration. Upon inspection of equation (15), it can be observed that b_1, the pension benefit paid to retirees in period one and onward, is unaffected by migration. In particular and somewhat surprisingly, the young generation at the time during which the migrants arrive (both its skilled and unskilled members) is not adversely affected by migration. Thus, the existing population (both young and old) in period zero will welcome migration.

Furthermore, by creating some surplus in the pension system in period zero (that is, by lowering b_0 somewhat), the gain that accrues only to the old in our setup could be spread over future generations as well. Thus, migration is a Pareto-improving change with respect to the existing and future generations of the native born.

We should emphasize that this result obtains even though the unskilled migrants may well be *net beneficiaries* of the redistributive pension system, in the sense that the present value of their pension benefits exceeds their pension contributions. To see this, let us calculate the net benefit to an immigrant. The present value of her benefit is $b_1/(1+r)$. The contribution is τqw. Substituting for b_1 from equation (15) we can rewrite the net benefit (denoted by NB) as:

$$NB = \frac{1+n}{1+r}\tau w\left\{\int_0^{e^*}(1-e)\,\mathrm{d}G + q[1-G(e^*)]\right\} - \tau qw. \qquad (16)$$

Using (2), it can be shown (see Appendix) that $NB \gtreqless 0$, if:

$$\frac{G(e^*)(e^* - e^-)}{1 - e^*} \gtreqless \frac{r - n}{1 + n}, \tag{17}$$

where e^- is the mean ability parameter of the skilled workers. Note that $e^* > e^-$, because e^* is the upper bound of the ability parameter of skilled individuals, while e^- is its mean. Thus, the LHS of (17) must be positive. Hence, if $r < n$, then *NB* is certainly positive, that is the migrants are net beneficiaries of the pension system. However, for dynamic efficiency considerations, it is typically assumed that $r > n$.[8] In this case, if a large share of the population is skilled, then *NB* is still positive. To see this, observe that when the share of the skilled population (e^*) approaches one, then the LHS of (17) increases without bound. Hence, the LHS of (17) will exceed its RHS. In this case, migrants are net beneficiaries of the pension system. However, when r is significantly larger than n, the share of skilled in the native-born population (namely, $G(e^*)$) is low, and the relative productivity of unskilled (namely, $q = 1 - e^*$) is high, then *NB* will be negative. The intuition for how low-skilled migrants can still be net contributors to a progressive pension system is grounded in the dynamic feature of the PAYG system. The benefits to which the migrants are entitled at old age grow in a PAYG system only at the rate of population growth rate, n. However, in order to compare these benefits to the taxes paid by the migrants at their working age, we have to discount these benefits by the market rate of interest, r. Thus, *ceteris paribus*, the larger is the gap $r - n$, the smaller is the present value of the net benefit of the migrants. Now, if migrants and the native born were all similar (that is, $q = 1$, $e^* = 0$ and $G(e^*) = 0$), then no redistribution is implemented by the social security system and the migrants, like all the native born, are net contributors to the system. By continuity, it can be concluded that if the migrants are not substantially different from the native born (that is, q is not significantly below one, e^* is not substantially high and $G(e^*)$ is not very large), then they are still net contributors to the pension system in the dynamically efficient case of $r > n$.

What we have established in this section is that regardless of whether or not the migrants are net consumers of the pension system, all existing and future generations may gain from migration. In our simple parable, migration was a one-time episode. Naturally, if this one-time immigration episode repeats itself in the future to generate a steady flow of immigrants in each period, the gain that we showed to exist for the contemporaneous old generation would repeat itself for all future old generations. Thus, a steady

[8]See also the discussion in Hemming (1998) about the role of r and n in the transition from a PAYG-DB pension system to a fully funded, defined-contribution system.

flow of low-skilled migrants would generate a steady flow of benefits to the native born.

Interpretation

An important lesson from this work is that in a static setup, one cannot fully grasp the implications of migration for the welfare state. Earlier studies by Wildasin (1994) and Razin and Sadka (1995), among others, emphasize the burden that low-skill migration imposes on the native-born population. However, in a dynamic context, this net burden could change into a net gain because the burden imposed by the migrants, who typically are net beneficiaries of the welfare system, may be shifted forward indefinitely. If, hypothetically, the world would come to a full stop at a certain point in time, the young generation at that point would bear the cost of current migration.

To illustrate this point we may construct a finite-time (two-period) modified version of our model. Suppose the young generation of period zero and the migrants that arrive then bear no children and the world ceases after period one. Suppose further that the social security contribution (tax) rate remains τ in period zero. Hence, b_0 does not change (see equation (13)) and, as before, the old living in period zero benefit from migration.

In period one, the last period, there will be no young people, no labour supply and no social security benefits. National output is $(1 + r)K$. The young born in period zero and the migrants live off their period-zero savings (namely $(1 + r)K$). Obviously, the young of period zero are not affected by migration. The migrants paid their social security taxes in period zero, receiving no benefits in return in period one. That is, the migrants are net contributors to the pension system (which ceased after period zero); they helped finance the increased benefit to the old of period zero with no compensation to themselves. In sum, the effect of migration is as follows: the old of period zero benefited, the native-born young generation was not affected and the migrants financed in full the gain to the old. In essence, it is a zero-sum game. If, in this zero-sum environment, the migrants are compensated in period one in some way or another for their social security contributions in period zero, it must be at the expense of the native-born old of period one (the native-born young of period zero).

III. Pension and Migration: Variable Factor Prices

We have shown in the preceding section that in an everlasting economy, the migrants make a positive contribution to the existing old and possibly all other generations as well. In this simplified account of migration, the larger the number of migrants, the better-off everyone is. This can be seen from equation (13) where the larger the m, the larger is b_0. Thus, the native-born population would opt for having as many migrants as possible. However, when factor prices are variable, migration will generate a downward pressure on wages. This may overturn the welfare calculus of the preceding section.

The Dynamics of the Model

Formally, national output is now given by a constant-returns-to-scale production function:

$$F(K_t, L_t) = L_t F(K_t/L_t, 1) \equiv L_t f(k_t), \tag{11a}$$

where $k_t = K_t/L_t$ is the capital–labour ratio.

This production function gives rise to the following factor price equations:

$$1 + r_t = f'(k_t), \tag{18}$$

and

$$w_t = f(k_t) - (1 + r_t)k_t. \tag{19}$$

At period zero, the capital–labour ratio is given by:

$$k_0 = K_0/L_0, \tag{20}$$

where L_0 is given by (8). In period one, the stock of capital (K_1) consists of period-zero savings (of the native-born young and the migrants). This K_1 is given by equation (10) with w_0 replacing w. The capital–labour ratio is hence:

$$k_1 = L_1^{-1}\frac{\delta}{1+\delta}w_0(1-\tau)\left\{\int_0^{e^*}(1-e)\,\mathrm{d}G + q[1 - G(e^*) + m]\right\} - L_1^{-1}\frac{b_1(1+m)}{(1+\delta)(1+n)}. \tag{21}$$

The supply of labour is given by:

$$L_t = (1+m)(1+n)^t\left\{\int_0^{e^*}(1-e)\,\mathrm{d}G + [1 - G(e^*)]q\right\}, \quad t \geqq 1. \tag{22}$$

Henceforth, the capital–labour ratio is given by:

$$k_t = \frac{1}{(1+n)(1+\delta)}\left[\delta(1-\tau)w_{t-1} - \frac{\tau w_t(1+n)}{1+r_t}\right], \quad t \geqq 2. \tag{23}$$

Note that the dynamics of k_t from $t = 2$ and on is different from the earlier periods ($t = 0$, 1) because the composition of the skilled–unskilled population, which affects the savings of each period, does not depend on m for $t \geqq 2$ as the offspring of the migrants are fully integrated in society.

The social security benefit in period zero, b_0, is given by (13) with w_0 replacing w; that is:

$$b_0 = (1+n)\tau w_0\left\{\int_0^{e^*}(1-e)\,\mathrm{d}G + q[1-G(e^*)+m]\right\}. \tag{13a}$$

Similarly, b_t for $t \geqq 1$ is given by the RHS of (15) with w_t replacing w; that is:

$$b_t = \tau w_t\left\{\int_0^{e^*}(1-e)\,\mathrm{d}G + q[1-G(e^*)]q\right\}(1+n), \quad t \geqq 1. \tag{15a}$$

Finally, the net benefit from the redistributive pension system is given by:

$$NB = \frac{b_1}{1+r_1} - \tau q w_0. \tag{24}$$

Simulation Results

We resort to numerical simulations in order to illustrate the gains and losses from migration. The results are shown in Tables 1 and 2.

Suppose first that the economy is in a steady state with no migration, i.e., $m = 0$. This is described in the first row of the two tables as period -1. Then, at period zero, the economy is shocked by an influx of m low-skilled migrants. We describe the path of the economy until it reaches a steady state again in period ∞. Note that this new steady state is identical to the original one, as can be seen by the absence of m from equation (23), the dynamic equation of the model; compare the first and last rows in each table. The path of the capital–labour ratio (k), the social security benefit (b), and the welfare loss to members of each generation are reported for $m = 0.1$ and $m = 0.2$. This loss is measured as the percentage increases in lifetime consumption that will restore utility to its pre-migration level.

The calculations were carried out for a constant elasticity of substitution

(CES) production function. Table 1 presents the results for the Cobb–Douglas case (i.e., for $\sigma = 1$, where σ is the elasticity of substitution). The labour share is assumed to be $\frac{2}{3}$. The distribution of e is uniform over the interval [0, 1]. Productivity of unskilled labour is one-half that of skilled labour, i.e., $q = 0.5$. The subjective discount rate is 5 percent annually; each period lasts 25 years. The social security contribution rate is 30 percent. The annual population growth rate (n) is 2 percent.

As migrants arrive, the capital-labour ratio (k_0) falls naturally. Moreover, the pension benefit to the old (b_0) rises. The old of period zero gain on two grounds: first, b_0 rises; second, the rate of return to her capital ($1 + r_0$) rises, because k_0 falls. Thus, the old in period zero always gain from migration. Thereafter the capital–labour ratio rises monotonically back to its steady-state level. The pension benefit in period one falls below the steady-state level but then rises monotonically to its steady-state level.

In contrast to the fixed factor price case (i.e., $\sigma = \infty$), with variable factor prices and $\sigma = 1$, *all* income groups in every generation (except, of course, the retirees at period zero) lose from migration, as can be seen from the last four columns of Table 1. Furthermore, their loss is an increasing function of m. Note that the migrants are net contributors to the pension system, as $NB < 0$. Thus, their contribution does not even enhance the welfare of the old at the time of the migrants' arrival without hurting any other generation.

For a higher value of σ than in the Cobb–Douglas case, some income groups in some generations may still gain. Table 2 presents simulation results for $\sigma = 3.33$. Here again the retirees in period zero naturally gain from migration. But in this case the highest skilled people in the generation

Table 1. *The effects of migration with* $\sigma = 1$

	Capital–labour ratio		Social security benefit		Welfare losses of highest skilled (%)		Welfare losses of unskilled (%)	
Period	$m = 0.1$	$m = 0.2$	$m = 0.1$	$m = 0.2$	$m = 0.1$	$m = 0.2$	$m = 0.1$	$m = 0.2$
$-1 (m = 0)$	0.0096		0.0444		0		0	
0	0.0088	0.0082	0.0468	0.0491	1.99	3.89	2.09	4.06
1	0.0091	0.0088	0.0438	0.0432	1.23	2.34	1.23	2.34
2	0.0094	0.0093	0.0442	0.0440	0.40	0.77	0.40	0.77
3	0.0095	0.0095	0.0443	0.0443	0.13	0.25	0.13	0.25
4	0.0095	0.0095	0.0444	0.0444	0.04	0.08	0.04	0.08
5	0.0095	0.0095	0.0444	0.0444	0.01	0.03	0.01	0.03
6	0.0096	0.0095	0.0444	0.0444	0	0.01	0	0.01
⋮	⋮	⋮	⋮	⋮	⋮	⋮	⋮	⋮
∞	0.0096	0.0096	0.0444	0.0444	0	0	0	0

$$NB = \begin{cases} -0.0162 & \text{for } m = 0.1 \\ -0.0159 & \text{for } m = 0.2 \end{cases}$$

Table 2. *The effects of migration with* $\sigma = 3.3$

	Capital–labour ratio		Social security benefit		Welfare losses of highest skilled (%)		Welfare losses of unskilled (%)	
Period	$m = 0.1$	$m = 0.2$	$m = 0.1$	$m = 0.2$	$m = 0.1$	$m = 0.2$	$m = 0.1$	$m = 0.2$
$-1 (m = 0)$	0.0032		0.1595		0		0	
0	0.0030	0.0028	0.1721	0.1848	−0.09	−0.18	0.09	0.16
1	0.0031	0.0030	0.1594	0.1594	20.50	37.53	20.25	37.08
2	0.0032	0.0032	0.1595	0.1595	0.29	0.53	0.29	0.52
3	0.0032	0.0032	0.1595	0.1595	0	0.01	0	0.01
4	0.0032	0.0032	0.1595	0.1595	0	0	0	0
5	0.0032	0.0032	0.1595	0.1595	0	0	0	0
6	0.0032	0.0032	0.1595	0.1595	0	0	0	0
⋮	⋮	⋮	⋮	⋮	⋮	⋮	⋮	⋮
∞	0.0032	0.0032	0.1595	0.1595	0	0	0	0

$$NB = \begin{cases} -0.0173 & \textit{for } m = 0.1 \\ -0.0173 & \textit{for } m = 0.2 \end{cases}$$

born in period zero (i.e., when the migrants arrive) also gain. This group, which owns a larger share of the capital stock, is less affected than others by the downward pressure on wages exerted by migration. Unskilled people in all generations lose. Here again, the migrants are net contributors to the pension system as $NB < 0$. But their net contribution does not suffice to support the gain to the retirees in period zero and to the skilled people born at that time, so that all other people in all other generations are worse off.

IV. Conclusion

Migration has consequential implications for the financial soundness of the pension system, which is an important pillar of any welfare state. While it is common sense to expect that young migrants, even if low-skilled, can help society pay the benefits to the current elderly, it may nevertheless be reasonable to argue that these migrants would adversely affect the current young, since migrants are typically regarded as net beneficiaries of the welfare state which redistributes income from the rich to the poor.

In contrast to the adverse effects of migration in a static model, we adopted Samuelson's concept of the economy as everlasting machinery, even though its human components are only finitely lived, and showed that low-skill migrants may be either net beneficiaries of or net contributors to an old-age social security system which is inherently progressive. Regardless of whether or not the migrants are net contributors to this system, we showed that migration is a Pareto-improving measure. That is, all the existing income (low and high) and all age (young and old) groups living at the time of the migrants' arrival would be better-off. This result obtains when the economy has good access to international capital markets, so that migration exerts no major effect on factor prices. The effect of migration in this case is manifested entirely through the PAYG-DB pension system.

Therefore, in a dynamic model, with capital or goods mobility that freezes factor prices, the political economy equilibrium will overwhelmingly support migration. Evidently, this pro-migration feature can be weakened and possibly overturned when capital inflows or factor-price-equalizing trade are not sufficient to peg factor prices. In this case, even if migrants are net contributors to the pension system, their contribution does not suffice to support the increased benefit to the old at the time of the migrants' arrival; other people are worse off.

Appendix

In this appendix we prove that $NB \gtreqless 0$, when condition (17) holds. Substituting (2) into (16), we can see that:

$$NB = \frac{1+n}{1+r}\tau w\left\{\int_0^{e^*} \mathrm{d}G - \int_0^{e^*} e\,\mathrm{d}G + (1-e^*)[1-G(e^*)]\right\} - \tau w(1-e^*). \quad \text{(A1)}$$

Since

$$e^- = [G(e^*)]^{-1}\int_0^{e^*} e\,\mathrm{d}G$$

and

$$\int_0^{e^*} \mathrm{d}G = G(e^*),$$

it follows that $NB \gtreqless 0$, if:

$$\frac{1+n}{1+r}\{G(e^*) - G(e^*)e^- + 1 - e^* - G(e^*) + e^*G(e^*)\} \gtreqless 1 - e^*. \quad \text{(A2)}$$

Hence, $NB \gtreqless 0$, if:

$$\frac{1+n}{1+r}[(e^* - e^-)G(e^*) + (1-e^*)] \gtreqless 1 - e^*. \quad \text{(A3)}$$

Thus, $NB \gtreqless 0$, if:

$$(e^* - e^-)G(e^*) \gtreqless (1 - e^*)\left(\frac{1+r}{1+n} - 1\right), \tag{A4}$$

which yields condition (17).

References

Altonji, J. G. and Card, D. (1991), The Effects of Immigration on the Labor Market Outcomes of Less-skilled Natives, in J. Abowd and R. Freeman (eds.), *Immigration, Trade and the Labor Market*, 201–234, University of Chicago Press, Chicago, IL.

Borjas, G. (1994), Immigration and Welfare, 1970–1990, NBER Working Paper no. 4872, Cambridge, MA.

Borjas, G. and Trejos, S. (1991), Immigrant Participation in the Welfare System, *Industrial and Labor Relations Review 44*, 195–211.

Brugiavini, A. (1999), Social Security and Retirement in Italy, in J. D. Gruber and D. A. Wise (eds.), *Social Security and Retirement Around the World*, University of Chicago Press, Chicago, IL.

Gruber, J. and Wise, D. A. (eds.) (1999), *Social Security and Retirement Around the World*, University of Chicago Press, Chicago, IL.

Heller, P. S. (1998), Rethinking Public Pension Reform Initiatives, IMF Working Paper 98/61, Washington, DC.

Hemming, R. (1998), Should Public Pensions be Funded? IMF Working Paper no. 98/35, Washington, DC.

Lalonde, R. J. and Topel, H. (1997), Economic Impact of International Migration and the Economic Performance of Migrants, in M. R. Rosenzweig and O. Stark (eds.), *Handbook of Population and Family Economics*, 1B, Elsevier, Amsterdam.

Razin, A. and Sadka, E. (1995), Resisting Migration: Wage Rigidity and Income Distribution, *American Economic Review, Papers and Proceedings 85* (2), 312–316.

Samuelson, P. A. (1958), An Exact Consumption Loan Model With or Without the Social Contrivance of Money, *Journal of Political Economy 66*, 467–482.

Wildasin, D. E. (1994), Income Redistribution and Migration, *Canadian Journal of Economics 27* (3), 637–656.

8

Early Retirement and Economic Incentives

*Erik Hernæs**

Marte Sollie

Steinar Strøm

I. Introduction

Up until 1989, the general retirement age in Norway was 67. In 1988, as a result of negotiations between trade unions and employers' organizations, an early retirement programme (AFP) was introduced. The main arguments in favour of lowering the retirement age, voiced by the parties involved in the negotiations, were to give workers other benefits than a rise in wages and to make room for younger people in the labour market. The unemployment rate in Norway had been increasing since mid-1986 and reached its highest postwar level in the early 1990s.

As of January 1, 1989, the early retirement age was set at 66 and has since gradually been reduced to age 62 in 1998. The programme, based on collective agreements between employers and employees, is now more widespread than in 1988 and covers 43 percent of all employees in the private sector and all employees in the public sector; see NOU (1998).

Public policy issues related to retirement are discussed at some length in the recent *OECD Employment Outlook* (1998). One important conclusion in this report is "... it appears likely that pension programs will be adjusted so that possibilities for early retirement are more limited or made relatively less attractive, and that workers will respond by seeking to delay retirement". The tone of the OECD report is quite optimistic; stronger financial incentives

*We thank two anonymous referees for helpful and constructive comments and suggestions. We also thank Ugo Colombino, Knut Røed and participants at the 1999 Norwegian *Forskermøte*, as well as participants at a seminar at Kansas State University, Manhatten, KS, for valuable comments. The usual disclaimer applies. Financial support from the Research Council of Norway and the Department of Health and Social Security is gratefully acknowledged. Parts of this paper were written when the first and third authors visited the International Centre for Economic Research, ICER, in Turin, Italy, and when the first author visited the National Bureau of Economic Research, Cambridge, MA. We thank ICER for financial support and both ICER and NBER for providing excellent working conditions.

to extend working life, combined with improved health of the elderly population, are expected to increase sharply the supply of older workers in coming decades.

Empirical estimates are needed to assess the policies aimed at achieving the increases in labour force participation called for in the OECD report. In this chapter, we estimate a model of retirement behaviour of individuals who became eligible for early retirement programmes in the 1990s, and use the estimated model in simulations to study how financial incentives can be used to extend working life. The analytical advantage of studying the retirement behaviour of this specific group is that we are able to identify the economic incentives. Based on our sample, we know in which year each individual qualifies for early retirement, the main components of his/her potential pension and when he/she actually retires. Earnings and potential pensions vary considerably among individuals and allow us to analyse the responsiveness of retirement behaviour to economic incentives. Although the AFP programme introduces variation in incentives between those who are covered by the programme and those who are not, much less is known about the latter group. In particular, some are covered by occupation-based programmes outside the AFP with lower retirement age and/or other pension levels, but we cannot identify these individuals. Likewise, many of the self-employed have additional, private pensions. We do not have a satisfactory basis for econometric analysis of retirement behaviour for those not eligible for AFP, but we do provide some descriptive statistics of retirement behaviour and labour force participation for the whole cohort.

As in Stock and Wise (1990) we analyse the impact on retirement of company-specific early retirement programmes beginning in 1989. In contrast to Stock and Wise (1990), because our data record all work activity, we observe not only retirement in relation to the company, but also any other work after (partial) retirement. In the sense that the early retirement programme was the outcome of negotiations between unions and employers in 1988, it may be regarded as an unanticipated change in retirement laws. Moffit (1984) argues that unanticipated changes in retirement programmes provide the best analytical basis for studying the impact of retirement rules on labour supply among the elderly. Others who have used unanticipated changes in retirement rules to analyse labour supply include Pedersen and Smith (1996) and Krueger and Pischke (1992).

We follow Blau (1994) and allow for three labour force states: full retirement, partial retirement/part-time work and full-time work. Like Pedersen and Smith (1996) we assume that full retirement is an absorbing state, which accords completely with observations. Moreover, we assume that partial retirement is partially absorbing; i.e., transition from partial retirement to full-time work is not allowed. Again, this accords with observations. We observe the labour force states in 1990 and 1992 of all individuals aged

63–65 in 1990 and eligible under the early retirement programme. Note that the social security age is 67, at which age early retirement benefits are replaced by social security benefits.

Based on observations of the labour market transitions between 1990 and 1992, we estimate a three-state, competing-risk model. As in Blau (1994) the individuals are assumed to move among states according to utility maximizing behaviour. We assume that the random utilities are extreme value distributed, thereby obtaining a multinomial logit model. We observe all types of pensions actually received: benefits from early retirement, social security benefits, private pensions and savings. Prior to retirement, we observe the major part of pension rights. Unlike previous studies, we are able to calculate taxes, which are considerably lower on low or middle incomes if all or part of the income is a pension. We also account for the earnings-tested reduction in retirement benefits in the part-time work/partial retirement case. Thus, our budget constraint variable is disposable income in the different states.

In order to estimate the model, we had to assess disposable income in all feasible states, including states not currently occupied by the individual. Pension and wage equations were estimated as functions of observed characteristics (education, working experience, gender and age). In contrast to Blau (1997) income is assumed to be evaluated in the same way regardless of its source. Spouse's income was not included, since this might have introduced an endogeneity bias. Following Blau (1997), we assume that the deterministic part of the utility function is a linear function of disposable income and leisure. In addition, observed socio-demographic characteristics such as age, gender, education, marital status and industry affiliation, were introduced into the utility function to capture effects on retirement decisions—in excess of budget constraint variables—that others have argued are important; see Krueger and Pischke (1992) and Anderson, Gustman and Steinmeier (1997).

The main conclusions to be drawn from our study are first, that a majority took the opportunity to retire, partly or completely, at the earliest possible date. Second, the probability of retirement varies considerably with education, gender, marital status and industry affiliation. Third, economic incentives were found to influence early retirement, with a substantial effect of a bonus for delayed retirement.

II. Institutional Setting

Since benefits in the early retirement programme follow the rules of the public pension (i.e., social security) system, we briefly describe that system over our observation period. The backbone of the Norwegian public pension system is a mandatory, pay-as-you-go, defined-benefit public pension system, covering all permanent residents, established in its current form in

1967. The benefit consists of two main components. One is a minimum pension, paid to all persons who are permanently residing in the country. With less than 40 years of residence, the pension is reduced proportionally. This reduction mainly applies to immigrants, of whom there are very few in the sample. In what follows, this feature of the system is disregarded. The other main component is an earnings-based pension.

A crucial parameter in the system, used to define contributions as well as benefits, is the basic pension, denoted *G*. In 1991, which in our chapter is the base year for calculating potential pension, *G* was NOK 34,100 (approximately USD 4,250) from January to April and NOK 35,500 (USD 4,450) between May and December. In the private sector, the earnings-based pension depends on *G* and on the individual's earnings history in several respects. Each year, earnings above the basic pension are divided by the basic pension to give pension "points" for that year. Earnings of more than 12 times the basic pension do not carry points, and earnings of between 8 and 12 times the basic pension are reduced to one-third before points are calculated. Yearly points are then multiplied by 0.45, after which average yearly points over the 20 best years are calculated. These points multiplied by the basic pension make up the earnings-based component, which is then added to basic pension to give the total public pension. With less than 40 years of earnings above the basic pension, the earnings-based pension is reduced proportionally.

Two other features of the public pension system have been taken into account in our calculations of potential pensions. First, since the system is still immature, a special "overcompensation" programme is in effect for those born before 1928. Second, those without any earnings-based pension component receive a supplementary pension equivalent to a minimum pension level of 1.605 times the basic pension. Keeping the 1991 regulations constant, the maximum future pension level will be 4.75 times *G*, i.e., NOK 168,625 (USD 21,100). This pension level will require 20 years of earnings of at least NOK 426,000 (USD 53,250) and another 20 years of earnings of at least NOK 35,500 (USD 4,450). Although the tax system also has a redistributive effect on pre-retirement earnings, this effect is much stronger after retirement. The after-tax pension for a pre-retirement earnings flow up to about 3 *G* (USD 13,300) is actually higher than after-tax earnings. The replacement ratio (defined as after-tax pension divided by an after-tax earnings stream which is constant in relation to the basic pension each year) falls sharply from one at an income level of 2.344 *G*, below which the earnings level does not affect the public pension. In 1992, the replacement ratio for earnings which exactly qualify for the maximum pension was 0.396.

Public sector employees have alternative ("government") pensions, coordinated so that benefits will amount to the maximum of public and government pensions. The government pension is based solely on the earnings level immediately prior to retirement and full pension is 66 percent of the sum of earnings up to 8 *G* and one-third of earnings between 8 and 12 *G*. Thirty years of public sector service is required in order to obtain full pension. The maximum government pension is 6.16 times *G*, giving a replacement ratio at that level of 0.51. In addition, there are other kinds of employer-based and individual pensions (tax deductible and widespread). Coverage is directly observed in our data but accrual is not.

Prior to 1989, persons who worked for employers that participated in the early retirement programme (AFP) and who met individual requirements (set out in the Appendix) could retire at an earlier age than the ordinary 67. As of January 1, 1989, the AFP age was 66. It was lowered to 65 in 1990, to 64 in 1993, to 63 in 1997 and to 62 in 1998. The AFP pension is the same as the ordinary old-age public pension (i.e., social security benefits) received from age 67. In addition to pension points accrued at the time of early retirement, pension points based on a projection of earnings up to age 67 are also taken into account when calculating the pension level. Hence, in the period up to age 67, unless earnings increase from the level immediately prior to early retirement and thereby improve the basis for the ordinary old-age pension, taking early retirement does not entail any loss in the pension level after age 67.

The central and local governments finance the AFP in the public sector. In the private sector, 10 percent of the benefits are paid directly by the employer, and the rest is split equally between the central government and the participating employers, by means of a fund. Non-government contributions to the fund are proportional to total wages paid by the employers covered; see NOU (1994).

Even in combination with other income, pensioners' income below a stipulated minimum pension (60.5 percent above *G*) is not taxed, and tax on income exceeding this minimum pension is capped at 55 percent; see Hernæs and Strøm (2000). In contrast, earnings equal to the minimum pension are taxed at 27 percent. Furthermore, there is an additional tax-exempt pension of NOK 11,400 in the private sector, and a higher but taxed additional pension in the public sector. This results in a negative income tax on pensions up to about three-quarters of the average AFP pension.

III. Retirement Rates by Year, Age, and Gender

The AFP scheme introduces a difference in incentives among those who are covered by the programme and those who are not. Unfortunately, we do not have enough information about the incentives for those not covered to conduct an econometric analysis. According to NOU (1998), about one-third of the employees of local and central government, such as nurses and policemen, are covered by early retirement schemes other than AFP. In the private sector, only a few percent have this option. Moreover, since the AFP has requirements about work history, it seems likely that the transition to disability will be higher among those not covered by AFP. Thøgersen, Bratberg and Holmås (1998) point out that those who retire due to disability differ in important respects from those who take early retirement. Therefore, the group not covered by AFP differs in many more respects than lack of coverage, and does not constitute a suitable reference group for econometric analysis.

In spite of this we will try to provide some additional information about the impact of the AFP. As seen from Table 1, the transition rates for all employees indicate a considerable frequency of early retirement also among the non-AFP-eligible. This is probably due to the special retirement rules for, say, policemen and nurses etc. referred to above. Still, retirement is considerably higher in the AFP group, indicating a substantial impact of the AFP scheme on aggregate labour force participation.

Turning now to the time-series data, we expect to find the largest impact from AFP on male labour force participation, since a much smaller proportion of females are covered by the AFP due to the work history requirements. Moreover, the historically rising labour force participation of females tends to increase labour force participation across cohorts of females. In Table 2, the AFP affects the cohorts below the lines. Among males aged 60–64, the downward trend from the 1980s is reversed in the mid-1990s; see Wadensjö (1996). Both the level and the trend of labour force participation at age 60 place Norway midway in the list of OECD countries; see Gruber and Wise (1997). Looking at single age groups, the sample size implies standard errors of the order of 10 percentage points in labour force participation and introduces considerable variation, even if participation declines with age; see Statistics Norway (1993). Furthermore, the decline may also be due to gradual diffusion of information and gradual adjustment of behaviour to a new regime. With declining labour force participation and a heterogeneous

Table 1. *Transition percentages from full-time work in 1990*

	All employees; age in 1992			AFP-eligible; age in 1992		
Status in 1992	65	66	67	65	66	67
Employed	59	52	13	39	30	3
Partially retired	19	19	57	30	28	55
Retired	5	12	26	4	23	35
Other	17	17	4	27	19	7

Source: Hernæs *et al.* (1997).

Table 2. *Labour force participation, 1989–1998, percent*

Year	60–64	65–66	60	61	62	63	64	65	66
				Males					
1989	*65.2*	*48.7*	73.8	70.8	67.3	60.6	53.2	52.3	44.7
1990	*63.9*	*43.9*	73.1	69.9	67.7	53.0	54.1	47.0	40.8
1991	*63.0*	*42.3*	73.9	73.3	62.3	57.1	46.9	50.3	33.7
1992	*63.5*	*39.1*	72.7	69.6	64.7	57.7	53.2	41.7	36.7
1993	*61.9*	*38.6*	73.5	66.4	64.3	53.0	53.3	46.1	31.9
1994	*61.5*	*36.6*	71.8	67.2	62.5	58.0	47.4	40.2	33.3
1995	*62.2*	*48.1*	69.6	73.9	63.5	57.5	48.1	41.2	27.5
1996	*62.4*	*38.1*	77.0	60.8	66.4	58.3	48.8	41.5	34.8
1997	*63.8*	*35.9*	78.5	71.2	62.2	58.5	47.3	38.8	33.1
1998	*62.9*	*31.7*	72.4	76.3	63.1	54.2	44.2	33.2	30.3
				Females					
1989	*44.1*	*29.1*	53.1	53.5	42.9	38.0	34.5	32.9	25.0
1990	*46.2*	*28.6*	53.6	49.6	51.5	39.6	37.0	31.2	26.3
1991	*47.1*	*28.2*	52.5	53.3	45.8	43.2	39.0	30.9	25.7
1992	*45.5*	*26.9*	51.3	49.5	47.4	38.7	40.1	31.4	22.7
1993	*45.9*	*29.6*	55.2	49.5	48.7	40.5	37.0	35.6	22.6
1994	*46.3*	*26.6*	52.6	47.3	51.0	42.6	39.4	26.2	27.1
1995	*48.1*	*24.9*	56.2	51.8	46.5	47.7	40.0	30.2	19.6
1996	*48.5*	*26.4*	55.7	48.2	50.9	50.1	39.5	29.4	23.3
1997	*48.5*	*25.4*	55.6	55.7	50.6	44.7	36.3	29.3	20.8
1998	*48.6*	*25.0*	62.6	55.6	50.2	42.3	31.1	25.9	24.0

Source: Statistics Norway (1989, . . . , 1998).

supply of labour, the labour force will be increasingly "employable", which tends to slow any downward trend in participation. On balance, and recalling the upturn in the labour market from 1993/1994 onwards, the decline in labour force participation in Table 2 may be interpreted as indicating an impact of AFP on aggregate labour force participation.

IV. The Model

The three states specified in our model are full-time work (state 3), partial retirement (2) and full retirement (1). Details on how these states are defined and observed are given in Hernæs and Strøm (2000). Let U_{kt} denote the utility derived from consumption and leisure when the individual is in state k at time t. The individual is assumed to maximize utility and hence prefers state j at time t, given that he occupied state i at time $t-1$, if the following holds:

$$[U_{j,t}|\text{state } i \text{ at } t-1] > [U_{k,t}|\text{state } i \text{ at } t-1]. \qquad (1)$$

State 1, full retirement, is assumed to be an absorbing state. If $i = 2$ (partial retirement) at time $t - 1$, then j and k are allowed to be $\{1, 2\}$. This follows from the assumption that partial retirement is partially absorbing, in that individuals are not allowed to exit from partial retirement to full-time work. If $i = 3$ at time $t - 1$, then individuals are permitted to exit to all states. Thus, in this case, $j, k = 1, 2, 3$.

Preferences are assumed to vary across individuals with a deterministic element that captures the effects of consumption and leisure on individual welfare and with a stochastic taste shifter that accounts for the impact of unobserved variables. The deterministic part of the utility function is allowed to vary with both the exiting and destination states. Thus,

$$[U_k | \text{state } i \text{ at time } t-1] = v_{ik} + \varepsilon_{ik} \tag{2}$$

where v_{ik} is the deterministic part of the utility function and ε_{ik} is the stochastic part. The deterministic part is assumed to be a linear function of consumption, C_k, leisure L_k and socio-demographic variables (denoted Z_s) such as gender, age, education, marital status and industry affiliation (see Table 3). Thus,

$$v_{ik} = \alpha_i C_k + \gamma_i L_k + \sum_s \beta_{iks} Z_s, \tag{3}$$

where the subscripts attached to the coefficients in front of the consumption and leisure variables indicate that we allow for different impacts of these two variables on household welfare depending on the state previously occupied by the individual. If the empirical results imply that these coefficients vary across states, then this result might indicate state dependence in preferences. As alluded to above, and as suggested by Krueger and Pischke (1992), we assume that socio-demographic variables may have an impact on the movements of individuals among the labour market states, in excess of their effects on labour income and pensions. Assuming that the stochastic variables are extreme value i.i.d. across states, we obtain the following probability distribution function:

$$P(\varepsilon_{ik} \leqslant y) = \exp(-e^{-y}). \tag{4}$$

This assumption, together with the utility maximizing behaviour governing the movements of individuals among states, (1), and the specification of the utility function, (2), yield a multinomial logit model for the transition probabilities. These probabilities are addressed below.

Transition Probabilities Given that State 2, Partial Retirement, is the Initial State

Given that the individual is in state 2 at time $t-1$, the only feasible destination states are 1 (full retirement) and 2 (partial retirement). Let Q_{2k} denote the probability that state $k = 1, 2$ is chosen, given that state 2 was the initial state. After normalization we get

$$Q_{22} = \exp(v_{22} - v_{21})/[1 + \exp(v_{22} - v_{21})] \tag{5}$$

$$Q_{21} = 1 - Q_{22}. \tag{6}$$

From the specification in (3) it follows that

$$v_{22} - v_{21} = \alpha_2(C_2 - C_1) + \gamma_2(L_2 - L_1) + \sum_{s=0}(\beta_{22,s} - \beta_{21,s})Z_s$$

and by noting that partial retirement is associated with an individual working a fixed number of hours a year, say, M, with that many hours less leisure, we further get

$$v_{22} - v_{21} = \alpha_2(C_2 - C_1) + (\beta_{22,0} - \beta_{21,0} - \gamma_2 M) + \sum_{s=1}(\beta_{22,s} - \beta_{21,s})Z_s. \tag{7}$$

With no measured variation in hours worked in partial retirement, the leisure term is absorbed in the constant for each state, and cannot be identified.

Transition Probabilities Given that State 3, Full-time Work, is the Initial State

Similarly, the transitions to full-time work are, after normalization:

$$Q_{33} = \exp(v_{33} - v_{31})/[1 + \exp(v_{32} - v_{31}) + \exp(v_{33} - v_{31})] \tag{8}$$

$$Q_{32} = \exp(v_{32} - v_{31})/[1 + \exp(v_{32} - v_{31}) + \exp(v_{33} - v_{31})] \tag{9}$$

$$Q_{31} = 1 - Q_{32} - Q_{33}. \tag{10}$$

Rewriting, while assuming M hours of work in partial retirement, we obtain for the choice between full and partial retirement:

$$v_{32} - v_{31} = \alpha_3(C_2 - C_1) + [\beta_{32,0} - \beta_{31,0} - \gamma_3 M] + \sum_{s=1}(\beta_{32,s} - \beta_{31,s})Z_s \tag{11}$$

and for the choice between continued full-time work and full retirement, assuming a constant N hours of work in full-time work:

$$v_{33} - v_{31} = \alpha_3(C_3 - C_1) + [\beta_{33,0} - \beta_{31,0} - \gamma_3 N] + \sum_{s=1}(\beta_{33,s} - \beta_{31,s})Z_s. \tag{12}$$

Although we allow the impact of consumption on transition probabilities to vary across initial states, we would not expect α_3 and α_2 to be very different. Both coefficients are the marginal utilities of consumption, which are positive according to economic theory. Positive α_3 and α_2 mean that an increase in consumption as a part-time or full-time worker relative to consumption as fully retired will reduce the transitions to full retirement. Stock and Wise (1990) allow, and also estimate, different effects of consumption in work and in retirement. An important component of this difference is probably due to leisure, of which neither Stock and Wise nor we have any direct observations. In our approach the leisure term is absorbed in the intercept terms.

From (7), (11) and (12) we observe that individuals are assumed to choose among states according to the level of consumption only in year t. This limitation is motivated by the fact that persons included in our sample are aged 65–67 when the retirement decision is observed. Since the pension level after age 67 is unaffected by early retirement, future income streams beyond age 67 cancel out at the individual level and our estimates are based on individual variation in income in year t only.

V. Results

As outlined in Section IV, the model consists of two separate blocks depending on the initial state in 1990. These two blocks are estimated separately. When the initial state is partial retirement, the likelihood equals the product-sum of the probabilities Q_{22} and Q_{21}. When the initial state is full-time work, all three states are permitted as destination states. In this case the likelihood equals the product-sum of Q_{33}, Q_{32} and Q_{31}.

When reading the results below, it should be kept in mind that we have normalized all probabilities with the utility values related to full retirement.

Estimation Results when Partial Retirement is the Initial State

From Table 3 we observe that only state-specific consumption and age 65 in 1990 have a significant impact on the transitions from state 2, partial retirement.

The estimates given in Table 3 can be used to calculate the impact of an increase in state-specific consumption on the transition probabilities. Thus, if $(C_2 - C_1)$ is increased by NOK 10,000 in 1992,[1] the mean probability of exiting to full retirement would be reduced by 3.7 percentage points, from 0.640 to 0.603. Or, if a person with mean characteristics is partially retired in 1990, the chances that he or she will extend his or her partial retirement throughout 1992 would be increased by 3.7 percentage points.

Estimates of the age coefficient imply that the probability of a person aged 65 in 1990 exiting to full retirement is higher than that of a person aged 63. The difference in exit probabilities is rather large. If a 63-year-old is predicted to have a 50–50 chance of exiting from partial to full retirement, then a 65-year-old, with the same personal characteristics other than age, is predicted to have a 69 percent chance of exiting to full retirement.

It should be noted that although we follow all persons over a three-year period, they obviously reach the age of eligibility at different times during this period. If we assume that no one will go into retirement, for example on a private pension, before AFP eligibility, then the age effect can be interpreted as reflecting gradual retirement after the date of eligibility. As emphasized by Blau (1994) this indicates that more insights into the retirement process would be gained by studying changes over a shorter time period than a whole year. Furthermore, some 65-year-olds became eligible

Table 3. *Transition probabilities from state 2, partial retirement into state 1, full retirement and state 2, partial retirement*

Variables	Coefficients from (7)	Estimates	*t*-Values
Consumption: $C_2 - C_1$	α_2	0.159×10^{-4}	4.1
Intercept	$\beta_{22,0} - \beta_{21,0} - \gamma_2 M$	−0.598	−1.6
Age 64 in 1990	$\beta_{22,1} - \beta_{21,1}$	−0.236	−0.7
Age 65 in 1990	$\beta_{22,2} - \beta_{21,2}$	−0.810	−2.9
Education at least 12 years	$\beta_{22,3} - \beta_{21,3}$	0.281	1.1
Female	$\beta_{22,4} - \beta_{21,4}$	0.157	0.5
Married	$\beta_{22,5} - \beta_{21,5}$	0.085	0.3
Service industry affiliation	$\beta_{22,6} - \beta_{21,6}$	0.371	1.6

Notes: No. of observations: 425; log-likelihood: −256, means $Q_{21} = 0.64$, $Q_{22} = 0.36$.

[1]This is around 15 percent of the average disposable pension per person in the population of all retired persons in Norway in 1992.

during 1990, and those who were working full time throughout that year may, of course, be a select group.

Estimation Results when Full-time Work is the Initial State

Comparing Tables 3 and 4, we see that the estimates of α_2 and α_3 differ somewhat. However, we cannot reject the hypothesis that they are equal, when tested against the hypothesis that they are different. Thus, we cannot reject the hypothesis that the marginal utility of consumption is the same across initial states.

To check the robustness of the estimate of economic responsiveness, we carried out an estimation of retirement behaviour on the sample of persons in full-time work and reaching normal retirement age; see Hernæs *et al.* (1997) for details. Taxes were not included, but we have comparable estimates based on pre-tax earnings. Among persons reaching normal retirement age, the coefficients for income, α_2 and α_3, were estimated at the same value which, in addition, was approximately 90 percent of the similarly estimated value for the AFP group.

The estimates in Table 4 imply that an increase in consumption of NOK 10,000 as a full-time employee, initially working full time and with average characteristics, will reduce the probability of exiting to full retirement by 2 percentage points. Moreover, it will also reduce the probability of exiting to partial retirement by nearly 3 percentage points. Consequently, it will increase the probability of staying in the state of full-time work by nearly 5 percentage points. The same increase in consumption as partially retired will have similar impacts on the transition rates, although the transition rates of partial retirement will increase and the probability of remaining in full-time work will decline. Elasticities of the transition probabilities with respect to consumption in the different states are given in Table 5.

To illustrate the partial impact of individual characteristics on the transition probabilities, we first set all dummy variables equal to zero and then included them one at a time. Disposable income in full-time work and partial retirement are set at the same value, close to sample averages in these two states for those who initially occupied the state of full-time work. The intercepts are set equal to zero. (As seen from Table 4 they are not significantly different from zero.) The results are given in Table 6. In the reference situation, the probability of staying in the state of full-time work and the probability of moving to partial retirement are the same, and equal to 0.40, while the probability of exiting to full retirement is 0.2. Note that the effects reported in Table 6 are partial. Some of the individual characteristics, like education, also have a strong impact on income and pensions, and hence on disposable income. Keeping disposable income constant, we only as-

Table 4. *Transition probabilities from state 3, full-time work into state 1, full retirement, state 2, partial retirement and state 3, full-time work*

Variables	Destination states (j)					
	State 2, partial retirement			State 3, full-time work		
	Coefficients from (11)	Estimate	t-Value	Coefficient from (12)	Estimate	t-Value
Consumption: $C_j - C_1$	α_3	0.208×10^{-4}	4.8	α_3	0.208×10^{-4}	4.8
Intercept	$\beta_{32,2} - \beta_{31,2} - \gamma_3 M$	−0.270	−0.1	$\beta_{33,2} - \beta_{31,2} - \gamma_3 M$	0.382	1.4
Age 64	$\beta_{32,1} - \beta_{31,1}$	−0.758	−3.6	$\beta_{33,1} - \beta_{31,1}$	−1.281	−6.4
Age 65	$\beta_{32,2} - \beta_{31,2}$	−0.636	−3.0	$\beta_{33,2} - \beta_{31,2}$	−2.638	−10.6
Education at least 12 years	$\beta_{32,3} - \beta_{31,3}$	0.683	3.2	$\beta_{33,3} - \beta_{31,3}$	−0.903	4.0
Female	$\beta_{32,4} - \beta_{31,4}$	−0.134	−0.6	$\beta_{33,4} - \beta_{31,4}$	0.611	2.7
Married	$\beta_{32,5} - \beta_{31,5}$	0.290	1.3	$\beta_{33,5} - \beta_{31,5}$	0.535	2.1
Service industry affiliation	$\beta_{32,6} - \beta_{31,6}$	0.710	3.5	$\beta_{33,6} - \beta_{31,6}$	0.357	1.6

Notes: No. of observations: 1,125; log-likelihood: −1,098; means: $Q_{33} = 0.384$, $Q_{32} = 0.362$, $Q_{31} = 0.253$.

Table 5. *Elasticities of transition probabilities with respect to consumption, evaluated at mean values*

	Elasticities of transition probabilities from initial state 2: partial retirement		
With respect to:	Q_{21}	Q_{22}	
C_1	0.57	−1.01	
C_2	−0.72	1.26	
	Elasticities of transition probabilities from initial state 3: full time work		
With respect to:	Q_{31}	Q_{32}	Q_{33}
C_1	1.53	−0.52	−0.52
C_2	−0.93	1.64	−0.94
C_3	−1.01	−1.02	1.63

Table 6. *Impacts of partial variation in individual characteristics on transition probabilities from full-time work*

Variables	Staying in full-time work, Q_{33}	Exiting to partial retirement, Q_{32}	Exiting to full retirement, Q_{31}
Reference: all dummies are zero	0.40	0.40	0.20
Age 64 in 1990	0.23	0.37	0.40
Age 65 in 1990	0.07	0.48	0.45
Education at least 12 years	0.50	0.40	0.10
Female	0.57	0.27	0.16
Married	0.48	0.38	0.14
Service industry affiliation	0.36	0.51	0.13

sessed the partial impact of individual characteristics on the transition probabilities.

According to Table 6, age has a strong impact on the transition structure. The probability of exiting to full retirement increases from 20 percent in the reference age group, 63 years in 1990, to 40 percent among 64-year-olds and 45 percent among 65-year-olds. Most of the increase in retirement is accounted for by a decreased probability of remaining in full-time work.

The education variable indicates that the higher the educational level, the longer full-time work is extended. Women are predicted to extend their full-time work longer than men do, while the opposite is indicated for part-time work. The net result with respect to the probability of retirement is that women are predicted to have lower probabilities than men do. The number of females eligible for AFP is less than one-fifth of the entire group, due, of course, to historically low female labour force participation in this age group. Fewer women meet the requirements for AFP with respect to labour market history, in particular regarding the number of years with sufficient earnings. The results indicate that those women who do qualify tend to extend their full-time work longer than males, other things equal. Married persons also extend their full-time work more than their unmarried counterparts.

Finally, employment in the service industry seems to favour transitions to partial retirement to the extent that the propensity to retire fully is drastically reduced. Again, it should be emphasized that the effects reported here are partial. For instance, women are likely to be overrepresented in the service industries. We have controlled for gender, and the combined effect of gender and industry affiliation may well imply a higher transition to partial retirement for females than males. Moreover, incomes and pensions are kept constant. The total impact of variations in individual characteristics on the transition structure cannot be assessed without accounting for the effects of these variations on incomes and pensions.

VI. The Simulated Effects of Offering a Bonus to Delay Retirement

We used the estimated model to simulate the transition effects of strengthening the financial incentives to extend working life among those who were eligible to retire early and who worked full time in 1990. Based on full-time work in 1992, the annual pension from 1993 onwards is increased by 7.2 percent. This increase is equivalent to a wealth increase amounting to 72.34 percent of the annual disposable pension, when pensions are evaluated at sample means. Wealth is defined as the discounted value of future annual disposable pensions. Expected remaining lifetime was then set at 18 years, which is close to the actual mean for people in the relevant age groups in 1992. We also assume that the real interest rate is 7 percent and that real incomes are constant over time.

It should be noted that our estimates here are based on variations in pensions and earnings in the near future. Owing to the age of the individuals in the sample and the rules of the social security system, each individual income stream beyond 1992 is unaffected by the state chosen in 1992. Variations in future income streams are outside the observation set. The validity of our policy simulation therefore depends on the assumptions that consumption is proportional to wealth, wealth is equal to the discounted value of future disposable incomes, the planning period is equal to the expected remaining lifetime, and real incomes and the real rate of interest are constant over time.

Table 7. *Effects of offering a bonus to delay retirement on transition probabilites from full-time work*

	Transition probabilities		
Alternatives	Staying in full-time work, Q_{33}	Exiting to partial retirement, Q_{32}	Exiting to full retirement, Q_{31}
Reference case	0.384	0.362	0.253
Annual pensions increased by 7.2% after 1992 if working full time in 1992	0.706	0.164	0.130
Annual pensions increased by 0.72% after 1992 if working full time in 1992	0.418	0.341	0.241

The bonus chosen accords with a bonus suggested by a government committee; see NOU (1980). To check the responses, we also simulated the impact of giving the retirees a smaller bonus, that is one-tenth of the bonus described above. We restricted the bonuses to those who worked full time in 1990. For each individual we used the estimated model—also the pension and income functions—to predict the choice probabilities. The aggregate transition probabilities shown in Table 7 are the average of the predicted individual probabilities.

A bonus that raises the annual pension by 7.2 percent, starting in 1993 and throughout the individual's remaining expected lifetime, will nearly double the probability of remaining in full-time work throughout 1992. This bonus reduces the probability of partial retirement relatively more than the probability of full retirement. Since we have assumed that all other real incomes are constant over time, an 7.2 percent increase in annual pension is a rather generous bonus. From Table 7 we observe, however, that a tenth of this increase has a rather modest effect on the transition probabilities.

Given the way we have specified the budget constraint, the bonus is defined in terms of disposable income. Hence, our simulations illustrate effects of an increase in total after-tax pensions, including employer-based and private pensions, which are endogenous. Even so, the estimated responses to economic conditions and the favourable taxation of pension income indicate a strong work disincentive in the tax system.

VII. Conclusion

In this chapter we have identified a group of 63–65-year-olds who qualified for a new early retirement scheme (AFP), and we have analysed their retirement behaviour during the period in which they became eligible (1990–1992). About one-third moved to each of the three destination states: continued full-time work, partial retirement and full retirement. Retirement behaviour differed widely with personal characteristics and incentives.

Among those who worked full time in 1990, the proportion that went into full retirement in 1992 was 20 percentage points higher among 64-year-olds than among 63-year-olds. Owing to the observation method, this reflects that retirement is drawn out over time, which can be explained both by the fact that the AFP scheme was fairly new and by a prolonged decision-making process on the part of potential retirees. However, information will spread and behaviour may gradually adjust to the new regime. Hence, the take-up rate is likely to increase over time, which indeed seems to have occurred; see Thøgersen *et al.*, (1998). Furthermore, since the age of eligibility has gradually been reduced, with the latest reduction to 62 years effective from 1998, retirement may be set to increase for many years, even in the absence of further changes.

Early retirement tends to be low among females, as well as among persons with more education and those who work in the service sector. The proportion of the workforce with these characteristics is likely to increase in the future. This may slow down the increase in early retirement.

Economic incentives appear to influence retirement behaviour, and the tax system dramatically reduces the economic incentives for full-time work. Earnings up to about three-quarters of the average pension are taxed at 27 percent, whereas a pension or even a combination of pension and earnings up to that level are not taxed at all. This may be part of the explanation for the high transition to partial retirement.

Illustrating the response to economic incentives by an increase in the annual disposable pension for one more year of work, the number of individuals who worked full time an extra year increased by about 30 percentage points. We have not investigated the macroeconomic consequences of such a bonus.

Taking these effects into account and looking ahead, it appears that there are conflicting trends. Take-up rates may increase "on their own", particularly because of increases in early retirement coverage. Meanwhile, changes in the composition of the workforce, with more people working in service industries, and a higher educational level may tend to decrease take-up rates. As regards the OECD (1998) call for policy measures, we have found responsiveness to economic incentives as well as strong work disincentives in the tax system. This might point to the tax system as a candidate for reducing early retirement, but this aspect has not been studied to any large extent in this chapter.

Assessing trends which affect the future of the pension system, it should also be kept in mind that 40 percent of the Norwegian labour force are not covered by the AFP scheme and thus have not been studied here. This group consists mostly of the self-employed and employees of small companies not participating in the AFP scheme. Their earnings, potential pensions and hence also their retirement behaviour may well deviate from the trends discussed above regarding the AFP, and should be a topic for further analysis.

Appendix. Empirical Specification of the Model

Data Sources and Sample

The empirical analysis is based on register files from Statistics Norway. All of these files are compiled using a so-called personal identification number, which allows them to be linked to different types of information and time periods. For the purposes of this study, we extracted information covering the period 1990–1992 for a 30 percent sample in the 1990 Population Census. The 1991 official files contained a serious error in the data on pensions, so we had to analyse transitions from 1990 to 1992. The demographic information extracted is gender, age, marital status and educational qualifications. The labour market data cover spells of employment and unemployment as well as the local unemployment rate; the tax files cover wage earnings and pensions and the social security files include accumulated public pension rights.

This sample consists of persons who were an employee in 1990 of a firm where some of the employees took AFP in 1992; aged 65–67 in 1992; had 10 years of earnings at least equal to the basic pension since age 50; had 10 years of earnings twice that level since 1967; had a labour income level at least corresponding to the basic pension both in the calendar year when AFP was taken and in the preceding calendar year. We were unable to implement the requirement that eligibility implies not having received a pension beforehand and having been employed by the company for the last three years. Given the eligibility requirements, practically no one in the sample is unemployed, retired or disabled. Hence, aggregation into the three states used in the analysis is trivial except for the partly retired group. Here, we include both those who went from work to retirement during 1992 and those who combined work and retirement, without being able to distinguish the two groups. Eleven persons who went from part-time to full-time work were dropped from the sample.

Potential Pre-tax Income

Full-time work in 1992 is an alternative only for those who also worked full time in 1990. We observed earnings in 1990 and assumed potential earnings in full-time work in 1992 to be the same as in 1990.

Potential public pension: The potential public pension of all persons in the sample was predicted from the sequence of public pension points observed since the start of the present system in 1967. The main structure is described in Section II and details are available in Hernæs and Strøm (2000).

Full potential pension: In addition to a public pension, people in the sample may be entitled to employer-based pensions and may have private pensions. Information on these other pensions is not available. However, we do know the full pension of those who have already retired. In order to avoid selection bias, we estimated the relationship between predicted public pension and full pension in the 30 percent census sample of 66,010 retired persons aged 68 or above in 1992. We obtained the following regression, which was used to predict the full pension, Y_1, for persons in our sample (t-values in parentheses):

$$Y_1 = \underset{(-53.237)}{-31{,}030} + \underset{(227.426)}{1.6135} \cdot B + \underset{(53.763)}{24{,}268} \cdot Educ12 - \underset{(-1.149)}{280} \cdot Female, \quad R^2 = 0.62$$

where *Educ12* is a dummy variable for at least 12 years of education and *Female* is a dummy variable for females. This procedure preserves the individual variation in predicted public pensions, but does not add any other variation. The main effect is therefore to scale the coefficient estimates.

Potential income as partly retired: For those who were partly retired in 1990, we assumed that potential income as partly retired in 1992 was the same as in 1990. For those who worked full time in 1990, we predicted potential earnings and pensions in 1992 (the two income components as partly retired) based on two regressions run for those who actually went from full-time work to partial retirement.

$$\begin{aligned} Y_2 &= \textit{Potential earnings} + \textit{Potential pension} \\ &= \underset{(1.695)}{36{,}555} + \underset{(3.313)}{0.3338} \cdot \textit{Earnings 1990} + \underset{(0.981)}{0.2559} \cdot Y_1 \\ &\quad - \underset{(-0.687)}{7{,}941.6} \cdot \textit{Educ12} - \underset{(-5.797)}{46{,}295} \cdot \textit{Age 64} \\ &\quad - \underset{(-3.095)}{24{,}423} \cdot \textit{Age 65} + \underset{(0.674)}{7{,}632.4} \cdot \textit{Female} - \underset{(1.314)}{12{,}878} \cdot \textit{Married} \\ &\quad - \underset{(-2.278)}{-33{,}372} + \underset{(4.204)}{0.2876} \cdot \textit{Earnings 1990} + \underset{(1.1631)}{0.2889} \cdot Y_1 \\ &\quad + \underset{(0.118)}{922.9} \cdot \textit{Educ 12} + \underset{(5.361)}{29{,}071} \cdot \textit{Age 64} \\ &\quad + \underset{(2.778)}{14{,}887} \cdot \textit{Age 65} - \underset{(-0.104)}{797.6} \cdot \textit{Female} + \underset{(1.2786)}{8{,}493.1} \cdot \textit{Married} \end{aligned}$$

There are 408 observations. For the earnings regression, $R^2 = 0.1855$ and for the pension regression, $R^2 = 0.3532$. *Married* is a dummy for that civil status, *Age64* and *Age65* are dummies for those two ages and *Earnings1990* does not comprise any pension. By collecting terms, we get:

$$Y_2 = 3{,}183 + 0.6214 \cdot \textit{Earnings1990} + 0.5448 \cdot Y_1 - 7{,}018.7 \cdot \textit{Educ12}$$

$$- 17{,}224 \cdot \textit{Age64}$$

$$- 9{,}536 \cdot \textit{Age65} + 6{,}834.8 \cdot \textit{Female} - 4{,}384.9 \cdot \textit{Married}$$

Potential Disposable Income

Potential disposable income was obtained using detailed tax rules; see Hernæs and Strøm (2000) and Hernæs, Sollie and Strøm (1998). As shown in the top panel of Table A1, average potential pre-tax income is higher as partly retired than as retired. Taxes change the relative incomes across states and sharply increase the incentive to retire. For those who were partly retired in 1990, the decline in average potential pre-tax income if retiring in 1992 is NOK 54,324 (USD 7,423). The drop in disposable income is only NOK 16,110 (USD 2,148). For a person working full time in 1990, the reduction in pre-tax income from retiring in 1992 is NOK 62,257 (USD 8,301). However, the drop in disposable income of moving from full-time work in 1990 to full retirement in 1992 is only NOK 17,340 (USD 2,312). It is even more striking that average disposable income is higher when moving from full-time work to partial retirement than to continuing full-time work. As alluded to above, these are sample averages of disposable income obtained by applying tax rules on the individual level. At this level, differences in potential income between alternatives move in the "right" direction sufficiently often.

Table A1. *Average potential state-specific income, before and after tax*

	State in 1992		
State in 1990	Retired	Partly retired	Full-time work
	Pre-tax income, NOK		
Retired	100,281	—	—
Partly retired	114,158	168,482	—
Full-time work	118,532	165,906	180,789
	Disposable income, NOK		
Retired	99,452	—	—
Partly retired	107,691	123,801	—
Full-time work	110,383	132,053	127,723
	Average tax as a percentage of income		
Retired	0.8	—	—
Partly retired	5.7	26.5	—
Full-time work	6.9	20.4	29.4

Summing up, the tax rules favour retirement, and application of special tax rules to a combination of pension and earnings particularly favours partial retirement. This structure illustrates the need to account for both actual tax rules and individual heterogeneity when analysing retirement behaviour.

References

Anderson, P., Gustman, A. and Steinmeier, T. (1997), Trends in Male Labor Force Participation and Retirement: Some Evidence on the Role of Pensions and Social Security in the 1970s and the 1980s, NBER Working Paper no. 6208, Cambridge, MA.

Blau, D. M. (1994), Labor Force Dynamics of Older Men, *Econometrica 62* (1), 117–156.

Blau, D. M. (1997), Social Security and the Labor Supply of Older Married Couples, *Labour Economics 4*, 373–418.

Gruber, J. and Wise, D. (1997), Social Security Programs and Retirement Around the World, NBER Working Paper, no. 6134, Cambridge, MA.

Hernæs, E., Sollie, M. and Strøm, S. (1997), Økonomiske betingelser og pensjonsbeslutning (Economic Conditions and Pension Decisions), SNF-rapport 37, Oslo.

Hernæs, E., Sollie, M. and Strøm, S. (1998), Virkninger på arbeidstilbud i yrkesaktive år av alternative pensjonsopplegg (Effects of Different Pension Schemes on Labor Supply), in *Fondering av Folketrygden* (*Funding Social Security*), NOU 1998: 10, Oslo.

Hernæs, E. and Strøm, S. (2000), Empirical Specification of the Model in "Early Retirement and Economic Incentives", Working Paper no. 01/00, Ragnar Frisch Centre for Economic Research, Oslo (www.frisch.uio.no).

Krueger, A. B. and Pischke, J.-S. (1992), The Effect of Social Security on Labor Supply: A Cohort Analysis of the Notch Generation, *Journal of Labor Economics 10* (4), 412–437.

Moffit, R. A. (1984), Trends in Social Security Wealth by Cohort, in X? Moon (ed.), *Economic Transfers in the United States*, Studies in Income and Wealth, Vol. 49, University of Chicago Press, Chicago and London.

NOU (1980), Deltidspensjon og førtidspensjon fra folketrygden (Partial and Early Social Security Pensions), NOU 1980: 54, Oslo.

NOU (1994), Fra arbeid til pensjon (From Work to Retirement), NOU 1994: 2, Oslo.

NOU (1998), Fleksibel pensjonering (Flexible Retirement), NOU 1998: 19, Oslo.

OECD (1998), Work-force Aging: Consequences and Policy Responses, Chapter 4 in *Employment Outlook,* June.

Pedersen, P. J. and Smith, N. (1996), Duration Analysis of the Decision to Retire Early, in E. Wadensjø (ed.), *Leaving the Labour Market Early in the Welfare State*, North-Holland Elsevier, Amsterdam.

Statistics Norway (1989, . . . , 1998), Grunntabeller, Arbeidskraftundersøkelsene (AKU) 1989–1998 (Basic Tables, Labour Market Survey), Oslo.

Statistics Norway (1993), Labor Market Statistics (AKU) 1992, NOS C 87, Oslo.

Stock, J. and Wise, D. E. (1990), Pensions, the Option Value of Work, and Retirement, *Econometrica 58* (5), 1151–1180.

Thøgersen, Ø., Bratberg, E. and Holmås, T. H. (1998), Normer incentiver og tidligpensjonering (Norms, Incentives and Early Retirement), SNF-rapport 33, Oslo.

Wadensjö, E. (ed.) (1996), *Leaving the Labour Market Early in the Welfare State*, North-Holland Elsevier, Amsterdam.

9

The Political Economy of Social Security

*Georges Casamatta**

Helmuth Cremer

Pierre Pestieau

I. Introduction

The determination of social security benefits and contribution rates is often studied in majority voting models. This approach was initiated by Browning (1975), who considers a society where people differ only according to age. Within that framework, the decisive voter is the median age individual. The voting equilibrium then leads to an excessive social security budget.

It is increasingly recognized that the political forces involved in the debate on social security cannot be represented along a single age axis. There are other dimensions, particularly that of income and, more specifically, income heterogeneity *within* generations. The income dimension is likely to be important when the social security system redistributes not only from younger to older generations, as the pay-as-you-go (PAYG) system often does, but also from high- to low-wage workers. In other words, introducing differential earning capacities is particularly important when the benefit rule is redistributive rather than actuarially fair.

The voting outcome also depends on the alternatives available for financing old-age consumption. Consider the hypothetical case where private savings are not available. Then, all individuals vote for a positive tax rate: the old because it determines their benefit level and the young to ensure themselves some consumption during retirement. However, when private savings are available and when their rate of return is higher than that offered by the social security system, individuals will vote against social security. This can occur for at least three reasons. First, if the social security system is of the PAYG type, and the rate of interest is higher than the rate of

*Financial support from the Belgian SSTC and the European Commission is gratefully acknowledged. We thank Philippe De Donder, Louis Gevers, Stéphane Rottier and, particularly, the two referees for their helpful comments. The third author wrote part of this paper while visiting CES at the University of Munich.

population growth, private saving is more attractive, at least for a young worker. Second, if the payroll tax implies some deadweight loss, the same bias may occur. Third, if the social security system is redistributive, those who pay for redistribution, namely workers with earnings above the average level, will prefer private saving. Conversely, workers with lower than average earning capacities benefit from redistribution. Consequently, they may vote in favour of social security, even when there are some distortions and when the rate of interest is higher than the rate of population growth.

In this chapter, we adopt a steady-state setting with given rates of interest and population growth. We also assume that the benefit rule is given. Some countries, labelled Bismarckian, such as Germany or France, offer replacement ratios that are stable across income levels, whereas others, labelled Beveridgean, such as Canada or the Netherlands, tend to have replacement ratios that fall as income increases. Table 1 illustrates this distinction for nine countries.

The assumption that the benefit rule is given implies that we concentrate on one specific aspect of the problem. In other words, our model is intended as a building block in a more ambitious set-up, encompassing a broader range of decision variables. This is a meaningful approach, for instance, if the decision process is inherently sequential. It may be noted that while the redistributive character of a system (i.e., its more or less Bismarckian or Beveridgean design) and its size are both essential features of a retirement system, they are not exactly symmetric. Its redistributive character is, to a large extent, an integral part of the very definition of the system itself. Regardless of whether systems are Bismarckian or Beveridgean, they imply specific institutional and administrative arrangements which cannot be overturned in the short run. By now, the Bismarckian system is solidly anchored in the traditions of countries like Germany and France. On the other hand, the tradition is Beveridgean in the UK.

Table 1. *Size and redistributiveness of social security*

	Half of average	Average income	Twice average	Regime*	Spending as % of GDP
Canada	76	44	25	BE	5.4
France	84	84	73	BI	12.5
Germany	76	72	75	BI	12.8
Italy	103 ($\frac{1}{4}\times$)	90	84 (3×)	BI	15.6
Japan	77	56	43	MI	6.6
Netherlands	73	43	25	BE	5.2
New Zealand	75	38	19	BE	5.4
UK	72	50	35	MI	4.4
USA	65	55	32	MI	4.6

*BI: Bismarckian; BE: Beveridgean; MI: mixed.
Source: Johnson (1998).

In the concluding section, we briefly discuss the choice of the benefit rule at an earlier, "constitutional", stage. Decisions at this stage can be made either by a welfare-maximizing authority or through a voting procedure. In either case, decisions in the first stage will be contingent on the induced outcome in the second stage. Consequently, characterization of the outcome for any given benefit rule is a necessary step in the analysis. A noteworthy observation that can be derived from analysing constitutional decisions is that, even from a pure Rawlsian viewpoint, it may be optimal to adopt a benefit rule that is not "too redistributive". Interestingly, the less redistributive than otherwise optimal benefit rule is not (or not only) adopted to mitigate labour market distortions but also to induce a majority to opt for generous retirement benefits.

Following Browning (1975), most of the subsequent literature assumes that individuals differ only in age and focuses on simple majority voting and the median voter outcome. Several variations on the Browning model have been considered; see Myles (1995) for a survey. While these studies have produced different specific results, the fundamental conclusion remains the same: majority voting tends to yield overspending on social security. Among the most representative variations, let us mention Hu (1982) who considers uncertainty of benefit receipts, Boadway and Wildasin (1989) who introduce an explicit capital market, and Veall (1986) who assumes intergenerational altruism.

A more drastic departure from Browning's setting is provided by Tabellini (2000). He assumes that individuals are altruistic (children towards parents and parents towards children) and introduces differences in income as a second source of heterogeneity, along with the traditional age differences. Another specific feature of his model is that there is no commitment to preserve past decisions in the future. The main result is that in such a setting, a coalition of the young poor and the retired may sustain a positive tax rate.

In our chapter, there are also two sources of heterogeneity. However, there is no altruism and we return to the conventional commitment assumption. Individual voters differ not only according to age but also according to productivity. In our setting, medium-wage workers, rather than those with the lowest wage, join the retirees to form a majority and vote for a positive level of social security. Furthermore, this level is often in excess of the one which maximizes lifetime welfare. The majority equilibrium level is also shown to depend on the difference between the rates of population growth and interest, as well as on the redistributiveness of the benefit rule.

II. The Model

Consider a small open one-sector economy with given interest rate, r_t. At each period of time t, two generations overlap: L_t workers and L_{t-1} retirees, with $L_t = L_{t-1}(1 + n_t)$, where n_t is the rate of population growth. Individuals differ in two ways: the generation they belong to and their wage w, a continuous variable with support $[w_-, w_+]$, mean $\overline{w}$ and median $w_m < \overline{w}$. Individual labour supply is given and normalized to 1.

The pension benefits that an individual earning w expects to receive is $p_{t+1}(w)$. We assume that $p_{t+1}(w)$ consists of two parts: a contributory part which is directly related to individual earning, w, and a non-contributory part which depends on average earnings, $\overline{w}$. With a pay-as-you-go (PAYG) scheme, the average return of the social security system is given by the population growth rate. These properties yield the following expression for $p_{t+1}(w)$:

$$p_{t+1}(w) = (1 + n_{t+1})\tau_{t+1}(\alpha w + (1 - \alpha)\overline{w}). \tag{1}$$

The parameter α is the Bismarckian factor, that is the fraction of pension benefits that is related to contributions; we assume $0 \leqslant \alpha \leqslant 1$. When $\alpha = 1$, the pension scheme is purely Bismarckian or contributory; when $\alpha = 0$, pension benefits are uniform and the scheme is Beveridgean. Moreover, throughout the chapter, we assume dynamic efficiency: $r_t \geqslant n_t > 0, \forall\, t$.

We first analyse the optimal saving decision of a working individual born in period t with earning w. He is subject to a payroll tax τ_t and expects the future tax rate to be τ_{t+1} when old. He can then allocate his disposable income between consumption c_t and saving s_t. When he retires, his consumption d_{t+1} is equal to the gross return of his saving, $(1 + r_{t+1})s_t$, and a pension p_{t+1}. Formally, he solves the following programme:

$$\max_{s \geqslant 0} U_t = u(c_t) + \beta u(d_{t+1}) \tag{2}$$

subject to:

$$w(1 - \tau_t) = c_t + s_t \tag{3}$$

and

$$d_{t+1} = (1 + r_{t+1})s_t + p_{t+1}(w). \tag{4}$$

In (2), $u(.)$ is strictly concave and $\beta \leqslant 1$ is a factor of time preference. Let σ denote the elasticity of substitution between c_t and d_{t+1}. We assume throughout the chapter that σ is constant and that $\sigma < 1$, which means that there is not much substitution in consumption, a widely accepted assumption. The coefficient of relative risk aversion, $R_r(x) = -xu''(x)/u'(x)$ is thus also constant and equal to $\varepsilon = 1/\sigma$. We restrict savings to be non-negative.[1]

The first-order condition associated with an interior solution of s_t is the following:

$$-u'(c_t) + \beta u'(d_{t+1})(1 + r_{t+1}) = 0. \tag{5}$$

Denoting $s_t^A \geqslant 0$ the optimal value of s_t, we can define the (indirect) utility function of an individual with income w as:

$$V_t(\tau_t, \tau_{t+1}, w) = u(w(1 - \tau_t) - s_t^A) + \beta u((1 + r_{t+1})s_t^A + p_{t+1}(w)). \tag{6}$$

We now determine the steady-state majority voting equilibrium tax rate. We consider α as given; the problem is therefore unidimensional and, under the condition that preferences are single-peaked, the median voter theorem, which ensures the existence of a Condorcet winner, applies. Individuals vote for τ believing that the value of τ chosen by the majority will hold for ever.[2] Formally, they expect that $\tau_{t+1} = \tau_t$, $\forall\, t$. We can thus remove all the time subscripts in the subsequent equations.

In the following, we first derive the preferred tax rate of the retirees and the workers, respectively. Then, to identify the Condorcet winner, we order these preferred alternatives. The Condorcet winner is the tax rate such that half of the population prefers a higher and half of the population a lower tax rate. For the time being, there is no tax distortion. Next, we derive the comparative statics of the majority voting solution with respect to some parameters of the model, namely α and n. We then compare the PAYG majority voting equilibrium tax rate with a (collective) fully funded (FF) solution, granted that both systems adopt the same benefit rule. Finally, we solve the problem when taxation generates (quadratic) distortions.

III. Preferred Tax Rates of the Different Agents

The Retirees

Each retiree has some non-negative private savings, s, with return r. Such private saving is the result of a past decision and the retirees have no control over it. The only variable they can affect is the tax rate which determines

---

[1] Allowing negative savings would generate extreme solutions. Young people in favour of the PAYG pension system would vote for a tax rate of 1 and would rely entirely on borrowing to finance their present consumption.

[2] Or that it will hold at least for the next two periods; the tax rate in later periods is of no relevance for these individuals.

their pension level. As there is no altruism, their preferred tax rate, τ^R, is the one which maximizes their consumption:

$$d = (1 + r)s + (1 + n)\tau(\alpha w + (1 - \alpha)\overline{w}). \tag{7}$$

The solution is given by $\tau^R = 1$ for all retirees.[3] In words, retirees want the tax to be as high as possible. This is because the current tax affects their pension level, but has no impact on their contributions (which were paid in the previous period).

The Workers

A worker with earning w chooses $\tau^A(w)$ which maximizes:

$$v(\tau, w) = u(w(1 - \tau) - s^A) + \beta u((1 + r)s^A + (1 + n)\tau(\alpha w + (1 - \alpha)\overline{w})), \tag{8}$$

where $s^A \geqslant 0$ is the optimal level of private saving and $v(\tau, w) = V(\tau, \tau, w)$.

Note that a worker will always be in favour of a zero tax if:

$$1 + r > (\alpha + (1 - \alpha)\overline{w}/w)(1 + n). \tag{9}$$

This means that the return from private saving is higher than the return from PAYG social security. Without tax distortions, these returns are independent of the tax rate. Consequently, a given individual will prefer either a zero tax rate and positive private saving if (9) holds or a strictly positive tax rate and no private saving in the opposite case.

In other words, an individual prefers private saving if his wage is higher than $\hat{w}$ defined as:

$$\hat{w} = \frac{1 - \alpha}{(1 + r)/(1 + n) - \alpha}\overline{w} \leqslant \overline{w}. \tag{10}$$

It can easily be checked that $\hat{w} = \overline{w}$ if $n = r$, $\partial\hat{w}/\partial n > 0$ and $\partial\hat{w}/\partial\alpha < 0$.

The solution to the worker's problem is characterized in

Proposition 1. *The preferred tax rates of the workers have the following properties:*

[3] This result is rather extreme, but introducing tax distortions or some degree of altruism from the old to the young would yield a value of τ^R smaller than 1.

(*i*) $\tau^A(w) = 0$ *if* $w > \hat{w}$ *and* $\tau^A(w) > 0$ *if* $w \leqslant \hat{w}$;

(*ii*) $\dfrac{\partial \tau^A(w)}{\partial w} > 0$ *if* $w < \hat{w}$;

(*iii*) $\max \tau^A(w) = \tau^A(\hat{w}) < \tau^R = 1$.

Proof: See Appendix.

The first point of the proposition recalls that only workers with a sufficiently low wage level want a positive tax rate. The second point says that preferred tax rates are increasing with income. This result arises because the intertemporal elasticity of substitution, σ, is smaller than one. Intuitively, the relationship between low intertemporal substitution and the property that the preferred tax rate increases with income is easily understood. Consider, for example, the extreme case where there is no substitution at all: individuals want to equalize their two-period consumptions. Because the rate of return of PAYG social security is decreasing with income, the high-wage workers would like to transfer a greater proportion of their income from the first period to the second period as compared to those with a low wage.[4] Finally, point (iii) states that the maximal preferred tax rate of the workers is lower than 1, the preferred tax rate of the retirees. This is simply due to the fact that individuals want to consume when young.[5]

IV. The Majority Voting Solution

Because their utility is increasing with the value of the tax rate, preferences of the retirees are obviously single-peaked. The objective function of the workers can easily be shown to be strictly concave, which implies that it is single-peaked; see the proof of Proposition 1. The workers are divided into two classes, those who prefer a zero tax rate and positive savings and those who prefer a positive tax rate and no savings. The utility of individuals in the first group decreases with the tax rate. For the second group, the preferred value of the tax rate is given by an interior solution.

Summing up, a fraction $1/(2+n)$ of citizens, the retirees, is in favour of $\tau^R = 1$. Further from Proposition 1, all workers with earnings above $\hat{w}$ are in favour of a zero tax. The preferred tax rate for the workers with earnings

---

[4]The property that preferred tax rates are increasing with income and may seem suprising. Within our framework, it results from the (realistic) assumption that the intertemporal elasticity of substitution is low. However, the assumption of a strictly proportional tax is crucial. If we had instead assumed that the poorest individuals are exempted from taxation, they would have a high preferred tax rate, thereby joining the retirees to sustain a generous social security system.

[5]Only for a linear utility function (which corresponds to an infinite intertemporal elasticity of substitution), would a corner solution with $\tau^A = 1$ be obtained.

below $\hat{w}$ increases with w. The profile of preferred tax rates is represented in Figures 1 and 2 for the cases $r = n$ and $r > n$, respectively. We can now determine the decisive voter and thus report the majority voting equilibrium tax rate in the following proposition.

Proposition 2. *If* $\int_{w_-}^{\hat{w}} f(w)\,\mathrm{d}w < n/2(1+n)$, *the majority voting equilibrium tax rate,* τ^*, *is* 0. *If* $\int_{w_-}^{\hat{w}} f(w)\,\mathrm{d}w \geqslant n/2(1+n)$, *the majority voting equilibrium tax rate is the rate preferred by the workers with earning* $\tilde{w}$ *defined as follows:*

$$\int_{\tilde{w}}^{\hat{w}} f(w)\,\mathrm{d}w = \frac{n}{2(1+n)}. \tag{11}$$

Proof: The Condorcet winner is the tax rate such that one-half of the total population prefers a higher tax rate and the other half a lower tax rate. The total number of individuals who prefer a tax rate higher than 0 is $L + L(1+n)\int_{w_-}^{\hat{w}} f(w)\,\mathrm{d}w$, where L is the number of old individuals. The total population is $L + L(1+n) = L(2+n)$. Consequently, if $L + L(1+n)\int_{w_-}^{\hat{w}} f(w)\,\mathrm{d}w < L(2+n)/2 \Leftrightarrow \int_{w_-}^{\hat{w}} f(w)\,\mathrm{d}w < n/2(1+n)$, less than one-half of the total population prefers a strictly positive tax rate and the Condorcet winner is 0. On the other hand, when $\int_{w_-}^{\hat{w}} f(w)\,\mathrm{d}w \geqslant n/2(1+n)$, the individuals who prefer a strictly positive tax rate constitute more than one-half of the total population and the Condorcet winner is strictly positive. It is the tax rate preferred by the individual with income $\tilde{w}$ such that those in the population who prefer a higher tax rate constitute half of the total population:

$$L + L(1+n)\int_{\tilde{w}}^{\hat{w}} f(w)\,\mathrm{d}w = \frac{L(2+n)}{2}. \tag{12}$$

Straightforward manipulations lead to (11). ■

The proposition first states that the majority voting equilibrium tax rate is zero when the number of working individuals in favour of a positive tax rate is too low. This may occur in particular when r is large relative to n. In this case, the redistributive effect of PAYG social security is dominated by the high return of private saving and even the poorest workers may prefer to save privately. The second part of the proposition states that when the Condorcet winner is strictly positive, the majority coalition consists of the retirees and of the workers with *medium* wages. This result is reminiscent of Epple and Romano's (1996) "ends against the middle" equilibrium in which there is a coalition made up of the tails of the income distribution; see also Casamatta, Cremen and Pestieau (2000). This property clearly hinges on our assumption on the elasticity of substitution. With $\sigma > 1$, preferred tax rates would be decreasing with income and the majority coalition would be composed of the retirees and the poorest working individuals.

V. Comparative Statics

The illustrative figures in Table 1 suggest that the size and the redistributive character of a system are inversely related. Put differently, the most generous systems also appear to be those which redistribute the least. To see whether this stylized fact is consistent with our model, let us now study the impact of the contributive part on the equilibrium tax rate. Consider the case where the Condorcet winner is strictly positive.

Differentiating (11) with respect to α yields:

$$\frac{\partial \tilde{w}}{\partial \alpha} = \frac{\partial \hat{w}}{\partial \alpha} \frac{f(\hat{w})}{f(\tilde{w})} \leqslant 0. \tag{13}$$

Furthermore, the first-order condition for τ^A, implies:

$$\frac{\partial \tau^A}{\partial \alpha}(\tilde{w}(\alpha), \alpha) = \frac{\beta(1+n)(\tilde{w} - \overline{w})u'(d)(1 - R_r(d))}{-D_\tau}. \tag{14}$$

Keeping in mind that $\tilde{w} < \overline{w}$ and that $R_r(.) > 1$, this expression is positive. Finally, recalling that $\tau^*(\alpha) = \tau^A(\tilde{w}(\alpha), \alpha)$ yields:

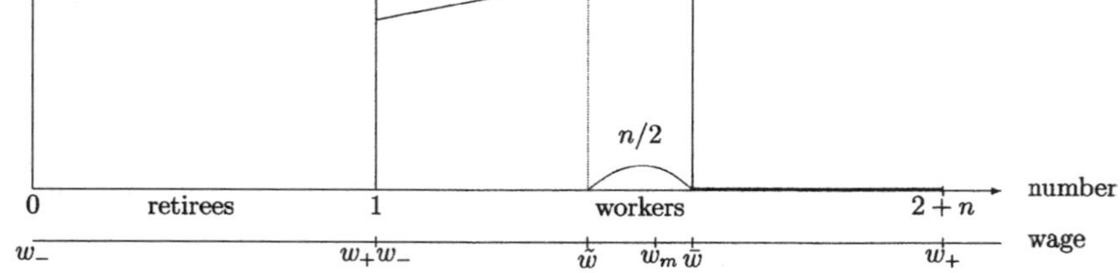

Fig. 1. Preferred tax rates when $r = n$

$$\underset{?}{\frac{\partial\tau^*}{\partial\alpha}} = \underset{+}{\frac{\partial\tau^A}{\partial\alpha}}(\tilde{w}(\alpha), \alpha) + \underset{+}{\frac{\partial\tau^A}{\partial w}}(\tilde{w}(\alpha), \alpha)\underset{-}{\frac{\partial\tilde{w}}{\partial\alpha}}. \tag{15}$$

Clearly the sign of $\partial\tau^*/\partial\alpha$ is positive when $r = n$; in that case the identity of the decisive voter does not depend on α and the second term vanishes. The first, positive, term then determines the sign of the expression and we get the expected positive relation between α and τ^*. When $r < n$, however, the sign of (14) is ambiguous. There are now two opposite effects. When α rises, the preferred tax rate of the decisive voter rises. However, when α changes, the identity of the decisive voter changes as well. When α rises, PAYG public pension becomes less attractive to low-wage workers (who support this system). Some of them (the more productive) "switch" to the private sector and the new decisive voter is poorer than before. As preferred tax rates are increasing with income, the tax rate chosen by this new decisive voter is lower than before.

We should note, however, that when $r > n > 0$, the majority voting equilibrium tax rate jumps discontinuously to 0 for α high enough. This comes from the fact that, when α is sufficiently close to 1, the PAYG system brings about so little redistribution that even the poorest among the workers do not find it attractive any more and vote for the abandonment of the system.

Following the same approach, we can also study the comparative statics of $\partial\tau^*/\partial n$. The result is also ambiguous: the negative "direct" effect induced by the decrease in the rate of return of the PAYG system has to be balanced against an ambiguous "indirect" effect which arises because the identity of

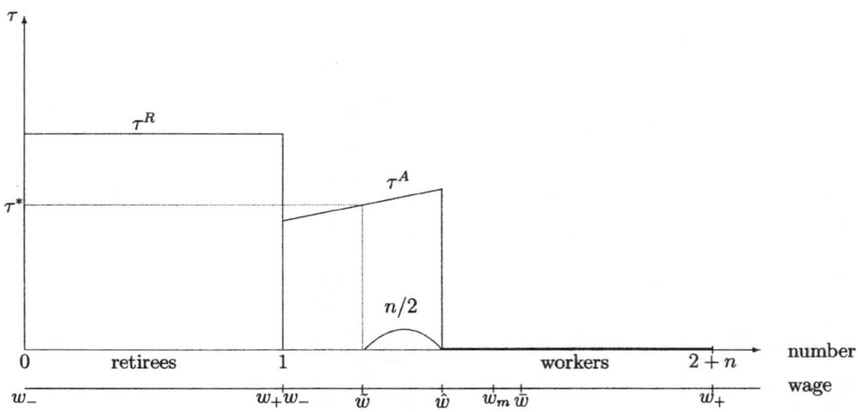

Fig. 2. Preferred tax rates when $r > n$

the decisive voter changes. Consequently, a decline in fertility *may* indeed result in an increase in the majority voting equilibrium tax.[6]

VI. Pay-as-you-go versus Fully Funded

So far, we have concentrated on voting with regard to PAYG systems. Let us now compare the majority voting equilibrium under PAYG and the equilibrium that arises with an "equivalent" fully funded (FF) scheme. We are not concerned with the transition from one to the other. We simply assume that voting takes place in two alternative steady states. To make the comparison fair we assume $r = n > 0$, so that the average return is the same under both systems. Furthermore, we consider identical benefit rules to ensure that the two schemes achieve the same degree of redistribution. In other words, we do *not* compare a redistributive PAYG system to a totally individualized FF system, as is often done in the literature on the privatization of social security.

The major difference between the two systems is that under an FF scheme, the retirees have no stake in the vote. All the decisions which are relevant for them have been taken in the past: private saving, s, and collective saving through pension funds, if any. Recall that the interest rate, r, and the Bismarckian factor, α, are also given.

Consequently, only the active population matters for determination of the voting equilibrium. Moreover, preferred tax rates of workers continue to be characterized by Proposition 1 and the decisive voter has earnings $\check{w}$ such that:

$$\int_{\check{w}}^{\overline{w}} f(w)\,\mathrm{d}w = \tfrac{1}{2}. \tag{16}$$

In other words, the young population is divided into two groups: those with earnings between $\check{w}$ and $\overline{w}$ and who want a tax rate higher than $\tau^A(\check{w})$, and those with earnings below $\check{w}$ or above $\overline{w}$ who want a lower tax rate. Note that $w_m < \overline{w}$ ensures that majority voting yields a strictly positive tax rate.

Comparing (16) and (11), while recalling that $r = n$ implies $\hat{w} = \overline{w}$, it

[6]For a "large" decline in fertility, however, the tax rate falls to zero, as long as the condition $w_- > \overline{w}/(1 + r)$ is satisfied. The explanation is simple: for n close to 0, $\hat{w}$ is close to $(1 - \alpha)\overline{w}/(1 + r - \alpha)$. Moreover, we know that $\hat{w}$ declines with α. Hence the maximal value of $\hat{w}$ when n tends to 0 is $\overline{w}/(1 + r)$. Therefore, if $w_- > \overline{w}/(1 + r)$, we are sure that the poorest individual does not support the PAYG pension system, so that a majority votes for abandonment of the system.

follows that $\check{w} < \tilde{w}$. Consequently, the decisive voter under the FF scheme has a lower wage than the decisive voter under the PAYG system. This leads to Proposition 3.

Proposition 3. *The majority voting equilibrium size of social security is larger under a PAYG than under an FF scheme.*

This result can be explained as follows. With a PAYG system, the retirees favour a payroll tax rate which is as large as possible. They do not have a majority, and the median voter is a worker who backs social security because of its redistributiveness. Nevertheless, it is clear that the vote of the retirees tends to increase the size of the social security system. With an FF system, on the other hand, the retirees do not have any leverage on the workers' tax payments.

In a sense, the voting under PAYG amounts to giving a larger weight to the older than to the younger generation. The current young will be old in the next period and take this into account when voting. Consequently, they assign some weight to old-age consumption—as, of course, do the currently old. First-period consumption, on the other hand, affects only the currently young.

What about social welfare? In the setting with heterogeneous individuals, the comparison is not straightforward and depends on which welfare function is used. With a Rawlsian criterion, FF always dominates PAYG, as it gives the decisive vote to workers with lower earnings (recall that, $\check{w} < \tilde{w}$).[7] With a general utilitarian criterion, the comparison is ambiguous.

VII. Extension: Distortionary Payroll Taxation

Up to now the tax system was assumed to imply no efficiency loss. Let us now briefly examine the implications of distortionary taxation. For simplicity, we use a quadratic loss function so that the steady-state relationship between contributions and pensions is now given by:

$$p(w) = (1+n)\tau(\alpha w + (1-\gamma\tau)(1-\alpha)\overline{w}), \tag{17}$$

where $\gamma > 0$ is the distortion factor. Note that the distortion applies only to the non-contributory part of social security. In other words, voters see

[7]Welfare depends on (*ex ante*) lifetime utilities.

through the budgetary veil and realize that the fraction α of their tax payment is given back to them with a return of n.[8]

The Retirees

It is straightforward to show that the preferred tax rate of a retiree with (past) wage w is given by:

$$\tau^R(w) = \min\left\{\frac{1}{2\gamma}\left(1 + \frac{\alpha}{1-\alpha}\frac{w}{\overline{w}}\right), 1\right\}. \tag{18}$$

The retiree chooses the tax rate that maximizes his pension under the constraint that $\tau \leqslant 1$. Note that $\tau^R(w)$ is increasing in w. This is because tax distortions are related to the Beveridgean part of pensions. Consequently, poor retirees suffer more from a tax increase than the rich.

The Workers

The problem of the workers is drastically modified when tax distortions are introduced. The rate of return of the PAYG system now depends on the value of the tax rate. Consequently, it is now possible that a given individual prefers the PAYG system to private saving for some values of τ and that his preferences change in favour of private saving for some other values. This individual will then choose a positive tax rate, such that the rates of return of public pension and private saving are equalized, and will supplement these mandatory public savings with private savings. Consequently, the possibility of a mixed choice—public pension supplemented with private savings—can no longer be ruled out.

Formally, the preferred tax rate, $\tau^A(w)$, and the savings, $s^A(w)$, of a worker are the solutions to the following problem:

---

[8]This specification is a reduced form of a more general (and complicated) model where labour supply is endogenous. Indeed the first-order condition for an interior value of τ would be:

$$-yu'(c) + \beta(1+n)(\alpha y + (1-\alpha)\overline{y})u'(d)$$

$$+\beta\left(\tau(1+n)(1-\alpha)\int_{w_-}^{w_+} w\,\partial l^A/\partial\tau f(w)\,\mathrm{d}w\right)u'(d) = 0,$$

where $\overline{y} = \int_{w_-}^{w_+} yf(w)\,\mathrm{d}w$, $y = wl^A(w)$ and $l^A(w)$ is the optimal labour supply of an individual with productivity w. It appears clear that tax distortions are associated with the third term of this first-order condition.

$$\max_{\tau,s} U = u(c) + \beta u(d) \tag{19}$$

subject to:

$$w(1-\tau) = c + s$$

$$d = (1+r)s + (1+n)\tau(\alpha w + (1-\alpha)(1-\gamma\tau)\overline{w}) \tag{20}$$

and

$$\tau \geqslant 0, \quad s \geqslant 0. \tag{21}$$

The next proposition states that low-wage individuals want a positive tax rate but no private savings, middle-wage individuals will make a mixed choice, with both PAYG social security and private saving, and higher-wage individuals will prefer to rely only on private saving.

Proposition 4. (*i*) $\max \tau^A(w) < \min \tau^R(w)$.
Moreover, there exists a value of w, $w' < \hat{w}$ (defined in (10)), such that:
(*ii*) *if $w \leqslant w'$, $\tau^A(w) > 0$, $s^A(w) = 0$;*
(*iii*) *if $w' < w < \hat{w}$, $\tau^A(w) > 0$ and $s^A(w) > 0$;*
(*iv*) *if $w \geqslant \hat{w}$, $\tau^A(w) = 0$ and $s^A(w) > 0$;*
(*v*) *if $w < w'$, $\partial\tau^A(w)/\partial w > 0$ and if $w' < w < \hat{w}$, $\partial\tau^A(w)/\partial w < 0$.*

Proof: See Appendix.

The first point in Proposition 4 says that the maximial preferred tax rate of the workers is lower than the minimal preferred tax rate of the retirees. The underlying idea is the same as in the case without distortions: workers do not want the tax to be too high because it decreases the first-period consumption. The other points imply that $\tau^A(w)$ is first increasing and then decreasing with w; it is equal to zero when $w = \hat{w}$. For workers with $w < \hat{w}$, social security is attractive up to a certain point; its relative return is now equal to $(\alpha + (1-\alpha)(1-\gamma\tau)\overline{w}/w)$, which can be lower than $1 + r$ for some τ. For workers with wage close to w_-, ther is no saving and the preferred tax rate increases with w. Figure 3 shows these results for the case where $r = n$, so that $\hat{w} = \overline{w}$.

The Majority Voting Solution

It can easily be shown that the objective function of each worker is concave relative to its arguments, τ and s. Therefore, preferences over τ are single-peaked and the median voter theorem applies. In the next proposition, we

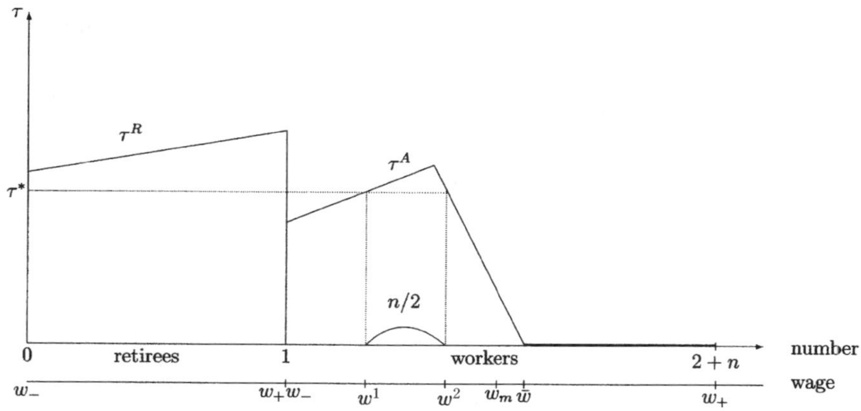

Fig. 3. Preferred tax rates with quadratic tax distortions when $r = n$

characterize the Condorcet winner. For this purpose, we define w^* as the income level satisfying $\tau^A(w_-) = \tau^A(w^*)$.

Proposition 5. *When the non-contributory part of social security implies quadratic distortions, the majority voting equilibrium tax rate is characterized as follows:*

(i) If $\int_{w_-}^{\hat{w}} f(w)\,\mathrm{d}w < n/2(1+n)$, *the majority voting equilibrium tax rate,* τ^*, *is* 0.
(ii) If $\int_{w_-}^{w^*} f(w)\,\mathrm{d}w \leqslant n/2(1+n) \leqslant \int_{w_-}^{\overline{w}} f(w)\,\mathrm{d}w$, *the majority voting equilibrium tax rate is the rate preferred by the workers with wage* w^p *defined as follows:*

$$\int_{w_-}^{w^p} f(w)\,\mathrm{d}w = \frac{n}{2(1+n)}. \tag{22}$$

(iii) If $\int_{w_-}^{w^*} f(w)\,\mathrm{d}w > n/2(1+n)$, *the majority voting equilibrium tax rate is the rate preferred by the workers with wage* w^1 *or* w^2 *satisfying:*

$$\int_{w^1}^{w^2} f(w)\,\mathrm{d}w = \frac{n}{2(1+n)} \quad \text{and} \quad \tau^A(w^1) = \tau^A(w^2). \tag{23}$$

The proof goes along the same lines as that of Proposition 2, so we do not develop the formal argument here. The idea is to find a sufficient number of individuals in the working population to form a majority coalition with the retirees and sustain a positive equilibrium tax rate. Under the condition in (i), the number of young who favour a positive tax rate is not sufficient to form a majority coalition with the old, and the PAYG pension system is not sustainable in the steady state. In (ii), the number of young individuals who favour the PAYG scheme is sufficient but there are not enough young with income between w^1 and w^2 to form a majority coalition with the old. Therefore, some young people with income $w > w^2$ also belong to that majority. Finally, in (iii), there are enough people in the interval $[w^1, w^2]$ and workers with income $w > w^2$ belong to the minority in favour of a tax rate lower than $\tau^A(w^1) = \tau^A(w^2)$. It is then clear that the set of workers who join the retirees to form a majority in favour of a positive tax rate is different from what it was without distortion. In particular, when $\int_{w_-}^{\hat{w}} f(w)\,\mathrm{d}w$ is not close to $n/2(1+n)$, those with earnings equal or just below $\hat{w}$ do not belong to that majority.

VIII. Concluding Comments

Throughout the chapter, the more or less Bismarckian feature of the social security system was regarded as given. A natural extension of our analysis would be to study the determination of α. A possible approach is to assume that the benefit formula is determined by a welfare-maximizing authority at a first, constitutional stage. This approach is in line with the sequential nature of the decision process alluded to in the Introduction. It has been adopted by Casamatta *et al.* (2000) but within a different context, namely social insurance. In that chapter the choice of the Bismarckian parameter, α, is made at the constitutional level, on the expectation that the payroll tax is determined later through majority voting. One of the main results is that a positive Bismarckian parameter can be desirable, even though the constitutional planner, with full control of α and τ, would set α equal to zero. This result arises because the redistributive character of the system has an impact on its political support. Specifically, when α is positive, the decisive voter chooses a tax rate that better fits the preferences of the low-wage individuals. A Rawlsian constitutionalist can then favour such a positive α.

Alternatively, one could consider a setting where both α and τ are chosen by majority voting. In this two-dimensional collective choice problem, a Condorcet winner does not generally exist. Therefore, the political process has to be given more structure. Some examples, again in the context of social insurance, can be found in Casamatta (1999), who studies sequential voting procedures, or in De Donder and Hendricks (1998), who study (two-party) electoral competition.

Another extension would be to study the properties of our setting out of the steady state. In particular, it is interesting to examine the transition following the occurrence of a shock such as, for example, a sudden drop in fertility or in productivity. In such a setting, the issue of voting is more complex and depends to a large extent on how expectations are formed. Moreover, the degree of redistributiveness can be very important when considering social security reforms. It is often observed that the resistance to change by vested interests is related to entitlements founded on the contributory part of social security. In other words, the choice of α has an effect not only on political support in the steady state, but also on political resistance out of the steady state when reforms are contemplated. But this is clearly another story.

Appendix

Proof of Proposition 1

First, observe that some straighforward algebra is sufficient to show that $v(\tau, w)$ is a concave function of τ. To prove (*i*), we differentiate $v(\tau, w)$ at $\tau = 0$:

$$\left.\frac{\partial v}{\partial \tau}\right|_{\tau=0} = -wu'(c) + \beta(1+n)(\alpha w + (1-\alpha)\overline{w})u'(d). \tag{A1}$$

At $\tau = 0$, everyone saves. Hence, substituting (5) in the previous expression, we obtain:

$$\left.\frac{\partial v}{\partial \tau}\right|_{\tau=0} = u'(c)\left(\frac{(1+n)}{(1+r)}(\alpha w + (1-\alpha)\overline{w}) - w\right). \tag{A2}$$

This expression is greater than 0 iff $w \leqslant \overline{w}$. Therefore, only these individuals will have a strictly positive preferred tax rate.

To prove (*ii*), let us write the first-order condition for τ for an individual with income $w < \hat{w}$

$$-wu'(c) + \beta(1+n)(\alpha w + (1-\alpha)\overline{w})u'(d) = 0. \tag{A3}$$

Differentiating this expression with respect to w, we obtain:

$$\frac{\partial \tau^A}{\partial w} = \frac{\beta(1+n)(1-\alpha)(\overline{w}/w)u'(d)(1-\epsilon)}{D_\tau}, \tag{A4}$$

where $D_\tau < 0$ is the second order derivative of $v(\tau, s)$ with respect to τ. Clearly, under our assumption that $\sigma < 1$, the preferred tax rate of individuals with income below $\hat{w}$.

To prove (*iii*), we note that the first-order condition $\partial v/\partial \tau = 0$ for $w < \hat{w}$ implies that workers with less than a break-even level of earnings oppose too high a tax rate because it decreases their first-period consumption. Indeed, when $\tau \to 1$, $u'(c) \to +\infty$ whereas the limit of $u'(d)$ is finite, which implies that the first-order condition cannot be satisfied.

Proof of Proposition 4

The first-order conditions associated with the programme of a working individual are:

$$-wu'(c) + \beta(1+n)(\alpha w + (1-\alpha)\overline{w}(1-\gamma\tau))u'(d) + \lambda_\tau = 0 \tag{A5}$$

and

$$-u'(c) + \beta(1+r)u'(d) + \lambda_s = 0, \tag{A6}$$

where λ_τ and λ_s are the Lagrange multipliers associated with the non-negativity constraints on τ and s, respectively.

To solve the programme, we have to consider different cases, depending on which constraint binds.

Case 1: $\lambda_\tau = \lambda_s = 0$.

Here, none of the non-negativity constraints bind, which means that we have an interior solution for both τ and s. Substituting (A6) into (A5), we obtain:

$$\tau^A(w) = \frac{(1+n)(\alpha w + (1-\alpha)\overline{w}) - w(1+r)}{2\gamma(1-\alpha)\overline{w}(1+n)}. \tag{A7}$$

A necessary and sufficient condition for $\tau^A(w)$ to be positive is that

$$w < \hat{w} = (1+n)(1-\alpha)\overline{w}/((1+r) - \alpha(1+n)).$$

All the people with earnings above this threshold will have a preferred tax rate of 0 and will choose to rely exclusively on private savings. For people with a wage lower than $\hat{w}$ who save privately, we have:

$$\frac{\partial\tau^A}{\partial w} = \frac{\alpha(1+n) - (1+r)}{2\gamma(1-\alpha)\overline{w}(1+n)} < 0. \tag{A8}$$

Consequently, preferred tax rates are decreasing with income.

Using (A6), we obtain:

$$\begin{aligned}\frac{\partial s^A(w)}{\partial w} &= -\frac{(-(1-\tau^A) + w[\partial\tau^A/\partial w])u''(c)}{u''(c) + (\beta(1+r))^2 u''(d)} \\ &\quad - \frac{\beta(1+r)([\partial\tau^A/\partial w](1+n)(\alpha w + (1-\alpha)\overline{w}) + \alpha(1+n)\tau^A)u''(d)}{u''(c) + (\beta(1+r))^2 u''(d)} \\ &= \frac{\alpha((1+n)(\alpha w + (1-\alpha)\overline{w}) - w(1+r))}{\gamma(1-\alpha)\overline{w}}.\end{aligned} \tag{A9}$$

This expression is positive for individuals with a wage below $\hat{w}$. The function $s^A(w)$ is thus increasing. Moreover, from (A6), it is negative for w sufficiently close to 0 and positive for w sufficiently close to $\hat{w}$. Therefore, there exists a value of w, w', such that each individual with income above this value has strictly positive savings and for those with income below w', the constraint $s \geqslant 0$ is binding.

To sum up, we have found that all the people with earnings between w' and $\hat{w}$ have an interior solution for both τ and s. These solutions are given by (A7) and (A6), respectively. The other individuals have either a positive preferred tax rate with no savings or positive savings and a zero preferred tax rate. We now analyse these two cases.

Case 2: $\lambda_\tau = 0$, $\lambda_s > 0$.

As already shown, individuals with earnings less than w' will choose a strictly positive tax rate and no savings. The value of the optimal tax rate is given by the condition (A5).

Case 3: $\lambda_\tau > 0$, $\lambda_s = 0$.

The richer individuals (those with earnings above $\hat{w}$) will rely exclusively on savings, the value of which is given by (A6).

In order to determine the majority voting solution, we must know how the preferred tax rates vary with income for individuals below w'. We obtain from (A5) that:

$$\frac{\partial \tau^A}{\partial w} = \frac{(1-\varepsilon)(\beta\alpha(1+n)u'(d) - u'(c)) - \alpha(1-\alpha)\beta\gamma\tau^2(1+n)^2\overline{w}u''(d)}{-D_\tau}. \tag{A10}$$

For those people who do not save privately, we know from (A6) that $u'(c) > \beta(1+r)u'(d)$ which implies that $u'(c) > \beta\alpha(1+n)u'(d)$. Hence, when $\varepsilon > 1$, this expression is positive, so that preferred tax rates are increasing with income.

Finally, we show that the maximal preferred tax rate of the workers is lower than the minimal preferred tax rate of the retirees. The maximal preferred tax rate of the workers is:

$$\tau^A(w') = \frac{(1+n)(\alpha w' + (1-\alpha)\overline{w}) - w'(1+r)}{2\gamma(1-\alpha)\overline{w}(1+n)}, \tag{A11}$$

and, assuming an interior solution, the minimal preferred tax rate of the retirees is:

$$\tau^R(w_-) = \frac{1}{2\gamma}\left(1 + \frac{\alpha}{1-\alpha}\frac{w_-}{\overline{w}}\right). \tag{A12}$$

Therefore, the condition for the maximal preferred tax rate of the workers to be higher than the minimal preferred tax rate of the retirees is

$$\tau^A(w') > \tau^R(w_-) \Leftrightarrow w'(\alpha(1+n) - (1+r)) - \alpha w_-(1+n) > 0.$$

Knowing that $\alpha(1+n) < 1+r$, this is impossible. Hence the result.

References

Broadway, R. and Wildasin, D. (1989), A Median Voter Model of Social Security, *International Economic Review 30*, 307–328.

Browning, E. K. (1975), Why the Social Insurance Budget is Too Large in a Democracy, *Economic Enquiry 13*, 373–388.

Casamatta, G. (1999), The Political Economy of Social Protection and Redistribution, Ph.D. dissertation, University of Toulouse.

Casamatta, G., Cremer, H. and Pestieau, P. (2000), Political Sustainability and the Design of Social Insurance, *Journal of Public Economics 75*, 341–364.

Conde Ruiz, J. I. and Galasso, V. (1999), Positive Arithmetics of the Welfare State, mimeo, Universidad Carlos III de Madrid.

De Donder, P. and Hendricks, J. (1998), The Political Economy of Targeting, *Public Choice 95*, 177–200.

Epple, D. and Romano, R. (1996), Public Provision of Private Goods, *Journal of Political Economy 104* , 57–84.

Hu, S. C. (1982), Social Security, Majority Voting and Dynamic Efficiency, *International Economic Review 23*, 269–287.

Johnson, P. (1998), Pension Provision and Pensioner's Incomes in 10 OECD countries, mimeo, ISF, London.

Myles, G. (1995), *Public Economics*, Cambridge University Press, Cambridge.

Tabellini, G. (2000), A Positive Theory of Social Security, *Scandinavian Journal of Economics 102*(3), 523–545.

Veall, M. R. (1986), Public Pensions as Optimal Social Contracts, *Journal of Public Economics 31*, 237–251.

10

A Positive Theory of Social Security

*Guido Tabellini**

I. Introduction

In many countries, social security comprises a large fraction of the government budget. Social security expenditures account for over a third of total government spending in most industrialized countries. Since the early 1980s, social security programs have grown in size almost everywhere. Yet, it is difficult to explain why a social security system exists, let alone why it is so large. At any given point in time, the number of recipients of social security benefits is smaller than the number of contributors. So, why do a large majority of citizens support a system that redistributes towards a minority?

The literature provides two answers to this question. The first stresses the intensity of preferences and forms of political participation other than through voting. Concentration of benefits among a few and diffusion of costs among many may explain why retired individuals successfully lobby to preserve the social security system.[1] But for this answer to be convincing, the costs of the program to the average taxpayer must be relatively small. This cannot be said of the social security systems currently prevailing in many countries.[2] It seems unlikely that such programs would be politically viable without the support of a large number of working individuals.

The second answer provided by the literature attempts to explain why workers who pay taxes may favor social security. The explanation is based on the assumption of no future re-voting. If the current majority can commit future majorities to preserving the law, then even a worker would support

*I wish to thank Torsten Persson for several discussions on the topic of this paper, as well as two anonymous referees and Casey Mulligan for helpful comments, Tom Harris, Pablo Sanguinetti and Alessia Amighini for excellent research assistance, and the NSF and the Center for Pacific Rim Studies for financial support.

[1]This explanation is proposed in e.g. Patton (1978). Hansson and Stuart (1989) study an overlapping-generations model that implicitly relies on this idea. The same assumption, that the old choose the equilibrium policy, is also used in Loewy (1988) and it is implicit in the work of Verbon (1988). More recently, Mulligan and Sala-i-Martin (1999a) have argued that the old are more successful at lobbying, because among other things they have more free time.

[2]For instance, according to Boskin, Kotikoff, Puffert and Shoven (1987), more than half of the workers in the US pay more in OASDHI contributions than they pay in personal income taxes.

social security, provided that his retirement age is sufficiently near.[3] But the assumption of no future re-voting is clearly counterfactual. Society cannot precommit its future decisions on social security legislation. And in practice, such legislation has been changed repeatedly over time.[4]

This paper suggests an alternative explanation as to why the social security system is politically viable. The central idea is that a social security program redistributes both across and within generations. The contributions to the system are linked to wage income, but the benefits are not (or are linked to a much smaller degree). As a result, a social security system also redistributes from high- to low-income households; for the US, this fact has been extensively documented by Boskin *et al.* (1987), Ferrara and Lott (1985) and Galasso (1998). Hence, poor workers/taxpayers may be in favor of the program, since the gain to their retired parents is larger than the cost to them.

In the first part of this paper, I study this idea in a simple overlapping-generations model with heterogeneous individuals and exogenous population growth. The social security program is chosen in each period under majority rule. All the generations currently alive are entitled to vote. Thus, there is no commitment and in any period the social security legislation could be repealed. The absence of commitment implies that future voting decisions are taken as given by today's voters. This breaks the link between current contributions and future benefits. In any period, a vote on the social security program is a vote on how much to transfer from the current young to the current old, with no repercussions on future legislation. A central feature of the model is that there is bidirectional altruism: parents care about their children, and children care about their parents. However, this altruism is sufficiently weak that no private transfers occur in equilibrium. Altruism plays a role only in the political equilibrium.[5] A young voter trades off his tax burden from financing the program against the benefits received by his parent, and so does an old voter.

---

[3]This point has been explored in several papers; see e.g. Browning (1975) and more recently Boadway and Wildasin (1989a, 1989b), and Cukierman and Meltzer (1989). Persson and Tabellini (1999, 2000) survey the literature.

[4]Some interesting papers, including Kotlikoff, Persson and Svensson (1988), Sjoblom (1985), Boldrin and Rustichini (1996), Aziariadis and Galasso (1997), and Cooley and Soares (1999) argue that "reputation" can substitute for commitment. Succinctly, if a young generation reneges on a social security program, it can be punished by the succeeding generation that refuses to reinstate the program. The threat of this punishment may deter each young generation from reneging. These reputation equilibria are extensively and critically discussed in Persson and Tabellini (1990, 1999) who, in particular, point out that some of the equilibria considered in this literature are not renegotiation-proof.

[5]Altonji, Hayashi and Kotlikoff (1989) provide empirical support for this assumption.

The main analytical result is that, with sufficient inequality in labor income, a social security program is supported in equilibrium by a majority of the voters. Moreover, with aggregate shocks to the income of each generation, the political equilibrium mimics an *ex-ante* optimal policy of intergenerational risk sharing, such as that characterized by Gordon and Varian (1988).

The analysis also yields two positive implications: in equilibrium, the size of social security is larger, the greater is the pre-tax income inequality and the larger is the fraction of elderly people in the population. In the second part of the paper, I explore these two empirical implications. I compare the size of social security programs in more than 40 countries by means of simple cross-country regressions. I find that cross-country differences are in fact well explained by the inequality of pre-tax income and by the age composition of the population, according to the predictions of the theory. This finding is robust to alternative specifications and to the possibility of measurement error in the explanatory variables.

The outline of the paper is as follows. The model is described in Section II. Section III characterizes the economic equilibrium. The voters' preferences are set out in Section IV, while Section V characterizes the political equilibrium. The empirical evidence is explored in Section VI. Section VII concludes.

II. The Model

The economy is populated by overlapping generations. Each generation lives for two periods; hence, two generations are alive in every period. Members of the old generation are called "parents"; members of the young generation are called "kids". Every parent has $(1 + n)$ kids; thus, $n > 0$ is the rate of population growth. Parents and kids are linked by mutual altruism. Specifically, let i denote the ith household. The preferences of the ith kid born in period t are represented by:

$$J_t^i = \max\left[\frac{\gamma}{1+n} H_t^i + U(c_t^i) + E_t H_{t+1}^i\right], \tag{1}$$

where c_t^i is consumption of the ith kid in period t, $U(\cdot)$ is a well-behaved utility function, E_t is the expectations operator and H_t^i is the indirect utility function of the period t parent in the ith household. The parameter $1 > \gamma > 0$ represents the degree of kids' altruism. Since a period t kid becomes a parent in period $t + 1$, he does not discount the utility function H_{t+1}^i. The preferences of the period t parent in the ith household are:

$$H_t^i = \max[d_t^i + \delta(1+n)J_t^i], \tag{2}$$

where d_t^i is the consumption of the ith parent in period t and $1 > \delta > 0$ is a parameter that measures parents' altruism. According to (1) and (2), altruism depends on family size. As n grows, parents become less selfish and kids more selfish.[6]

Different households have the same preferences but different endowments. At the beginning of his life, the ith kid receives an endowment $w_t(1 + e_t^i)$. The individual-specific endowment e_t^i can be either positive or negative and is distributed in the population according to a known function $G(\cdot)$, with bounded support $[\underline{e}, \overline{e}]$ inside the unit circle, zero mean and negative median. The aggregate endowment w_t is drawn at random from a known distribution with support $[\underline{w}, \overline{w}]$. The variables w_t and e_t^i are mutually uncorrelated, and their period t realizations are known to everyone at the start of period t. The serial correlation properties of w_t and e_t^i do not matter. Hence, in particular, it does not matter whether the incomes of parents and kids belonging to the same household are correlated with each other or not. As will become clear below, this is because of the linearity of consumption in the parents' preferences.

Each kid pays a non-negative social security tax proportional to his endowment and may receive a non-negative bequest, $b_t^i/(1+n)$, from his parent. He can consume, save and leave a non-negative gift to his parent. Hence, the budget constraint of the ith kid in period t is:

$$w_t(1 + e_t^i)(1 - \tau_t) + \frac{b_t^i}{1+n} \geqslant c_t^i + s_t^i + f_t^i, \tag{3}$$

where τ_t is the social security tax rate and s_t^i and f_t^i denote savings and gifts, respectively. Individuals can freely borrow or lend. Hence, savings can be positive or negative.

In the second period of his life, each individual receives an endowment a from nature and a non-negative lump-sum social security benefit g_t from the government, plus any gift from his kids. Hence, the budget constraint of the ith parent in period t is:

$$a + g_t + R_{t-1}s_{t-1}^i + f_t^i(1+n) \geqslant d_t^i + b_t^i, \tag{4}$$

[6]The specification of preferences is plausible and simplifies the algebra, but is not crucial for most of the results. Equally unimportant is the assumption that individuals care about the indirect utility (rather than the consumption) of their relatives.

where R_{t-1} is the rate of return on the savings accumulated (loans contracted) in period $t-1$. By the non-negativity constraints on private transfers, $f^i_t, b^i_t \geqslant 0$, all i, t.

Output is non-storable and there are no outside assets (such as fiat money or government debt). Hence, in every period the kids' aggregate savings must be zero in equilibrium:

$$\int s^i_t \,\mathrm{d}F_t(s^i_t) = 0, \tag{5}$$

where $F_t(\cdot)$ is the period t distribution of savings among the kids' population (to be derived below).

Finally, the government budget must be balanced in every period. Since the mean of e^i_t is zero, the government budget constraint is:

$$g_t = (1+n)w_t\tau_t. \tag{6}$$

Two features of this model are worth noting. First and most important, the social security program redistributes from parent to kid as well as from rich to poor. This occurs because the benefit g_t is lump sum, whereas the contribution is proportional to income. This feature of the model reflects the redistributive character of existing social security programs. Since there is no crucial discontinuity in the model, the results hold even for less extreme asymmetries between contributions and benefits. Second, the linearity of consumption in the parents' welfare implies that all income effects are absorbed by this term. This in turn implies that private intergenerational transfers are the same for all households, irrespective of their relative incomes. While this feature considerably simplifies the description of the political equilibrium, it is not crucial for the qualitative results.

Events unfold according to the following timing. At the beginning of each period, the policy (τ, g) is chosen under majority rule. By the government budget constraint, only one of the two policy instruments, say τ, can be freely set. Then private agents make their economic decisions. A political–economic equilibrium must satisfy two conditions: (i) economic equilibrium: for any given policy, economic decisions are optimal for private agents and markets clear; (ii) political equilibrium: the policy is (weakly) preferred by at least 50 percent of the voters to any other policy in a pairwise comparison.[7]

[7]Meltzer and Richard (1981) have analyzed the determinants of the size of redistributive policies in a related framework. However, they study a static model, in which the issues of intergenerational redistribution and commitment do not arise.

III. Economic Equilibrium

Consider first the economic equilibrium for a given policy. The first-order conditions with respect to gifts and bequests imply (a subscript denotes a partial derivative);

$$1 \geqslant \delta U_c(c_t^i) \geqslant \delta\gamma \tag{7}$$

where the first (second) inequality is strict if the non-negativity constraint on bequests (gifts) is binding. Throughout the paper I assume that altruism is sufficiently weak that private transfers never occur, irrespective of the policy or of the realization of aggregate output. Specifically, I assume that:

$$\frac{1}{U_c(0)} > \delta, \quad U_c(\overline{w}(1+\overline{e})) > \gamma. \tag{8}$$

Under (8), the inequalities in (7) always hold as strict inequalities, so that $f_t = b_t = 0$. Relaxing this assumption would make it more likely that the political equilibrium involves a positive transfer through the social security system (since voters would be more altruistic), even though it would complicate the description of the voters' preferences.

The optimal amount of savings is determined by the first-order condition:

$$R_t = U_c(c_t^i), \quad \text{all } i. \tag{9}$$

Imposing the equilibrium condition (5), and exploiting the budget constraints, we then obtain a complete description of the economic equilibrium as a function of the policy τ_t:

$$\begin{aligned}
c_t^i &= w_t(1-\tau_t) \quad \text{all } i \\
s_t^i &= e_t^i w_t(1-\tau_t) \\
d_t^i &= a + (1+n)w_t\tau_t + R_{t-1}w_{t-1}(1-\tau_{t-1})e_{t-1}^i \\
R_t &= U_c(w_t(1-\tau_t)).
\end{aligned} \tag{10}$$

IV. The Voters' Preferences

I now turn to a description of the voters' preferences for the policy. Throughout the rest of the paper, by policy I mean a social security tax rate, τ_t. The government budget constraint then determines g_t residually.

Insert the equilibrium expressions (10) into the utility function of kids and parents. After some transformations, we obtain their utility as a function of past, current and future policies:

$$J_t^i = \frac{1}{1-\delta\gamma}\bigg\{U(w_t(1-\tau_t)) + \gamma w_t\tau_t + R_t w_t(1-\tau_t)e_t^i$$

$$+\frac{\gamma}{1+n}R_{t-1}w_{t-1}(1-\tau_{t-1})e_{t-1}^i + (1+n)E_t w_{t+1}\tau_{t+1}$$

$$+\mu + \delta(1+n)E_t J_{t-1}^t\bigg\}$$

$$H_t^i = a + (1+n)w_t\tau_t + R_{t-1}w_{t-1}(1-\tau_{t-1})e_{t-1}^i + \delta(1+n)J_t^i, \qquad (11)$$

where $\mu = \gamma a/(1+n) + a$. Although rather complicated, these expressions are linear in the individual specific parameters e^i. This is because all income effects are absorbed by consumption when old, d^i, which in turn enters linearly into the utility of each generation. This property of the utility function considerably simplifies the characterization of the political equilibrium.

Since there is no outside asset and the voters' preferences are additively separable in τ_t, there is no intertemporal link in the voters' optimization problem: the policy optimal for voter i in period t is independent of previous and future voting decisions.

Consider the effect of changing τ_t on the ith kid and parent welfare at time t. Differentiating (11) with respect to τ_t and simplifying:

$$J_{\tau_t}^i = \frac{w_t}{1-\delta\gamma}\left[\gamma - R_t - \frac{(1-r)}{1-\delta\gamma}R_t e_t^i\right] \qquad (12)$$

$$H_{\tau_t}^i = (1+n)[w_t + \delta J_{\tau_t}^i], \qquad (13)$$

where $J_{\tau_t}^i$ and $H_{\tau_t}^i$ denote the partial derivatives of J_t^i and H_t^i with respect to τ_t, respectively, and $r_t = -U_{cc}(c_t)c_t/U_c(c_t) > 0$ is the coefficient of relative risk aversion of $U(\cdot)$. Throughout the rest of the paper, I assume that $r_t < 1$ for any c_t.

For the average voter (i.e., if $e_t^i = 0$), equation (12) can be shown to imply $J_{\tau_t} < 0$ and $H_{\tau_t} > 0$ for any $1 \geqslant \tau_t \geqslant 0$.[8] This is not surprising. For the average voter, the social security programme only redistributes across generations, with no intra-generational consequences. Hence, average kids want no social security, and their parents want as much of it as possible.

But for non-average kids (i.e., if $e_t^i \neq 0$), the policy also has intra-generational effects, since it redistributes from rich to poor households. Specifically, if the ith kid is richer than the average (if $e_t^i > 0$), then he will be even more opposed to the social security system, while his parent will be less strongly in favour (or may even oppose it, if e_t^i is sufficiently large). And conversely, a poor kid may support the social security system, while his parent will be even more strongly in favour of it.

More generally, by (12) and (13), the voters' preferences can be ranked according to the kids' relative income, e_t^i: the larger the kids' income, the lower the preferred social security tax, for both kids and parents.[9] But the parents always prefer a higher social security tax than their kids. Under the additional assumption that the second-order conditions of the voting problem are satisfied for every voter, we can then conclude that the voters' preferences are single-peaked. The political equilibrium is thus given by the policy preferred by the median voter.[10]

To identify the median voter, we have to combine the two groups of voters, parents and kids. Consider a kid with endowment e_t^k. By (12) and (13), the optimal value of τ_t for this kid is the same as for the parent of a kid with endowment e_t^p, defined by:[11]

[8] If $e_t^i = 0$, (12) and (13) reduce to:

$$J_{\tau_t} = \frac{w_t}{1 - \delta\gamma}(\gamma - R_t)$$

$$H_{\tau_t} = \frac{(1+n)w_t}{1 - \delta\gamma}(1 - \delta R_t).$$

Combining (7)–(9), we see that $J_{\tau_t} < 0$ and $H_{\tau_t} > 0$ for any $1 \geqslant \tau_t \geqslant 0$.

[9] Note that all that matters here is the kids' relative income and not that of their parents. This is because the social security tax is proportional to the kids' income, and parents have a constant marginal utility of consumption.

[10] As in any optimal taxation problem, the second-order conditions of the policy optimization problem are more restrictive than just concavity of the utility function. Since the voters' utility functions are linear in the individual specific parameter e^i, they belong to the class of intermediate preferences defined by Grandmont (1978). Preferences in this class are single peaked.

[11] Equation (14) has been obtained by setting the RHS of (12) and (13) equal to zero and simplifying.

$$e_t^p = e_t^k + \frac{(1-\delta\gamma)^2}{\delta(1-r_t)R_t}. \tag{14}$$

Equation (14) enables us to match each kid with a parent who votes exactly like he does. As expected, the pth parent is wealthier than the kth kid, since parents always tend to favor the social security system more than their own kids.

We are now ready to identify the median voters. Recall that each parent has $(1+n)$ kids, and that e^i is distributed according to the function $G(\cdot)$. The median voters are a kid with endowments e_t^{mk} and the parent of a kid with endowment e_t^{mp} such that e_t^{mk} and e_t^{mp} satisfy (14) and are defined implicitly by:

$$(1+n)G(e_t^{mk}) + G(e_t^{mp}) = 1 + \frac{n}{2}. \tag{15}$$

The first term on the LHS of (15) is the number of kids poorer than the median voter kid (who thus prefer higher social security taxes); the second term is the number of parents poorer than the median voter parent. If (15) is satisfied, an equal number of voters lies on the opposite side of e^{mk} and e^{mp}. Let e^m be the median value of e^i. Since $G(\cdot)$ is increasing and $e_t^{mk} < e_t^{mp}$ by (14), we have $e_t^{mk} < e^m < e_t^{mp}$: the income of the median voter kid is below the median income, whereas the opposite is true of the median voter parent.[12]

V. Political Equilibrium

The equilibrium policy is the value of τ_t preferred by the median voters. Consider first an interior optimum for the median voters. It is convenient to express the equilibrium in terms of the kids' consumption, rather than in terms of the policy. Let c^* be the kids' consumption in the political equilibrium. Then, c^* is found by setting the RHS of (12) and (13) equal to zero, for $e^i = e^{mk}$ and $e^i = e^{mp}$, respectively. Doing that and using (10) we obtain that c^* must satisfy:[13]

[12] Recall though that e_t^{mp} is the endowment of the kid of the median voter parent.

[13] Since e^{mk} and e^{pk} satisfy (14), the same value of c^* enters both expressions of (16). Moreover, since $e^{mk} < e^m$ and $e^m < 0$ (by hypothesis), we have $e^{mk} < 0$. By (7), (9) and (16), we then also have $e^{mp} > 0$.

$$
\begin{aligned}
e^{mk} &= \frac{(1-\delta\gamma)(\gamma - U_c(c^*))}{U_c(c^*) + c^* U_{cc}(c^*)} \equiv E^k(c^*) \\
e^{mp} &= \frac{(1-\delta\gamma)(1-\delta U_c(c^*))}{\delta[U_c(c^*) + c^* U_{cc}(c^*)]} \equiv E^p(c^*).
\end{aligned} \tag{16}
$$

The political equilibrium is characterized by the condition:

$$(1+n)G[E^k(c^*)] + G[E^p(c^*)] = 1 + \frac{n}{2}. \tag{17}$$

The function $G(\cdot)$ is strictly increasing. Differentiating (16) with respect to c^* and invoking the second-order conditions, it can be shown that $E^k(c^*)$ and $E^p(c^*)$ are also strictly increasing.[14] Hence, equation (17) identifies a unique equilibrium value c^*. The equilibrium policy, τ_t^*, is then defined by:

$$\tau_t^* = 1 - \frac{c^*}{w_t}. \tag{18}$$

Thus, if the political equilibrium is at the median voters' interior optimum, the kids' consumption is constant and does not depend on the aggregate endowment. The equilibrium social security tax moves in the same direction as w_t, and fully insures the kids against any aggregate shock. All aggregate risk is borne by the parents' generation.

Under what conditions does the political equilibrium involve a positive amount of social security transfers? This is equivalent to asking: when are the median voters not at the corner $\tau_t^* = 0$? The answer is easily obtained from (17) and (18). Since the LHS of (17) is strictly increasing in $c*$, the median voters are *not* at the corner $\tau_t^* = 0$ if and only if:

$$(1+n)G[E^k(w_t)] + G[E^p(w_t)] > 1 + \frac{n}{2}. \tag{19}$$

Whenever (19) is satisfied, the equilibrium involves a positive amount of

[14] Alternatively, the sign of $E_c^k(c^*)$ and $E_c^p(c^*)$ can be determined as follows. Let τ_t^k and c_t^k be the tax rate and kids' consumption preferred by the kth kid. Set the RHS of (12) equal to zero, for $e_t^i = e_t^k$. By the implicit function theorem and the second-order conditions, it can be shown that $\mathrm{d}\tau_t^k/\mathrm{d}e_t^k < 0$ at an interior optimum. Hence,

$$\frac{\mathrm{d}c_t^k}{\mathrm{d}e_t^k} = \frac{\mathrm{d}c_t^k}{\mathrm{d}\tau_t^k}\frac{\mathrm{d}\tau_t^k}{\mathrm{d}e_t^k} = -w_t\frac{\mathrm{d}\tau_t^k}{\mathrm{d}e_t^k} > 0.$$

Finally, note that $E_c^k(c^*) = (\mathrm{d}c^k/\mathrm{d}e^k)^{-1}$ for $e^k = e^{mk}$. The same procedure can be used to show that $E_c^p(c^*) > 0$.

transfers through the social security system. Whether or not this occurs thus depends on the parameter values as well as on the realization of aggregate output, w_t.

By (16)–(18), the equilibrium size of the social security system depends on two central features of society: (i) the proportion of young people in the population, n; and (ii) the distribution of labour income among taxpayers—the function $G(\cdot)$. Consider first a change in the proportion of young people in the population, n. Applying the implicit function theorem to (17), it can be shown that $\mathrm{d}c^*/\mathrm{d}n > 0$.[15] Hence, by (18), the social security tax rate is negatively related to n. Intuitively, if there are more kids in the population, a larger fraction of the voters will be opposed to the social security system; hence the equilibrium size of τ_t^* is smaller.

Next, consider the effect of changing the distribution of labour income among the kids. The more unequal is the distribution of labour income, the lower are e^{mk} and e^{pk} (since the cumulative distribution $G(\cdot)$ would rise more rapidly for low values of e). Hence, the median voters correspond to poorer individuals, who in turn prefer a larger social security system (see equations (12) and (13)). Thus, the size of the social security system is larger in societies with greater income inequality. These two predictions of the theory are tested in the next section.

I close this section by comparing this equilibrium against a normative benchmark. There are two relevant dimensions. First, how is aggregate risk shared among generations? Second, how is consumption allocated on average between the young and old generations? On the first dimension, the political equilibrium exactly mimics the *ex ante* optimal policy of inter-generational risk sharing; see Gordon and Varian (1988). Since the parents are risk neutral, the optimal policy shifts all aggregate risk onto the parents, as in the political equilibrium. Thus, the *ex ante* optimal policy can be implemented under majority rule, even in the absence of commitments.[16] On the second dimension (the average allocation of consumption between young and old), the normative comparison is ambiguous. Here we need a stronger

[15]By the implicit function theorem,

$$\frac{\mathrm{d}c^*}{\mathrm{d}n} = -\frac{G[E^k(c^*)] - \frac{1}{2}}{g(E^k(c^*))e_c^k + g(E^p(c^*))E_c^p}.$$

The denominator is positive. Since E^k is smaller than the median e^i, $G[E^k(c^*)] < \frac{1}{2}$. Hence, $\mathrm{d}c^*/\mathrm{d}n > 0$.

[16]Note that a similar finding would also hold if the parents were risk averse. In this case, the political equilibrium would be more difficult to characterize, but it would have the feature that aggregate shocks are borne by both generations currently alive. Naturally, the political equilibrium would exactly implement the *ex ante* optimal risk sharing only for particular parameter values.

criterion than Pareto efficiency. Since there is heterogeneity between rich and poor and young and old, the nature of the optimal allocation of consumption depends on the weights given to different individuals. Depending on how these weights are chosen, the equilibrium allocation of c^* to every kid may be too large or too small compared to the optimum.

VI. The Empirical Evidence

The theory has predictions for both time-series and cross-country data. But the time-series predictions (that social security tax rates are positively correlated with aggregate income) are not robust to minor changes in the model. In particular, increasing the risk aversion of the old compared to that of the young reverses the time-series predictions. For this reason, in the remainder of the paper I test the predictions of the theory by comparing the size of the social security programs of a large number of developing and industrialized countries.

The Data

The closest observable counterpart to the average social security tax rate—the variable in the model—is the ratio of social security contributions to GNP. This ratio is displayed in the first column of Table 1 for a number of

Table 1. *Social security contributions and expenditures*[a]

Country	Contributions		Expenditures	
	% of GNP	% of govt revenues	% of GNP	% of govt spending
South Africa	–	1.21	–	–
Jamaica	–	3.66	–	–
Madagascar	–	9.94	–	–
Ecuador	–	–	–	1.07
Niger	–	4.19	–	1.89
Nigeria	–	–	–	2.48
Sierra Leone	–	–	–	3.28
Morocco	–	5.08	–	5.15
Senegal	–	3.75	–	5.58
Peru	–	–	0.03	0.17
Philippines	–	–	0.27	2.11
Sudan	–	–	0.28	1.72
Bolivia	–	–	0.31	2.79
Tanzania	–	–	0.34	1.17
Pakistan	–	–	0.48	2.65
El Salvador	–	–	0.64	3.80
Zambia	–	–	0.78	2.30
Fiji	–	–	0.80	2.97

Table 1. *(continued)*

Country	Contributions		Expenditures	
	% of GNP	% of govt revenues	% of GNP	% of govt spending
Côte d'Ivoire	1.32	5.47	0.97	3.05
Burma	–	–	0.98	6.21
Malaysia	0.12	0.46	1.10	3.81
Korea	0.19	1.05	1.13	6.46
Venezuela	1.21	4.32	1.75	6.76
Trinidad & Tobago	0.65	1.64	1.87	5.92
Costa Rica	4.66	25.89	1.95	8.86
Tunisia	3.04	9.51	2.83	8.54
Mexico	2.26	15.11	3.03	16.01
Colombia	1.40	10.43	3.03	20.06
Panama	6.04	23.11	3.30	9.58
Barbados	2.72	9.68	4.57	14.98
Sri Lanka	–	–	5.95	16.01
Argentina	3.67	22.34	6.29	32.38
Australia*	–	–	7.00	27.94
Brazil	6.60	27.80	7.03	35.25
United States*	5.77	28.40	7.53	33.96
Finland*	2.67	9.47	7.74	27.00
United Kingdom*	6.74	17.08	9.43	25.48
Greece*	8.10	26.98	10.21	28.35
Chile	4.15	12.79	10.39	33.96
Italy*	11.47	34.55	12.61	30.11
Norway*	10.07	23.47	12.90	33.89
Israel*	5.12	8.32	14.59	20.31
Germany, Fed.*	15.22	53.32	14.99	49.58
Denmark*	–	–	16.46	42.29
France*	16.64	42.57	17.56	44.12
Sweden*	12.34	33.40	19.48	47.89
Netherlands*	18.34	36.67	19.95	37.09

Sources: International Monetary Fund, GFS and IFS.

[a]In the first two columns, the numerator is 100 ∗ social security contributions, and the denominator is indicated above. In the other two columns, the numerator is 100 ∗ social security plus welfare expenditures, and the denominator is indicated above. All the ratios are averaged over the period 1978–1982.

*indicates an industrialized country.

countries. Since the sample includes very heterogeneous countries, which certainly also differ in the availability of observable tax bases, the second column of Table 1 reports a different measure of the size of social security: the ratio of social security contributions to total government revenue. This second variable, although not literally related to the model, is perhaps more meaningful than the first. The reason is that its variation across countries is less likely to be affected by the difficulties of administering tax collections or general political attitudes towards the size of government, which are difficult to control for.

Data on social security contributions are missing for many countries. On the other hand, a larger group of countries report comparable data on social security and welfare spending.[17] Moreover, if the social security system is unbalanced and financed with general government revenues, social security expenditures as a fraction of GNP are perhaps a better measure of the variable in the model. This measure is displayed in the third column of Table 1. Finally, and for the same reasons discussed above, the last column of Table 1 also reports social security and welfare spending as a fraction of total government spending.

All the variables in Table 1 are averaged over the period 1978–1982 (or whatever fraction of it is available). The data sources are described in more detail in the Appendix. The sample of countries is determined by data availability, also taking into account the variables described below.

Table 1 underscores the extent to which the size of social security differs across countries. Most of the industrialized countries (indicated by an asterisk) have relatively large social security programmes; but this is also true of some of the developing countries, particularly when social security is scaled to total government revenue or spending. Can these differences be explained by the theory formulated in the previous sections?

According to the preceding model, the size of social security is related to the relative proportions of taxpayers and retirees among voters, and to the distribution of income. I measure the former by the proportion of individuals over 65 years of age in the total population ("*prop65*"), and the latter by the fraction of pre-tax income received by the top 5 percent of the population (*Top5*). Other measures of income distribution are also used, as described below.

The Cross-country Regressions

To test the predictions of the theory, I estimated the following regression:

$$y = \beta_0 + \beta_1 prop65 + \beta_2 top5 + \beta_3 \mathbf{x} + u \tag{20}$$

where y is the size of social security as measured by one of the variables listed in Table 1, u is the error term and $\mathbf{x}$ is a vector of additional explanatory variables neglected by our theory, but which may nevertheless contribute to explaining international differences in the size of social security. Our theory predicts that β_1 and β_2 are positive. Hence, the null hypothesis to be tested is: H_0: $\beta_1 = \beta_2 = 0$.

The vector $\mathbf{x}$ of additional explanatory variables includes a dummy

[17]The breakdown of social security and welfare is missing for most countries. But when available, welfare is generally a small proportion of social security plus welfare.

variable taking a value of 1 for industrialized countries and 0 otherwise (industrial), and real per capita income (per capita income), as a general proxy for the stage of development. Below I also report the results of including other variables in **x**, such as the size of the agricultural sector or of the urban population, which may be related to the cost of administering tax collections.

Table 2 contains the summary statistics and the correlation matrix among the variables mentioned above. Note that all the measures of social security are highly positively correlated with each other.

The estimated coefficients for alternative specifications, for different samples of countries, and for alternative measurements of the dependent variable are reported in Tables 3 and 4. Table 3 refers to all countries, while Table 4 splits the sample into industrial and developing countries.

Consider Table 3 first. Since there is evidence that the absolute size of the estimated residuals is correlated to per capita income, the coefficients were estimated by weighted least squares, with per capita income as weight. The unweighted estimates are very similar. For all measures of the dependent variable and all sample sizes, the regression fit is extremely good, considering the large variance in the dependent variable. The estimated coefficients of the variables of interest (*top5* and *prop65*) are always of the correct sign and are generally significantly different from zero.

Table 2. *Summary statistics*

Variables	Mean	Std. Dev.
S.S. Contrib. (% of GNP)	6.02	5.25
S.S. Contrib. (% of govt. revenue)	16.51	13.88
S.S. Exp. (% of GNP)	6.07	6.12
S.S. Exp. (% of govt. spending)	16.25	15.23
Prop65	0.07	0.05
Top5	26.63	8.92
Per capita income	4,114	3,675

Partial correlation matrix

	S.S. cont. (% rev.)	S.S. exp. (% GNP)	S.S. exp. (% sp.)	*Prop65*	*Top5*	P.C. income
S.S. cont (% GNP)	0.90	0.89	0.80	0.71	0.03	0.64
S.S. cont (% rev.)		0.72	0.83	0.64	0.07	0.62
S.S. exp (% GNP)			0.91	0.86	−0.36	0.80
S.S. exp (% sp.)				0.84	−0.29	0.83
Prop65					−0.43	0.89
Top5						−0.48

Table 3. *All countries*[a] *(1978–1982)*

Dependent variable	S.S. cont. (% GNP)	S.S. cont. (% rev.)	S.S. exp. (% GNP)	S.S. exp. (% sp.)	S.S. cont. (% GNP)	S.S. exp. (% sp.)
Explanatory variables						
Intercept	−8.814	−26.99	−3.603	−11.971	−10.828	−16.161
	(−2.427)	(−3.108)	(−1.247)	(−2.040)	(−2.610)	(−2.691)
Prop65	36.259	118.286	70.071	214.312	73.541	204.885
	(1.120)	(1.513)	(2.654)	(3.943)	(2.503)	(4.231)
Top5	0.362	1.147	0.118	0.502	0.343	0.533
	(3.219)	(4.415)	(1.341)	(2.760)	(2.789)	(2.974)
P.C. income	–	–	–	–	0.37E(−3)	1.33E(−3)
					(0.911)	(2.032)
Industrial	6.786	16.516	4.940	8.490	–	–
	(2.111)	(2.130)	(1.848)	(1.540)	–	–
$\overline{R}^2$	0.586	0.632	0.655	0.731	0.517	0.743
S.E.	280.970	683.879	253.850	524.008	303.397	512.401
No. obs.	25	28	38	40	25	40

[a] All regressions were estimated by weighted least squares, with P.C. income as the weight; *t*-statistics in parentheses.

Table 4. *Industrial and developing countries*[a] *(1978–1982)*

	Industrial countries			Developing countries		
Dependent variable	S.S. cont. (% GNP)	S.S. cont. (% rev.)	S.S. exp. (% sp.)	S.S. exp. (% GNP)	S.S. cont. (% rev.)	S.S. exp. (% sp.)
Explanatory variables						
Intercept	−3.648	−19.687	−3.439	−2.839	−10.387	−10.092
	(−0.426)	(−1.086)	(−0.298)	(−1.302)	(−1.101)	(−1.230)
Prop65	30.372	111.754	197.553	19.640	70.693	317.987
	(0.508)	(0.883)	(2.372)	(0.887)	(0.706)	(3.073)
Top5	0.471	1.598	0.578	0.170	0.635	0.211
	(2.004)	(3.214)	(1.675)	(2.795)	(2.458)	(1.032)
$\overline{R}^2$	0.228	0.523	0.439	0.314	0.206	0.225
S.E.	4.460	9.436	6.859	1.727	8.209	8.985
No. obs.	11	11	13	14	17	27

[a] Estimation method: ordinary least squares; *t*-statistics in parentheses.

Similar results are obtained in Table 4, when the regressions were estimated separately for industrialized and developing countries.[18] Note, however, that now the variable *prop65* loses significance in both samples when the dependent variable is measured as contributions (rather than expenditures). This could be due to the small number of observations within each sample. Very similar results (not reported in the tables) are obtained when per capita income is included in the regressions as an additional explanatory variable, or when social security is measured as expenditures as a percentage of GNP.

Sensitivity Analysis

To further assess the robustness of the estimates, I tried alternative specifications besides those reported in Table 3, as well as alternative measures of the data. First, I replaced per capita income in Table 3 with the share of the agricultural sector in GDP and with a measure of urbanization. The coefficients of interest did not change even though the size of the urban population had a significant estimated coefficient in some specifications.

Second, I created a new dummy variable that distinguishes between democratic and non-democratic regimes. The new dummy variable was always insignificant when included as an additional variable, and the other estimated coefficients were generally not affected by it.

Third, I replaced the measure of income inequality, *top5*, by two other measures of income distribution: the Gini coefficient and the fraction of income received by the third quintile in the population (which includes median income). The Gini coefficient is a measure of inequality, and the expected sign of its coefficient is positive as for *top5*; the third quintile is a measure of equality, and its expected sign in the regression is thus negative. The estimated coefficients of these variables always had the expected sign in all regressions, even though their *t*-statistics were generally slightly lower than for the variable *top5* (perhaps because they vary less in the sample).

Fourth, the same specification was estimated for more recent measures of all variables except income inequality. Thus the same variables listed in Table 3 were collected for the period 1988–1992 and the average was taken for each country over this same period (or whatever subperiod over which data where available). Income inequality is still measured by the same variable and with the same source used in Table 3. The number of countries for which data could be collected is somewhat smaller than for the regressions reported in Table 3. The new estimates are reported in Table 5 (the names of the variables are kept the same, even though they refer to

---

[18]Table 4 reports the unweighted estimates. Estimating with weighted least squares again makes little difference.

Table 5. *All countries*[a] *(1988–1992)*

Dependent variable	S.S. cont. (% GNP)	S.S. cont. (% rev.)	S.S. exp. (% GNP)	S.S. exp. (% sp.)	S.S. cont. (% GNP)	S.S. exp. (% sp.)
Explanatory variables						
Intercept	−10.939	−24.36	−7.038	−11.678	−13.686	−16.063
	(−2.041)	(−1.884)	(−1.922)	(−1.695)	(−2.338)	(−2.190)
Prop65	61.849	50.649	100.835	249.513	57.211	205.678
	(1.031)	(0.350)	(3.079)	(4.050)	(1.341)	(3.742)
Top5	0.418	1.296	0.188	0.537	0.447	0.640
	(2.342)	(3.094)	(1.526)	(2.320)	(2.507)	(2.775)
P.C. income	–	–	–	–	0.46E(−3)	0.80E(−3)
					(0.953)	(1.411)
Industrial	3.451	17.564	2.922	2.285	–	–
	(0.541)	(1.087)	(0.868)	(0.361)	–	–
$\overline{R}^2$	0.407	0.415	0.635	0.698	0.431	0.720
S.E.	482.997	1164.900	359.262	675.845	473.124	650.189
No. obs.	19	20	27	27	19	27

[a] All regressions were estimated by weighted least squares, with P.C. income as the weight; *t*-statistics in parentheses.

different periods). The results (and particularly the estimated coefficient of income inequality) are remarkably stable.

I conclude from these regressions that we cannot reject the predictions of the theory: social security is larger in countries with a more unequal distribution of pre-tax income and in countries with a greater proportion of elderly people in the population.

Finally, a central question is whether the earlier results are robust to errors in measuring the two explanatory variables of interest, *prop65* and *top5*. To answer it, I computed consistent bounds on their coefficients. Under the conventional hypothesis of the error in variables literature (namely the measurement error is not systematically related to any included regressor), even if these two variables are measured with error, their true maximum likelihood coefficients lie within these bounds.

Our procedure exploits the results of Klepper and Leamer (1984). Consider the first column in Table 3. First, I estimated the coefficients of *prop65* and *top5* by unweighted OLS and by alternatively interchanging each of them with the dependent variable (social security contributions as a percentage of GNP). I thus obtained three estimates for each coefficient, one of which corresponds to that reported in Table 3. For both variables, the signs of the three coefficients are the same across the three estimators. As shown by Klepper and Leamer (1984), I can then conclude that the true maximum likelihood coefficients lie within the convex hull of these three estimates. I then repeated the same procedure for the remaining five columns of Table 3. I find that for both variables, the three estimates always lie in the same orthant. Hence, I can compute the consistent bounds on the coefficients of *prop65* and *top5* for all the regressors reported in Table 3.

These bounds are reported in Table 6. The lower bounds always happen to coincide with the unweighted OLS estimator. Hence, if present, the measurement error tends to bias the results against the theory. I infer from this table that the findings of the preceding subsection are robust to the possibility of measurement error in income inequality and in the proportion of the population over 65 years of age.

VII. Concluding Remarks

This paper started with a question: why do a majority of voters support a social security system that redistributes income towards a minority of the population? To answer this question, I formulated a positive theory of social security that relies on a simple central idea. Social security redistributes both across and within generations. For this reason, it is supported by the recipients of social security benefits, as well as by the poorest taxpayers. When this idea is formalized in a simple overlapping-generations model, two positive implications are obtained. The size of the social security program is larger (i) the greater the proportion of retired individuals in the population; and (ii) the greater the inequality of pre-tax income. Both implications are strongly supported by the empirical evidence on cross-country data.

But the ideas studied in this paper lead to a second, deeper, question. Why

Table 6. *Errors in variables bounds*[a]

	Prop65		*Top5*	
Equation	Lower	Upper	Lower	Upper
(1)	33.800	558.660	0.268	40.080
(2)	115.990	1,414.430	0.905	2.400
(3)	70.110	383.000	0.027	5.263
(4)	272.816	874.126	0.243	4.437
(5)	64.577	308.070	0.254	1.072
(6)	199.223	877.193	0.284	3.640

[a]The equation numbers refer to the columns of Table 3.

is it that in many countries, most of the intra-generational redistribution occurs through the social security system? Outside this system there are not many purely redistributive programs; in most countries welfare expenditures are small compared to the size of social security. So, why do we observe that inter- and intra-generational redistributive policies are intertwined through a single policy instrument? The model analysed in this paper cannot answer this question. Specifically, suppose that in our overlapping-generations model we add one more instrument that enables the government to transfer a lump sum also to every young individual. This additional instrument breaks the link between inter- and intra-generational redistribution. Hence, in equilibrium all the kids would vote against any positive transfer to the parents, and the tax proceeds would only be redistributed among the kids; the equilibrium would then resemble that of Meltzer and Richard (1981), in which a majority of the voters favor a policy that taxes and redistributes. So, why is this extra instrument not used more systematically?

Perhaps, the answer is to be sought in a more complex model of political interaction. In this paper, the voters' preferences are single peaked and the political equilibrium is the policy preferred by the median voters. But in a more general environment, the political equilibrium would reflect the formation of different coalitions. A coalition of poor taxpayers and retirees would presumably support a social security program like that observed in most countries, and described in this model. So, the previous question could be reformulated as follows. Why is it that, in many countries, we observe the formation of this particular coalition of voters?[19] Considering that major reforms to most social security systems are fairly recent and date to the same postwar period, it is likely that the answer to this new question has much to do with particular historical circumstances. Galasso and Conde Ruiz (1999b) have recently addressed this question. They consider an overlapping-generations model combining two redistributive policy tools: a purely intra-generational scheme of redistribution, and a pension scheme that redistributes both within and across generations. In their model, preferences are no longer single peaked, and hence they study a structure-induced equilibrium as defined in Shepsle (1979). They find that both tools are used in equilibrium. But, consistent with the evidence, the intra-generational scheme turns out to be much smaller than the pension system. The reason is that the old constitute a large and homogeneous coalition which supports pensions but not other forms of redistribution. This intuition may also help explain why pensions are financed out of wages, with no explicit or implicit taxes on accumulated wealth (pension benefits are almost never conditional on individual wealth holdings): taxing wealth would break the homogeneity of the

[19] For instance, in Italy, slightly less than half of trade union members are retirees who currently receive pension benefits.

old generation *vis-à-vis* the policy, and reduce the size of a coalition in favor of larger pensions.

Another important policy dimension neglected in this paper is the age of retirement. Why is retirement compulsory in virtually all public pension systems? And what determines retirement age? Recent interesting work by Mulligan and Sala-i-Martin (1999a) and Galasso and Conde Ruiz (1999b) has begun to explore this important question.

Appendix. Variable Definitions and Data Sources

Social Security Contributions in Percent of GNP or of Total Government Revenues

First I take the ratio, and then I compute the average over the period 1978–1982 (or any year within that period for which data are available). *Sources*: Government Finance Statistics and International Financial Statistics, International Monetary Fund. In Table 5 the definition is the same, but the average is taken over the period 1988–1992.

Social Security Expenditures in Percent of GNP or of Total Government Spending

The numerator includes social security and welfare expenditures. The IMF classifies as social security expenditures the "transfer payments designed to compensate for reduction or loss of income or inadequate earning capacity". Health expenditures are not included in social security expenditures. The bulk of social security expenditures generally consists of pensions and retirement benefits. Welfare expenditures are defined by the IMF as "assistance delivered to clients or groups with special needs, such as the young, the old or handicapped". Welfare expenditures are generally much smaller than social security expenditures. *Sources*: Government Finance Statistics and International Financial Statistics, International Monetary Fund. In Table 5 the definition is the same, but the average is taken over the period 1988–1992.

Prop65. Proportion of the total population over 65 years of age. *Source*: UN Demographic Yearbook. This variable is available every five years, and for different years in different countries. The year closest to 1980 was chosen. In Table 5, the source is the World Bank Savings database, and the average is taken over 1988–1992, on yearly data.

Top5. Fraction of pre-tax real income received by the richest 5 percent in the population. It refers to households' income. The data differs across countries, but generally refer to the early 1960s. The other measures of income distribution mentioned in the paper were taken from the same source, namely Paukert (1973).

Industrial. A dummy variable taking a value of 1 for the countries defined as industrialized (see Table 1), and 0 otherwise.

Per Capita Income. Real per capita income in 1985. *Source*: Summers and Heston (1988). In Table 5, this variable is defined as m_rgdpch: real GDP per capita in constant dollars (chain index) in international prices, base 1985, average 1988–1992. *Source*: Penn World Tables (PWT), available on the net.

Other variables used were: Urban population as a percent of total population. *Source*: World Development Report, 1988. And: fraction of the labor force employed in the agricultural sector. *Source*: World Development Report, 1988.

References

Altonji, J., Hayashi, F. and Kotlikoff, L. (1989), Is the Extended Family Altruistically Linked? Direct Tests Using Micro Data, NBER Working Paper no. 3046, Cambridge, MA.

Aziariadis, C. and Galasso, V. (1997), Fiscal Constitutions and the Determinacy of Intergenerational Transfers, Universidad Carlos III Working Paper no. 97–71, Madrid.

Boadway, R. and Wildasin, D. (1989a), Voting Models of Social Security Determination, in B. A. Gustafsson and N. A. Klevmarken (eds.), *The Political Economy of Social Security*, North-Holland, Amsterdam.

Boadway, R. and Wildasin, D. (1989b), A Median Voter Model of Social Security, *International Economic Review 30* (2), 307–328.

Boldrin, M. and Rustichini, A. (1996), Equilibria with Social Security, forthcoming in *Review of Economics Dynamics*.

Boskin, M., Kotlikoff, L., Puffert, D. and Shoven, J. (1987), Social Security: A Financial Appraisal Across and Within Generations, *National Tax Journal XL* (1), 19–34.

Browning, E. K. (1975), Why the Social Insurance Budget is Too Large in a Democratic Society, *Economic Inquiry 13*, 373–388.

Cooley, T. and Soares, J. (1999), A Positive Theory of Social Security Based on Reputation, *Journal of Political Economy 107*, 135–160.

Cukierman, A. and Meltzer, A. (1989), A Political Theory of Government Debt and Deficits in the Neo-Ricardian Framework, *American Economic Review 79*, 713–732.

Ferrara, P. and Lott, J. (1985), Rates of Return Promised by Social Security to Today's Young Workers, in P. Ferrara (ed.), *Social Security: Prospects for Real Reform*, Cato Institute, Washington, DC.

Galasso, V. (1998), The US Social Security: A Financial Appraisal for the Median Voter, mimeo, Universidad Carlos III, Madrid.

Galasso, V. and Conde Ruiz, J. I. (1999a), Early Retirement, mimeo, Universidad Carlos III, Madrid.

Galasso, V. and Conde Ruiz, J. I. (1999b), Positive Arithmetic of the Welfare State, mimeo, Universidad Carlos III, Madrid.

Gordon, R. and Varian, H. (1988), Intergenerational Risk Sharing, *Journal of Public Economics 37*, 185–202.

Grandmont, J. (1978), Intermediate Preferences and the Majority Rule, *Econometrica 46*, 317–330.

Hansson, I. and Stuart, C. (1989), Social Security as Trade Among Living Generations, *American Economic Review 79*, 1183–1195.

Klepper, S. and Leamer, E. E. (1984), Consistent Set of Estimates for Regressions with Errors in All Variables, *Econometrica 52*, 163–184.

Kotlikoff, L., Persson, T. and Svensson, L. (1988), Social Contracts and Assets: A Possible Solution to the Time Consistency Problem, *American Economic Review 78*, 662–677.

Loewy, M. (1988), Equilibrium Policy in an Overlapping Generations Economy, *Journal of Monetary Economics 22* (3), 485–500.

Meltzer, A. and Richard, S. (1981), A Rational Theory of the Size of Government, *Journal of Political Economy 89*, 914–927.

Mulligan, C. and Sala-i-Martin, X. (1999a), Gerontocracy, Retirement, and Social Security, NBER Working Paper no. 7117, Cambridge, MA.

Mulligan, C. and Sala-i-Martin, X. (1999b), Social Security in Theory and Practice (I): Facts and Political Theories, NBER Working Paper no. 7118, Cambridge, MA.

Mulligan, C. and Sala-i-Martin, X. (1999c), Social Security in Theory and Practice (II): Efficiency Theories and Implications for Reform, NBER Working Paper no. 7119, Cambridge, MA.

Patton, C. (1978), The Politics of Social Security, in M. Boskin (ed.), *The Crisis in Social Security*, Institute for Contemporary Policy Studies, San Francisco.

Paukert, F. (1973), Income Distribution at Different Levels of Development—A Survey of the Evidence, *International Labor Review, 108* (2), 97–125.

Persson, T. and Tabellini, G. (1990), *Macroeconomic Policy, Credibility and Politics*, Harwood Publishers, London.

Persson, T. and Tabellini, G. (1999), Political Economics and Public Finance, forthcoming in A. Auerbach and M. Feldstein, (eds.), *Handbook of Public Economics*, North-Holland, Amsterdam.

Persson, T. and Tabellini, G. (2000), *Political Economics—Explaining Economic Policy*, forthcoming, MIT Press, Cambridge, MA.

Shepsle, K. (1979), Institutional Arrangements and Equilibrium in Multidimensional Contracts Models, *European Economic Review 40*, 61–89.

Sjoblom, K. (1985), Voting for Social Security, *Public Choice 45*, 225–240.

Summers, R. and Heston, A. (1988), A New Set of International Comparisons of Real Product and Price Level Estimates for 130 Countries, 1950–85, *Review of Income and Wealth 1*, 1–25.

Verbon, H. (1988), *The Evolution of Public Pension Schemes*, Springer-Verlag, Berlin and Heidelberg.